Fearless Editing

Crafting Words and Images for Print, Web and Public Relations

Carolyn Dale

Tim Pilgrim

PEARSON

Boston • New York • San Francisco
Mexico City • Montreal • Toronto • London • Madrid • Munich • Paris
Hong Kong • Singapore • Tokyo • Cape Town • Sydney

Editor: *Molly Taylor*
Executive Editor: *Karon Bowers*
Editorial Assistant: *Michael Kish*
Senior Marketing Manager: *Mandee Eckersley*
Editorial Production Service: *Whitney Acres Editorial*
Manufacturing Buyer: *JoAnne Sweeney*
Cover Administrator: *Kristina Mose-Libon*
Electronic Composition: *Omegatype Typography, Inc.*

For related titles and support materials, visit our online catalog at www.ablongman.com.

Between the time Website information is gathered and then published, some sites may have closed. Also, the transcription of URLs can result in typographical errors. The publisher would appreciate being notified of any problems so that they may be corrected in subsequent editions.

Library of Congress Cataloging-in-Publication Data

Dale, Carolyn
    Fearless editing : crafting words and images for print, web, and public relations / Carolyn Dale, Tim Pilgrim.—1st ed.
        p. cm.
    Includes bibliographical references and index.
    ISBN 0-205-39354-3 (pbk.)
        1. Journalism—Editing. I. Pilgrim, Tim. II. Title.

PN4778.D36 2005
808'.06607—dc22

                                                                                    2004052461

Printed in the United States of America

10 9 8 7 6 5 4 3 2 1   09 08 07 06 05 04

Fearless Editing

Contents

4 *Working with Words—and Their Writers*   **65**

5 *Shaping Beautiful Writing*   **81**

7   *Editing Images*   121

8   *Color*   173

11   Layout and Design   237

Acknowledgments

The authors gratefully acknowledge the support from the people and organizations, which made preparation of this book possible:

- The Poynter Institute for Media Studies, St. Petersburg, Fla., which accepted both authors for the Visual Journalism Educators Seminar, one in June 1995 and the other in June 2000, and to whose teaching staff, particularly Pegie Stark Adam, Kim Elam, Monica Moses, Ann Glover and Ron Reason, the authors are indebted.
- The Herald (Everett, Wash.) and editor Stan Strick, along with Judy Stanley, Dan Bates, Justin Best, Michael O'Leary, Joe Nicholson and Drew Perine for many, many professional examples, photos, layouts and infographics.
- MSNBC, Redmond, Wash., which covered expenses for workshops conducted by one of the authors to test material in this book within the online news environment, and whose staff of editors, writers and producers provided helpful comment.
- The American Society of Newspaper Editors; Excellence in Journalism Education Fellowship for Carolyn Dale, summer 2000, which included a week-long seminar at American Press Institute, Reston, Va., living costs in Seattle during the summer, and the opportunity to work in a copy editing position at the Seattle Post-Intelligencer.
- The Seattle Post-Intelligencer, which through the ASNE fellowship program employed Dale during a six-week position as a copy editor in features and news departments and allowed us to reproduce a section cover page.
- Western Washington University, which granted professional leave that provided the time to research and write the manuscript; Carol Brach and Bill O'Neill for administrative and computer technical support; Shearlean Duke and John Harris, who provided helpful comments while using the text as a class manual.
- Jan Koutsky, Andy Purdue, Soon Beng Yeap, John Harris, Brian Plonka, Ed McDonald, Judy Smith, Kay Sardo, and Tom Griffin, all of whom generously helped with illustrations.
- Western Washington students, especially graduates Jennifer Collins and Laura Thoren, for layouts, photos, inspiration and class-testing of materials, and Western's student publications, Western Front newspaper, Klipsun magazine and The Planet magazine.

- Our families and friends, who smiled at our grouchiness and tolerated our absences.
- Karon Bowers and Molly Taylor at Allyn & Bacon for their belief in the project; Michael Kish, Marjorie Payne and Faye Whitney for their keen eyes for the production and copy editing.

We also thank our reviewers for their kind remarks and helpful suggestions, Barbara Bullington, East Carolina University; Judi Cook, Salem State College; James Ellis, University of Nevada, Reno; Stan Ketterer, Oklahoma State University; and Judith Pratt, California State University, Bakersfield.

Without the support of all of these folks, this book would still be a dream.

August, 2004

Introduction

Between us, we two authors have taught writing, editing, grammar and design to high school and college students and to adults for a combined total of about 50 years. We have taught and advised in magazine, newspaper and online journalism and have professional backgrounds in journalism and public relations. We have also done consulting for print media and online sites.

We are writing the book because we need this information all in one place between two covers. We have seen separate books for editing in separate media and books that teach working with words as an entirely separate process from arranging them on pages.

These are the primary reasons we have grown to believe such ways of approaching editing are unrealistic:

- Many of our students and alumni working in news and public relations edit in several different media during their day's work; indeed, media themselves are converging.
- Many books treat editing as a compilation of disparate skills, most of which apparently need to be memorized or simply executed from checklists. This treatment ignores the influences of a publication's goals and audiences, and limits development of editors' professional or artistic ability to initial skill stages.
- More visual skills are required of editors who now often work in teams with artists, photographers, writers and technical production staff. Working with words is not a process separate from deciding which components of a story need to be told in photographs, headings, information graphics, illustrations or video clips in order to provide the fullest, clearest meaning.
- The World Wide Web is part of our lives, with much journalistic content being presented by online editors, yet most editing texts deal with this growing area in a slim chapter tossed in just before the index.

So, our book has several goals.

We focus on the concepts that underlie all editing regardless of the medium and organize all our chapters around these concepts:

- Priority
- Community
- Clarity
- Unity
- Contrast
- Beauty

We show how the concepts apply specifically in media that offer pages of news. Our readers will see examples from newspapers, public relations, magazines and the World Wide Web all within one volume.

We link these concepts to underlying ideals in writing and design in order to create both cultural context and impetus for professional development.

Finally, we treat visual and verbal editing as being linked—companion processes that need to be treated together in each section of text.

The illustrations in the book go through stages of development, including thumbnail sketches of pages; they depict dummies and finished pages, early drafts, student media and professional work. We hope to show how editing skills develop in stages and how pages go through drafts before achieving their final form.

We offer this volume humbly. Like others who come from a word-laden, print-oriented age, we have struggled with visual concepts, and though we see changes in media around us, we are indebted to the clear, fresher vision of our students and to the experimenting and sharing of knowledge by colleagues working in the new medium of the Web.

A strong orientation toward language remains in the book because that focus too is basic to all contemporary editing. Editors of major online news media, when asked what are the standards of knowledge expected in new hires, answer simply: knowledge of grammar and the ability to work with the language.

Many writers use language intuitively, and this serves them well. Editing, however, requires this intuitive self-guidance to evolve into clearly articulated understandings and accurate, beneficial applications to work done by other people. The process cannot rely solely on intuition—fortunately, it can be learned.

Editing is often not treated as a conceptual or creative process. Yet we know that something special happens when a written story, photographs and artwork or design are pulled together into a polished whole before publication, and when the packages are crafted effectively to suit the medium.

In periods of rapid media change such as the present, with new media technologies and mergers that build multimedia conglomerates, editing has sometimes been given short shrift, its rewards being small staffs, little time and minimal recognition.

But, changes in access or delivery or company size do not eliminate the space and time of the conceptual process editing entails. It is good content that brings readers and viewers back to a publication or a Web page, and good content relies on good writing, accurate information and useful and attractive presentation.

Outline

The role of editors in different media is covered with **Chapter 1,** which details our conceptual approach and introduces the audiences' need for accurate, useful information in order to function as citizens in a democracy. The pressures—in terms of variety of tasks, economics, deadlines and changing media—are described for newspapers, magazines, public relations and the Web.

Chapter 2 covers the critical evaluation of news and feature stories and the expression of that value through headings and page layout. Streamlining story shapes for news and features, deciding on the prominence of the headings and placing the story units on pages are steps in a process that expresses priority. Modular design is explored as a way to express both priority and contrast on pages of differing sizes.

Chapter 3 discusses the language and construction of better, more poetic headings in a variety of media.

Words formed into sentences convey not only the meaning intended by the writer, but also potential unintended meanings and, occasionally, incoherence. Editing for clarity can help writers to convey only the meanings they intend. Heading type sizes and the interplay with line length are also discussed.

- After completing these beginning chapters, students will understand the visual dimensions of evaluating stories, placing them in an appealing and readable fashion on the printed or Web page and crafting headings that will attract readers to them.

Working constructively with writers and building a conceptually based approach to grammar and language structure are the emphases of **Chapter 4.** If an editor's directions to writers are to work, they must be specific about the nature of the problems as well as the way to fix them. Beginning editors often feel overwhelmed by the dense thicket of grammar rules to be mastered; this chapter shows how to develop a personal system for spotting errors and for building familiarity and ease with the labels used by grammar handbooks.

Chapter 5 covers the primary word editing areas necessary for unity and clarity: punctuation and English basics (such as tense, agreement, parallel structure, etc.). Other sentence essentials, such as length and voice, are discussed as ways to enhance beauty.

- Following completion of chapters 4 and 5, students will know that an omnipotent being did not part the clouds and say, "Some editors will know the basics of the language, and the rest must wander in darkness."

Instead, students will understand that superior editing skills include an ability to work constructively with writers and their writing and will know they must develop a personal editing system that allows them to catch the numerous errors possible in grammar, usage and punctuation—and be willing and able to turn to grammar guides or English handbooks in instances where their memories and systems fail.

Chapters 6 through 11 tie editing of text to editing of visuals because today's editors do more than simply proofread stories and write headings for them prior to printing. In media and public relations work, editors' responsibilities for visual presentation vary from doing design work themselves to working with artists who will do the major design.

Chapter 6 emphasizes graphics based on words and shows how editors must be able to envision stories in altered shapes and create text treatments that engage readers and expand their understanding of the story's topic or themes—including sometimes the reshaping of material to move it from one medium to another.

Since editors are at center stage for choosing, presenting, researching and producing "the look" of a publication's content, the chapter also incorporates the need for editors to be software savvy and adept and critical researchers of electronic sources to carry out their traditional functions as fact-checkers.

Visual elements convey emotion and draw readers to them, and **Chapter 7,** "Editing images," is guided by concepts of contrast and unity. It focuses on showing how editors decide how much of a story needs to be told in pictures, which photos (and in which sizes and shapes) best tell certain aspects of the story in a manner appropriate to community sensibilities, or if an artist should be asked to create an illustration.

Color is life, and when used in publications or online, the appeal of warmth, liveliness, coolness and poise are added to the written and visual content. **Chapter 8,** "Color," shows how editors use color, as well as black and white, and white space, to provide dimension, contrast and unity within designs, and how editors can grow adept at using different aspects of color—complements, intensity, contrast, placement, shading—to create a desired tone and mood.

The chapter explains how editing with color takes place at several levels because viewers respond to colors physiologically as well as culturally, because colors respond to each other and appear to alter each other, and because colors vary depending on whether they are created as ink on paper or as light waves on a monitor.

Chapter 9 deals with typography and emphasizes how editors work with typefaces to provide unity throughout a publication and to place emphasis by building in typographical contrasts. It discusses arranging display type within white space as well as with text. Be it in print or on the screen, editors choose type while keeping in mind proportion, balance and historical context.

Chapter 10 focuses on information graphics and the importance of presenting data clearly. Because graphics such as charts compactly and systematically present numbers that tell important parts of a story, editors must learn to be skillful in analyzing data and placing results as numbers in spatial arrangements that the eye can take in quickly, or can linger on to make comparisons. Included are guidelines editors can use to ensure that vital aspects of surveys and scientific studies are covered in stories.

Chapter 11 focuses on the editor's role in layout and how it intersects with overall publication design as well as with the role of a publication's art staff. The emphasis remains on content editing and on the broader scope design plays in a publication's look.

The chapter focuses on specific media while discussing some design issues, such as distinguishing between news and features, planning inside pages, covers and contents pages, exploring aspects unique to magazines or newsletters, and organizing a Web page.

Here, the underlying concepts of priority, clarity, beauty, contrast and unity can all be brought to bear; this chapter also draws on the earlier, more detailed treatment of photography, color, typography and graphics.

- Working with these chapters, students will be able to plan pages that communicate the personality and function of a publication or Web site through use of typographical elements. They will be able to select and edit photos, evaluate and create information graphics, and plan effective use of color. These concepts then can be applied to pages of differing sizes and purposes, with students understanding the modifications needed for each medium.

Editors press the final buttons that set decisions into type or light patterns on a monitor. As the last person to see a work, an editor is the final guard for the accuracy and reputation of the publication within its community. In the process of making numerous decisions on presentation, editors also set the tone and balance of a publication while making decisions involving legal issues, as well as issues of taste and ethics.

While elements of ethics are incorporated into earlier chapters, **Chapter 12,** "Balancing community interests: ethics and law," examines these two areas, which are characterized as "written limits" (law) and "unwritten limits" (ethics). Both are discussed specifically from the viewpoint of editors, rather than solely that of writers.

- A polished presentation—be it in print or on a Web page—is not just a happy accident, a meeting of talented creators who all happened to produce art and writing that flowed and gelled perfectly together. "Fearless editing" shows the creativity of a conceptually based editing process.

1

Concepts:
A Time for Editing

Readers are drawn to a page for its information and because of its beauty. In the chaos of constant, competing stimuli, this is a space where order shows through priority, where clarity results from a fellow human having studied the elements, checked their accuracy and value and prioritized them.

The page shows an editor has asked:

- What makes this story different from all others like it?
- What does this really mean to you who will come to this page?
- Which elements—words and visuals—can be combined to tell the story in the best possible way?

We may agree or disagree with that editor's ordering and emphasis but inwardly be grateful. A properly edited page provides us a standpoint in the enormous, rushing swirl of events and talk, a place to grab on to, a place to start our own interpretation, another human mind against which to test our knowledge and ideas so that we may nurture our understanding.

Good editing also lends a feeling of satisfaction from the time we spend with a page because of its physical beauty, the enjoyment of dense colors of ink balanced against white space, the movement of the eye as it is directed from item to item.

And, an element of trust is instilled in readers—a belief that the information will be accurate, true, and have been judged worthwhile on the merits of its ideas and information, and on its contribution to our understanding of the world, society, cosmos.

These feelings of interest, restfulness, trust and enjoyment are responses to good, consistent editing. The underlying concepts allowing readers to achieve such feelings are what should motivate us in our work as editors.

Six Concepts Guide Effective Editing

This book explains how editing is most effective when guided by six key concepts:

- **Priority**—with the readers in mind, the judging of importance of written and visual information, along with the ranking and displaying of that information.
- **Community**—knowing the public, or audience, to whom the publication is directed, and whose values and interests underpin the publication and the entire editing process.
- **Clarity**—providing content in a way that avoids any confusion and allows readers to understand the information quickly and accurately.
- **Unity**—being consistent or uniform in treatment of elements of design, writing, story approach and content so that clarity and reader trust in the publication are reinforced.
- **Contrast**—using skillful change in writing and design often enough to stir reader interest and direct attention.
- **Beauty**—presenting material that is pleasing to the intended audience and that appeals to the aesthetic senses.

(See Box 1.1 for a full discussion of these concepts.)

Applying these concepts to stories and images, an editor can gain confidence and ease, and can connect the tasks of editing words or designing visuals to intellectual traditions in language and art. Editing in a conceptual way enables editors to communicate more clearly with writers and artists while allowing them to observe and enjoy their own growth as professionals.

A love of the language keeps an editor enjoying its changing nuances and seeking out word derivations and meanings; a love of fine art encourages an editor to develop aesthetics and a sense for visual trends and changing tastes.

Love and aesthetics are perhaps vague and even mysterious-sounding, like qualities one either has or doesn't have. However, those who know and love language and art apply their knowledge through sets of ideas, or concepts, which are more specific.

Editing for Media

It may be that the best editing is the least apparent to the eye: What we notice as readers are the story that flows quickly and involves us in the telling, the photographs that invite us to stop, the typography and illustrations that enhance the meaning. Editors make the creative people they work with look good, and the nature of this process is not mechanical, but creative.

It also may seem like less competitive and individualistic work than writing. But, because editors must coordinate and elicit the best work from writers, artists

BOX 1.1 • *Using Concepts in Editing*

Priority—judgment of written and visual information and the subsequent process of ranking and displaying based on importance.
  Editing expresses priority through:

- placement of a story on a page or within a publication; placement of information within a story;
- placement of an idea within a sentence;
- use of heading size, number of lines, width, and bold or italic typeface;
- use of color, photos or illustrations;
- use of textual design elements such as pullquotes or fact boxes;
- length of story and shape and size of the overall package;
- selection of certain issues for editorial comment or analysis.

Community—the public or audience (and its values and interests) to whom the publication is directed and the working relationship that develops between the two.
  Editing for community involves:

- defining the audience for the publication, and how often to publish or update; defining the publication's profile, cost, role and geographic reach;
- defining standards for content created outside: advertising, letters to the editor, op-ed pieces, guest columns, etc.;
- defining internal standards or local style for treating sensitive issues;
- editing for truthfulness to maintain integrity and readers' trust;
- representing major voices in the community, including the unpopular ones;
- editing in the best interest of the audience and resisting self-interested pressures of advertisers or sponsors or even of editors exercising their personal values and tastes;
- avoiding unnecessarily harming others through libel, slander or invasion of privacy;
- giving credit to other writers and artists by respecting copyright practices;
- providing true information so that community members can function fully as citizens in a democracy;
- supporting freedom of speech within the United States and, as possible, abroad.

Clarity—presentation of content in a way that conveys the intended meaning, shows the publication's purpose and allows quick navigation.
  Editing a publication for clarity ensures:

- the purpose of a publication and identity of its publishers are stated;
- editorial content or news is differentiated from paid announcements;
- contents pages or navigation points provide ease of use;
- information most important to the audience is emphasized;
- each item appeals to some segment of the overall audience;
- content is ordered using news or feature writing values;
- information sought or obtained from readers is openly stated;

(continued)

BOX 1.1 • Continued

- irrelevancies, redundancies and inaccuracies are removed;
- missing information has been researched and gaps filled;
- a direct and informative style is used for stories, headings and captions;
- style is applied that prefers active voice, present or past tense, shorter paragraphs and sentences, but that varies these for effect or to preserve editorial voice;
- stories and packages show the relationship among elements;
- graphic elements are relevant and offer explanatory material.

Unity—consistent or uniform treatment of elements of design, writing, story approach and content. Unity shows the personality of the publication and builds the background or context against which variations will provide contrast. Over time, unity underscores reader recognition of the publication and trust in it.
   Editing for unity ensures:

- elements building the look of the publication are applied throughout;
- style, grammar, punctuation, typefaces, type sizes, column widths, placement of photos, illustrations and graphics and lengths of items are applied consistently;
- visual hierarchies (such as large type sizes) serve the content's meaning;
- an underlying template and a color palette are planned and used consistently;
- the same standards are used to evaluate visual and verbal items; the kinds of stories, the departments or sections and the voice used contribute to the publication's identity and role in the community.

Contrast—use of change in writing and design often enough to stir readers' interest and direct attention. Contrast is the exception to the rule; it must be used with restraint because it needs to stand out but not destroy the background it depends upon for effect.
   Editing for contrast creates tension between two opposites:

- In sentence structures: passive voice/active voice; compound or complex sentences/ short, declarative sentences;
- In voice: writer's voice/institutional voice; humorous tone/serious tone; opinion pieces/objective-style reporting; expert sources/readers' responses; following community tastes or sensitivities/challenging them;
- In page design: horizontal modules/vertical modules; rectilinear/round shapes; large image/small images; large headings/small headings; dominant or dark elements/white space;
- In use of color: black and white/color; white background/reversed or dark background; color complements/color contrasts; proportion/extension;
- In typography: plain type/bold, italic or cursive; serif/sans serif; capitals/lower case; justified type/ragged or centered type; standard column width/ narrower or wider columns; small leading/large leading.

Beauty—presentation of material in a manner that appeals to the aesthetic senses of the intended audience.

Editing for beauty ensures:

- unity of form plus excitement through contrast;
- use of content attractive to the community;
- avoidance of writing and design fads and gimmicks.

It pleases the eye through:

- providing high quality physical reproduction (ink, paper, monitor);
- planning visual and verbal presentations to complement each other;
- selecting photos and art that are well composed and executed;
- using regular shapes, such as modules;
- planning the length of paragraphs and sentences for visual appeal;
- using color with consideration for complementarity, contrast and restraint.

It pleases the reader's "ear" through:

- organizing the structure of each sentence;
- using a range of sentence structures to provide rhythm and variety;
- selecting precise words and creating phrases with cadence and flow;
- enhancing the voice of the writer or the publication;
- smoothing writing so it sounds great when read out loud.

and photographers, they often grow to seek and appreciate the skills of others as well as the management and organizational abilities needed to draw diverse people into a team and produce professional pieces on deadline.

As a process, editing begins with the thinking that lays the foundation, the decisions about what will be told in words or through visuals and about how parts will be reshaped for presentation in different media.

It goes on to apply specific concepts: Good writing is clear writing; an apt heading can be poetic; a page design balances dominant elements and guides the eye; an informed person has checked facts and decided what is important; the elements form a pleasurable whole that imparts value.

Editing Differs in Each of the Major Media

Editing means something different in each of our major media, which draw on differing combinations of skills:

- At a newspaper, it may refer to copy editing, headline writing and a final checking for errors, or it may encompass news editing, selecting from hundreds of foreign and national stories.

- At a magazine, it may mean guiding writers from story ideas through final drafts.
- In public relations, it may mean creating entire publications oneself, from research and writing to final design and layout.
- For World Wide Web pages, it may mean digesting large amounts of information for selective presentation or telling a single story in depth with audio and video in addition to text and photos.

To picture likely futures and careers in editing, it is helpful to understand where editing fits in different media now as well as the pressures in economics, shifting audiences and new technologies that are reshaping the nature of the work.

Newspapers

The imminent demise of newspapers has been often predicted, from Marshall McLuhan's forecasts of 30 years ago to current electronic editors referring to them as "legacy media." However, newspapers are persistent about surviving and still sell millions of copies daily.

Economic pressures come from competition by other media for advertising dollars, and from readers' preferences for news delivery in the morning. Urban daily newspapers often publish half a dozen times in a 24-hour cycle and maintain Web pages as well. These Web pages vary extensively in their nature and purpose.

Historically, both a newspaper's advertisers and readers have been in a defined geographic area. An editor may find it difficult to picture a typical reader of the newspaper where she works because it tries to reach everyone within that geographic area. Increasingly, newspapers reach the older members of their potential audience, and a Northwestern Media Management readership impact study in 2001 showed only a third of American adults to be heavy readers and a third to be non- or light-readers.

Larger newspapers offer local news as well as summaries of national and international events. With large and hierarchical staffs, editing is specialized.

Story editors work with reporters to develop the content and may work in a small group that includes a layout/design editor, photographer and artist. Copy editors give the final read, do fact checking, make corrections for grammar and consistency, and write headlines. They often also lay out pages by using templates based on the newspaper's design.

Editing is a career track that runs parallel to reporting. It can also be a route to management. Editors of the editorial page, for example, can have considerable influence in their communities and within the newspaper.

At all stages and in whichever capacities, the editors are concerned with accuracy, balance, ethics and legal safety. They also work under the constant pressure of deadlines and must struggle against the feeling that there is too little time to think in depth.

This pressure intensifies at the news desk, where editors read and select news stories that arrive on the wires, such as Associated Press, foreign services, and the offerings of newspaper groups, such as the Los Angeles Times or Washington Post wires. Here, editors often trim and combine stories or edit them severely to fit a digest format.

At smaller newspapers, which may publish weekly and serve a community rather than a larger area, editing is often done in one place, with the same person who directs story development also giving stories their final reading and checking. This person will also often write the headlines and design the pages.

This editor may write as well, and have to edit her own work at a later stage. She also must work closely with the photographer, even serving on occasion as back-up photographer. This editor often works without a newsroom artist, though someone on the advertising side may be able to help with charts or infographics.

The challenges are to be a master of both words and visuals and to bring a fresh editing eye to stories and photos worked on earlier. The editor who covers news most likely will not write the editorials, however, but rely on the newspaper's publisher or manager for those.

Editing a community newspaper may be exhausting work in its variety of demands but satisfying for the editor who likes to be independent, to have an impact on his community and who likes the range of tasks.

As the medium with the longest history in the United States, newspapering may be struggling against presentations that seem quickly outmoded by its electronic cousins. However, the common cultural base newspapers have set—such as organizing by departments or sections, distinguishing between news and features, defining the public's need to know, and many other conventions—forms the accepted, unarticulated basis underlying even new media formats and decisions.

Magazines

Magazines sprout like mushrooms after rain; each year in the United States, hundreds, if not thousands, are added to the total being published. The linking of the PC to a desktop printer, and later to external hard drives, was the key to placing magazine publishing in the hands of any ordinary person who wished to take it on.

Hence, many self-published newsletters bloom, and some cross the vague line that separates them from magazines, which are usually available on newsstands, carry advertising and reach for a broad subscriber base defined by interest instead of geographical area.

Contrary to a newspaper editor's difficulty in picturing the typical reader, the magazine editor knows quite specifically what her typical reader is like—not just by demographics, but also by what she wants to read because of how she pictures her identity.

The labor of editing is commonly divided between story editing, which will mean working with writers on story development through rewrite stages, and fact checking, which means doing research to verify every item to be printed.

Defining both functions is the practice of using free-lance writers—writers not employed full-time—for some portion of the articles.

Editors may also write short items and work up to writing longer pieces. The close mix of editing, writing and research functions leads to titles and roles such as "contributing editor." Challenges include working months ahead of production, foreseeing topics and developing stories and illustrations six months or more ahead of the publication date. Deadline pressures run in a cycle having both calm and intense times.

Visual presentation is considered from the beginning of the process, as this medium really shows off color design and photography. Larger magazines employ art directors, who determine the overall look of the publication and who design each editorial page.

Advertisers buy space and color inks, and the amount of advertising determines how thick the "book" will be. Historically, advertisers have been able to influence the content of some magazines, notably some women's magazines. Other magazines are heavily supported by subscribers; and some, such as Ms. and The Sun, are free of ads yet offered at newsstands for prices comparable to magazines with advertising support. Many small, special-interest magazines run with the help of an associated foundation or nonprofit group; some have experimented with taking only classified ads.

No one is predicting the demise of magazines as a medium, perhaps because of their successful compatibility with electronic media and their strong appeal to young people. Yet historically, this medium has gone through tough periods, such as the decline of mass-interest magazines during the years following the introduction of television.

World Wide Web

The Internet is a truly interactive medium in the amount of control and selection it gives to users. Web use of the Internet was free in early years, and briefly challenged corporation-dominated models of mass media, but soon began to mirror the existing commercially oriented broadcast model.

As the Web came of age and as the "digital divide" began to vanish (by 2002 about 30 percent of Americans, including those older than 50 used the Web), advertisements proliferated on most information sites, and a strategy of persuasion and selling lay behind most public relations and commercial sites.

Early on, some sites such as Microsoft's Slate magazine experimented briefly with a fee/subscription approach but found users would not pay because of the many free sites available.

However, the World Wide jury is still out regarding this aspect of the Web. In recent years, news sites have been exploring different ways (such as charging for archive or video-clip use) of using their online publications to bring in revenue. In 2001, consumers spent $675 million for online content, and by mid-2002, 1,700 sites (not including porn or gambling sites) charged for content.

Still, the Web is in transition as a medium and continues to develop potential for conveying vast amounts of information—and also much disinformation and misinformation—without the limitations of space encountered by magazines and newspapers. Because items can be added and updated in an electronic flash at any moment of the day or night, no real deadlines exist.

Instant feedback has become the norm, with many news outlets using the Web to conduct "instant" (unscientific) polls. Special news sites such as Jim Romenesko's MediaNews out of the Poynter Institute and the USC Annenberg Online Journalism Review allow immediate public forums regarding coverage of issues and events.

Though readers can rapidly and easily sift through and store images, videos and sound bites they want to keep, the Web is a medium relying most heavily on words and text, which also can be downloaded easily. They form the content that, if pleasingly presented, will most likely cause users to return.

A division of labor often exists in this medium between those who edit the content and the technical staffs who work with the software that gets that content onto the Web.

Here, editors may be in charge of creating content in a manner similar to a newspaper or magazine but more complex in that they may arrange for audio and video clips and sophisticated graphic elements that supplement the text that Internet users will read on the screen.

More often, Web editors may be busy with "shovelware"—a term that refers to putting existing printed material on to the Web. Editors in this medium struggle a bit because the audience being addressed on the Web is not as readily known as in most print media, though it can be targeted in a way, as with magazines and newspapers that have online versions.

Web editors must be aware of the limits inherent in the medium. Readers will not scroll endlessly down a page. They will not click endlessly through a maze of pages. They will not have infinite patience while waiting for images to appear on their screens. They usually hate to scroll laterally, and they learn to abhor blinking text, busy pages (especially those stuffed with swirling advertisements), text streaming across in reader-board fashion and blazing colors.

Public Relations

Public relations is a growing field, and has been since it began to emerge as a profession in the 1920s. Editing in public relations involves taking a message that carries the source's intent and shaping it for any of the mass media. It may be released to news media in hopes it will be treated like a news item and have its worth validated by that process. Or, it may be carried in the agency's or company's own internal newsletter or magazine, posted on its Web page or developed for internal broadcast.

The public relations professional is valued for the same skills she would use in news media, though she has chosen to use those skills to further a cause or issue, or to help an agency improve its fit within its community. Editors in this field are expected to produce items that look and sound enough like news articles or footage so that they appear virtually unchanged in a news medium. They also produce their own media, which should be of equal professional quality, for an audience unified by a cause or a commercial effort.

Editing challenges lie in the definition of audience and in whom one is serving; how much one discloses of internal operations to different groups, such as the general public, news media, investors or employees; in whether information is to flow two ways and express workers' views to management; and in assuring meaningfulness of content.

Editors in public relations sometimes fight outmoded concepts that would require "good PR" to be only fluff or partial truths, as though the public, drenched as it is in constant media messages, has somehow remained unsophisticated.

The source of funding for the internal publications and for the public relations department's paychecks is the agency wanting its image promoted, but the editor has to serve real audiences as well as the central interest. In the end, if the audience tunes out the message, nothing at all is communicated.

Many editors of newsletters serve nonprofit organizations. Often, the jobs include researching, writing, editing and designing. Budgets may or may not allow for photography and artwork to be hired, and printing may be only black and white. Like the editor at a community newspaper, the public relations person working alone in an organization needs to master a variety of skills and to enjoy that variety.

Editors in this field can enjoy considerable control over content and the mix of messages and media to develop for the client. Pressures or interests that influence decisions and make them different from news media decisions include less-frequent publication schedules, the intent of the message created, highlighting aspects of messages for different audiences and a client's overall comfort level with disclosing decisions and information.

Audiences and Ethics

Picturing the typical reader is a good way for editors to stay connected to the kinds of questions readers will bring to each piece and to their sense of whether that piece is complete. When editing for any medium, editors are wise to imagine specific kinds of people being interested in certain stories while skipping others. Young readers will tune into a story about CDs if it's about hip-hop artists; oldsters if it's about interest rates on certificates of deposit.

Who the audience is becomes a key question at two levels. It must be asked in order to define the publication's overall nature and purpose. And, it must be asked to challenge each story, photo or graphic: In what way does this item fulfill that purpose? Which segment of the audience will this appeal to?

All messages placed in the marketplace of ideas reach varying numbers of people and have some kind of effect. The importance of how to reach an audience and the problem of how to increase its size are ongoing.

Research organizations like Media Management Center at Northwestern University will continue to study how to grow readership and, perhaps, will urge, as it did in its 2001 study, more local, people-centered and lifestyle news.

At the core, however, the public, or body politic, must have a plethora of unvarnished pictures of events and of issue-oriented, true information so that they might function as citizens in a democracy and hold public officials accountable. This book is most oriented toward those messages that are seen to have intrinsic worth, that are in the marketplace because of their potential value as ideas or useful information for readers.

This includes material produced through public relations because it will be evaluated during an independent editorial process. But, this book does not discuss advertising or other messages that are in the marketplace because someone has paid to place them. The distinction is important because editors must be clear about their criteria when making news judgments or design decisions.

Those criteria are limited in this book to news and information, and presume an economic model in which the audience finds the messages useful enough to pay for them, either directly (for instance, through subscriptions to publications, cable TV or some Web services), or indirectly (for example, through using a medium that carries advertising, such as network broadcasting or Web news sites).

The codes of ethics for professional associations in news and in public relations, such as the Society of Professional Journalists, the Public Relations Society of America and the International Association of Business Communicators, require truthfulness and place primary importance on the necessity of accurate information and an informed citizenry in a democracy.

It is not at all clear, though, that mass audiences in the United States, at least, are continuing to make this distinction themselves, or to care greatly about it. More and more, traditional distinctions are blurred between news, entertainment, complementary copy, paid message placements and co-sponsorship arrangements.

This blurring results in many new ethical dilemmas in media, as Valerie Alia's "Deadlines & Diversity: Journalism Ethics in a Changing World" documents. Editors have the growing burden, as well as the duty, to distinguish among the content types and make ethical decisions. (See Chapter 12 for a full discussion of ethics.)

Conclusion

Clearly, new technologies allow audiences to select their sources of news and information from vast and changing possibilities. Some researchers fear this may mean the public will screen out bad news because of feelings of discomfort within our communities, will skip stories on taxes or zoning because they seem dull or dense, and will take public-relations and advertising messages at face value as being free of intent or slanting—and, thus, will fail to distinguish between news and marketing, or will grow so cynical about media performance that they cease to care.

Some researchers also fear that the continuing conglomeration of media leads to marketing and promotion parading as news, such as when a newsmagazine makes a cover story about a film one of its subsidiaries is producing.

Editing that is critical, creative and committed to democratic principles is needed to respond to these fears. Here are a few things that will contribute to fearless editing:

- Research shows people are exercising their choices among media, and good content is what brings them back.
- Editing remains a conceptual process in all media and through recent changes.
- Editing improves story direction before writing, and clarity and meaning after the writing is done.
- The editing process means visualizing the best combination of words, images, typography and infographics.
- Editing draws from intellectual traditions in literature and art, and offers the possibility of professional growth.
- The underlying concepts—priority, beauty, clarity, unity, contrast and community—can be applied to various editing tasks and in all media; they can be specifically identified, discussed and learned, and they function as ideals that inspire ever better editing.

Exercises to Apply Concepts and Develop Skills _____

1. Goal: To use the criteria discussed in this chapter to analyze printed pages, apply the concepts and grow comfortable with the vocabulary.

    Ask students to bring in a publication or address of a Web site they strongly like—or dislike. Examine several, using criteria such as priority (Which items are most important, and how is this communicated?) and community (To whom does this publication appeal? Which items in this publication appeal to which age group or social group?).

    Discuss their feelings and preferences using the concepts covered in this chapter. For example, an opinion that a page is cluttered can be explored as absence of priority and followed by discussion of how priority could be shown. A page students find boring can be discussed in terms of appeal to a particular audience or need to increase contrast in the design.

2. Goal: To discern how editing incorporates news values.

    Take a newspaper feature section or a section of a popular magazine and discuss likely origins of stories. How many originated from publicity or public relations for companies or celebrities? Which stories show reporting or research by the publication's writers? Are articles surrounded by complementary advertisements?

3. Goal: To evaluate Web sources for origin and purpose.

Visit Web sites and try to decipher from what appears on the opening page (or on a page no more than two clicks away) who the organization is, what it does, what the purpose of the site is, what information it asks from users, what information is available and what the organization's policy is regarding privacy for users.

4. Goal: To understand editing processes within a variety of media.

Invite professional editors from different media to visit class and describe their typical day or week of work. Arrange for students to visit the site of a large editing operation, such as a local newspaper.

Helpful Sources

The importance of visuals and the strong draw of content are key ideas in research done by staff of the Poynter Institute, St. Petersburg, Fla. See especially:

Adam, Pegie Stark and Mario Garcia, Edited by Edward D. Miller. "Eyes on the News," Poynter Institute publications, 1991; this summarizes the 1990 Color Research Project.

"The Editor's Guide to Newspaper Design" in The American Editor. Vol. 75, No. 3, Issue 808 (April 2000). See articles by Pegie Stark Adam, Mario R. Garcia, Monica Moses and Ron Reason. This guide is published by The American Press Institute, Reston, Vir.

Garcia, Mario. "Contemporary Newspaper Design." 3rd Ed. Englewood, N.J.: Prentice Hall, Inc., 1993.

Media Management Center at Northwestern University, Reader Institute. "The Power to Grow Readership: Research from the Impact Study of Newspaper Readership." April 2001.

Moses, Monica. "Readers Consume What They See," Design 74, Society of Newspaper Design. Spring 2000, pp. 39–41.

Moses, Monica. "Why Usability Matters." Poynter Institute Web Site (Aug. 12, 2002) at http://www.poynter.org

Poynteronline. This site provided by the Poynter Institute is located at http://poynter.org/ and has reference resources and articles, as well as results of the Poynter/Stanford eyetrack study from 2000.

Media structure and economics:

Bagdikian, Ben H. "The Media Monopoly." 6th Ed. Boston: Beacon Press, 2000.

Biagi, Shirley. "Media/Impact: An Introduction to Mass Media." 6th Ed. Belmont, Calif.: Wadsworth Publishing Co., 2002.

McChesney, Robert W. "Rich Media, Poor Democracy: Communication in Dubious Times." Urbana, Ill.: University of Illinois Press, 1999.

Online journalism and media convergence:

Benedetti, Winda. "Put your money where your mouse is: Net surfers are getting the message: Pay up," Seattle Post-Intelligencer, August 13, 2002, pp. E1, E3.

Cannon, Carl L. "The Real Computer Virus," American Journalism Review. April 2001, pp. 28–35.

Colon, Aly. "Three Media, One Site—The Multimedia Newsroom: Three Organizations Aim for Convergence in Newly Designed Tampa Headquarters," Columbia Journalism Review. May/June 2000, pp. 25–27.

Fulton, Katherine. "The Changing Nature of 'News,'" Columbia Journalism Review. July/August 2000, pp. 30, 35.

Hargrove, Thomas and Guido H. Stempel III. "The 'Digital divide' is shrinking," Seattle Post-Intelligencer. August 13, 2002, p. E2.

Houston, Frank. "Enjoy the Ride While It Lasts," Columbia Journalism Review. July/August 2000, pp. 22–25.

Majeri, Tony. "New Horizons, New Products, New Technologies." Address to the ASNE Institute for Journalism Excellence Seminar at the American Press Institute, Reston, Va., June 14, 2000.

McNamara, Tracy. "The Blurry Line Between Commerce and Content," Columbia Journalism Review. July/August 2000, pp. 31, 35.

Nielsen, Jakob. "Alertbox." Columns on effective Web use at http://www.useit.com/alertbox/

Reavy, Matthew. "Introduction to Computer-Assisted Reporting: A Journalist's Guide." Mountain View, Calif: Mayfield Publishing Co., 2000.

Robertson, Lori. "The Romenesko Factor," American Journalism Review. September 2000, pp. 28–31.

Romenesko, Jim. MediaNews. See the site at http://www.poynter.org/medianews/

Trombly, Maria. "The New Journalist: A Jack (or Jane)-of-all-trades," Quill. March 2000, pp. 13–15. See also an accompanying article, "A New Media Curriculum," by Ralph Langer.

USC Annenberg Online Journalism Review. See this site at http://www.ojr.org

Profession and practice of public relations:

Baskin, Otis and Craig Aronoff. "Public Relations: The Profession and the Practice." Dubuque, Iowa: Wm. C. Brown, 1996.

Edelman, Richard, et al. "The Art of Public Relations." Boston: Aspatore Books, 2003.

Newsom, Doug, Alan Scott and Judy VanSlyke Turk. 7th Ed. "This is PR: The Realities of Public Relations." Belmont, Calif.: Wadsworth Publishing Co., 2000.

Newsom, Doug and Bob Carrell. "Experts in Action: Inside Public Relations." 2nd Ed. Belmont, Calif.: Wadsworth Publishing Co., 1989.

Seitel, Fraser P. "The Practice of Public Relations." 7th Ed. Upper Saddle River, N.J.: Prentice Hall, 1997.

Newsom, Doug and Bob Carrell. "Public Relations Writing: Form & Style." 6th Ed. Belmont, Calif: Wadsworth Publishing Co., 2000.

The impact of consumer culture on media and their role in democracy:

Boihem, Harold and Chris Emmanouilides, producers. Directed by H. Boihem. "The Ad and the Ego (videorecording): truth and consequences." San Francisco, Calif.: California Newsreel, 1996.

Chomsky, Noam, et al., eds. "Understanding Power." New York: New Press, 2002.

Ewen, Stuart. "PR!: A Social History of Spin." New York: Basic Books, 1996.

Ewen, Stuart and Elizabeth Ewen. 2nd Ed. "Channels of Desire: Mass Images and the Shaping of American Consciousness." Minneapolis, Minn.: University of Minnesota Press, 1992.

Ewen, Stuart. "All-Consuming Images: The Politics of Style in Contemporary Culture." New York: Basic Books, 1988.

Gerbner, George, et al., eds. "Invisible Crises: What Conglomerate Control of Media Means for America and the World." Boulder, Colo.: Westview Press, 1996.

Herman, Edward S. and Noam Chomsky. "Manufacturing Consent." New York: Pantheon Books, 2002.

Jhally, Sut, writer and editor. "Advertising and the End of the World" (videorecording). Northampton, Mass.: Media Education Foundation, 1998.

Jhally, Sut, producer and director. "The Crisis of the Cultural Environment: Media and Democracy in the 21st Century" (videorecording). Northampton, Mass: Media Education Foundation, 1997.

Jhally, Sut, producer and director. "The Electronic Storyteller: Television and the Cultivation of Values" (videorecording). Northampton, Mass.: Media Education Foundation, 1997.

Jhally, Sut. "The Codes of Advertising: Fetishism and the Political Economy of Meaning in the Consumer Society." New York: Routledge, 1990.

Korten, David. "When Corporations Rule the World." 2nd Ed. West Hartford, Conn.: Kumarian Press, 2001.

Meiklejohn, Alexander. "Political Freedom: the Constitutional Powers of the People." New York: Harper, 1960.

Meiklejohn, Alexander. "Free Speech and Its Relation to Self-Government." New York: Harper & Bros., 1948.

Schiller, Herbert. "Culture, Inc.: The Corporate Takeover of Public Expression." New York: Oxford University Press, 1991.

Ethics:

Ethical expectations are outlined in media organizations' internal codes, and in codes of the major professional societies. See especially codes of ethics for the Society of Professional Journalists, Public Relations Society of America and International Association of Business Communicators, which is developing an international code. Citations for Web versions of these can be found in Chapter 12.

Alia, Valerie, et al. "Deadlines & Diversity: Journalism Ethics in a Changing World." Halifax, Nova Scotia: Fernwood Publishing, 1996.

Black, Jay, et al. "Doing Ethics in Journalism: A Handbook with Case Studies." 3rd Ed. Boston: Allyn & Bacon, 1996.

Christians, Clifford G., et al. "Media Ethics: Cases & Moral Reasoning." 6th Ed. White Plains, N.Y.: Longman, 2000.

Steele, Bob. "Why Ethics Matter." Poynter Institute Web site (August 9, 2002) at http://www.poynter.org

2

Priority: Shaping Stories on the Page

A writer working on a story and a copy editor later looking at that story both become absorbed in its intrinsic qualities.

They will ask whether its beginning, or lead, is vibrant and presents the most important angle, whether the body of the story flows in an organized fashion, whether people appear distinctly through direct and indirect quotations, and whether the facts are attributed to sources.

After the copy editors' fine-tuning and double-checking, they typically will write a headline to fit a size and line-length that another editor has ordered. This editor has been working on the overall page, section, newsletter or World Wide Web site and has been making a different level of decisions. She has been weighing the importance of stories relative to each other and deciding which will receive the most prominent play.

She also has been deciding how best to tell each part of a story by sorting through the text and its related components: stories, photos, graphics, illustrations, and, perhaps, audio and video clips.

The decisions to be made are these:

- What will run? Which are most important among the stories that will run? Which are the most compelling and relevant photos? The editor will choose the facts and information that best serve the audience. This also means excluding some potential stories and cutting or trimming others to fit the space available.
- What could run but is not ready yet? The editor will critically evaluate stories for accuracy and completeness.
- What is the best story mix? The editor will look at both news stories, which cover breaking events, and features, which emphasize human nature, show how people cope with trends, and aim to entertain. She will clarify the stories' shapes and organization.

- Which parts of the story can be told well visually, through photos, illustrations or graphics? She will sort through photographs and sketches for illustrations, and may ask for new graphics to be created.
- How much of the secondary material is there room for? The editor forms packages of stories, photos, headings and graphic items into modular or rectangular shapes but knows that the publication's overall design limits the number of modules on each page. A sense of priority helps her to decide to use the strongest pieces and to set the others aside.

Editors working at both levels—that of the individual story and that of the page, package or site—are applying the concept of priority. They ask what is most important and most meaningful to their readers or viewers and then ask how they can best express that importance visually.

Editors show the importance of items by:

- The length of a story, as an expression of the amount of space or time it merits;
- The size of its heading and the placement of that heading. Newspapers and newsletters generally place the most important item at the top left; World Wide Web pages place it high on a list and may include a summary and photo or video clip; a magazine may make it a cover illustration or mention it in a cover line.
- The complexity of an overall package. The number of photographs or illustrations included, graphics or text treatments such as boxes, time lines, Q&A, sidebars, or the number of links from a Web page to related topics all indicate that a story is multifaceted and has a significant impact on other, associated stories or events.

Copy Editors' Expanding Role

The copy editor who understands where his edited story and headline will be placed can picture its role in the overall scheme. This is increasingly important as copy editors produce additional pieces of the package. Copy editors write captions for photographs and explainers for graphics; they write break-out boxes that encapsulate key statements; they write the smaller headings that run under a title and tie the components of a package together. These elements are further discussed in Chapter 6.

Sometimes, they have had a role in planning all of these elements and are familiar with what the photographer or illustrator will be providing. But in breaking-news situations, they will quickly make decisions with material they have seen only for a matter of minutes.

Some news media and public relations organizations use teams to plan the newsgathering, writing, photography and illustrations at the same time, a concept the Poynter Institute in St. Petersburg, Fla., has developed under the acronym

WED, for writing, editing and design. Teamwork also arises in Internet news, where editors working with words collaborate with editors of visual and interactive components. For major packages, planning may start weeks ahead.

Regardless of the flow of news events, staff organization and mix of media to draw upon, an editor begins his day's work with one image in mind: the page that must be filled. He sees a rectangular space that can hold only so many smaller rectangular shapes, or modules.

Modular Design

Design is called modular when the units are shaped like squares or rectangles and fit together like wooden blocks within the frame of a child's puzzle.

This look has been around in American culture for nearly 200 years. Some of the earliest use of modular design was in Amish quilts, whose rectangles of vivid hues divide space into compelling patterns of horizontals and verticals, with emphases placed through varying deeper and lighter shades.

Americans live in a culture that reads left to right and top to bottom. This makes the top left portion of any page the spot where readers expect to begin. And, they expect to find the most important news items placed there.

When thinking about a modular layout, an editor will imagine placing dominant elements. These are the darkest areas of a page; it is easy to ascertain which elements are dominant by squinting at a finished page and letting the grayest, lightest, areas fade.

Dominant elements are photos, art and headings. They are the shapes we see when gazing at a newsstand's offerings from across the street.

A second consideration is how many modules will appear on the page. The front page of a broadsheet-size newspaper typically carries half a dozen major packages; the front page of a Web site may list summaries, headings or icons for three times as many, though they will be grouped into predictable, recurring rectangular areas of the screen. A newsletter on letter-size paper may have only two or three stories. Magazines devote an entire page or several pages to a major story before following with the next one. (See Illustration 2.1.)

The publication's overall design sets a model or even a formula that the editor follows for individual pages. This provides consistency and unity throughout a publication and allows the most important elements to be clearly identifiable.

The editor selects the top items; to do this well, he must know the audience and what these readers expect of the publication or the site.

Story Mix: News and Features

An editor tries for a mix of stories and photos on the front page that will appeal to the largest number of readers. Editors understand, though, that not all audience

Basic modules

Vertical rectangles require headings smaller in size, but with several lines stacked up in the narrow space.

Horizontal rectangles use a line or two of larger type running across the top of the module. Though these are basic modules, much variation is possible.

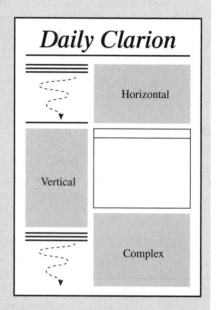

Daily Clarion

Horizontal

Vertical

Complex

Large Headline

A complex module

Before editors think about doing a final proofread of a story, they may have to make cuts or trims, or even divide out part of a story to become a sidebar. The graphic design of a package affects editors' work a great deal. To produce the complex module below, an editor had to write three headings, a caption for the photo and find an interesting item to run as a breakout—and then proofread copy.

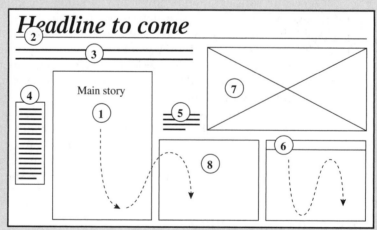

Headline to come

An editor's tasks:

1. story trimming
2. main heading
3. deck heading
4. breakout
5. photo caption
6. sidebar heading
7. photo sizing
8. final copy edit

Main story

ILLUSTRATION 2.1 *Modular Design.* Stories are packaged with their headings, photos and other related elements into rectangular or square shapes.

members will read or even be interested in each story. Chances are greater of pulling in more readers the more variety is shown. An editor of a public relations newsletter, for example, may intend that each of the several items on the front page will appeal to a different group among her readers.

Editors begin picturing this mix along several dimensions: local news versus national or international; breaking news versus features; general-interest versus special-interest areas such as sports, food or business. Magazine editors consider also the mix of voices and styles of their contributors and columnists.

Values within News Stories

Having narrowed the field to the most important items among the different categories of stories, the editor will ask which is the strongest story, and which is the best piece of art; in other words, which deserve placement in the top left quarter of the page. For a magazine, the placement involves questions of what will be on the cover and in the centerfold.

Editors of pages use the same news values that writers use in their reporting and that copy editors use when reworking a story. These values are consistently:

- consequence: the impact of events on readers' lives;
- prominence: the involvement of well-known people;
- proximity: events that have happened nearby;
- timeliness: events that are the most recent, or new;
- unusualness: events well out of the ordinary.

While these news values are common to newspapers, Web pages and time-oriented public relations writing, magazines and feature sections in newspapers and newsletters specialize in material showing other values.

The shift to a more relaxed, entertaining style of writing and subject matter is signaled by directing the eye more toward the middle of a features page, rather than to the top left. As Mario Garcia and other designers have explored, the eye may even make a circular motion, beginning with a very large photograph or illustration placed toward the middle of the page, then moving to either side for display-size typography, and then around to smaller items placed along the sides and in lower corners.

Values within Feature Stories

Feature stories are evaluated for their ability to show the following:

- human interest: how events play out in or affect people's lives; or, profiles that show the personal sides of newsmakers;
- trends: changes in lifestyles, generations or the way we live;

- entertainment: writing and subject matter that offer enjoyment and deal with the varied pleasures in life;
- analysis: the significance behind a series of related events, or how-to pieces on coping;
- voice, or the viewpoint and style that an author brings to a piece;
- narrative flow and engaging storytelling.

The fact that these patterns and values are not true for all cultures means that designers of magazines or Web pages intended for international markets need also to consider reading patterns and social values in their target cultures and whether the page will have an American visual identity.

Copy Editing and Visual Components

Editors laying out a page try to make it more lively by providing contrasts in shapes and sizes. They often will begin by sketching small "thumbnail" drawings of the page to work out ideas, and then "dummy" the page on electronic software.

After placing the most-dominant elements, editors place the lesser elements in the lower left and right of a page or screen, providing large enough headings and placing graphics to continue moving the reader's eye and to create a sense of balance and completion.

The stories, art, typography and white space are placed to form rectangular shapes, or modules. To create dynamism, the editor will vary the modules by making some strongly horizontal and others narrow and vertical.

The interplay of horizontal and vertical is so commonly understood that a photographer assigned to illustrate a story that is already written will ask the editor, "Do you want a horizontal or a vertical?" and will frame her shots to suit the photo's ultimate shape on the page. Artists will ask this as well when editors approach them for an illustration or graphic.

The copy editor can tell whether she is working on a horizontal or vertical package by the nature of the heading ordered. If it is for a large type size and will flow across a number of columns, she pictures the result as a horizontal package. Conversely, if the heading is narrow and to be written in several lines of small type, it is for a vertical.

In addition, as she writes photo captions, lines of subheads, explainers for graphics and a summary for a break-out box, she can picture the reader's eye moving from one element to the next. Awareness of the visual properties of her work allows her to order information logically. If the reader's eye moves from the heading to the caption and then to subheading and break-out, she knows each element must present a vital angle of the story and that the angles must pull together into a cohesive whole with the main text.

Though it may seem that horizontal headings are so large and dark they always are the most dominant, vertically shaped headings gain weightiness through adding to the number of lines. Both shapes will be points of emphasis. (See Illustration 2.2.)

News story

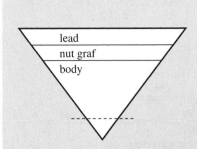

News stories are written in the shape of an inverted pyramid, with the most important information in the lead. Next comes the "nut graf," which carries context, and then the body of the story, which typically carries facts in descending order of importance.

The ending tapers off, which is an aid to editors; when they need to make a trim quickly, they can cut from the bottom without fear of losing essential facts.

Broadsheet news page

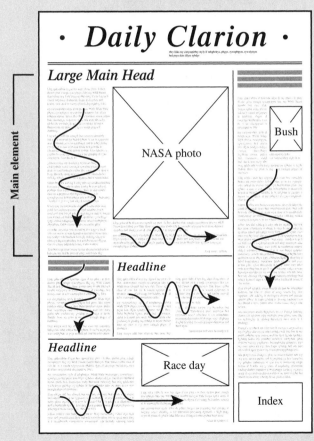

A news page draws the eye to the most important story, signaled by the largest headline and photo. The main story is placed at the top left or right, with stories of lesser importance lower on the page.

The reader gains a sense of the page being ordered, as the headlines and photos are run in smaller sizes lower on the page.

ILLUSTRATION 2.2 *Showing Priority.* Priority is expressed in news and feature stories through their organization, and on pages through their layout.

(continued)

Feature story

Feature stories are organized thematically. They often begin with an opening scene or anecdote followed by a paragraph or two of context. If the story needs to be shortened, editors will trim a subtheme and preserve the ending because it usually presents a scene or anecdote that refers to the opening and provides a sense of completion.

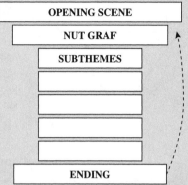

| OPENING SCENE |
| NUT GRAF |
| SUBTHEMES |

| ENDING |

Food

Sushi

Hand rolling

Main element

Circular reading pattern

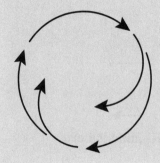

Feature pages aim for a sense of relaxation or enjoyment. They draw the eye to artwork placed very large and often positioned toward the center of the page. White space surrounds images and type that are larger than on news pages.

The eye may move in more of a circular pattern from the main element to lesser elements arranged around it. Readers feel they are invited to choose their topics and pace.

ILLUSTRATION 2.2   *Continued*

Expressing News Values through Editing

Just as a writer will think carefully about the audience and choose items for the lead that most affect and draw in readers, so an editor thinks about impact on audience in checking the leads of stories.

Balance and fairness are other professional values in journalism that help editors make decisions. Editors check that stories represent varieties of viewpoints. They also may show which viewpoints are supported by objective facts or other means of substantiation such as peer reviews, artistic reviews and endorsements by known organizations.

Editors evaluate more diverse material than most writers do because they prepare for publication a range of columns, letters to the editor, artistic reviews, analyses of events, and news items from far away.

An editor who reads widely or is well versed in another culture or in a certain discipline will be better able to make distinctions and to recognize, against the backdrop of common knowledge in that field or foreign country, what truly is news of priority.

The editor will also be reflecting the voice of the publication or protecting the voice of the writer, labeling pieces that are primarily opinion or comment to distinguish them from news, and looking at whether a source's commercial or financial interests in a publicity release throw the legitimacy of the news released into question.

It may be difficult for news editors to remain independent or uninfluenced by the climates in which they work, though they fiercely defend their independence and integrity. Within corporate culture, a news corporation that routinely grants "best of" awards within its chain demonstrates what kinds of topics are most suitable; a magazine that runs cover stories about movies or music produced by its corporate affiliates may be making news judgments reflecting its own realm of interests.

Editors exercising their own judgment will create pages that look different and set different priorities and emphases than each other's. Little reason exists that finished pages should be identical or even similar, especially if they are truly reflecting their own unique communities. Sameness is not the same as equality.

But, the reasons for news decisions are crucial: They are based on articulated news or features values, they place the audience's needs foremost, they draw on background knowledge, they offer balance, fairness and substantiation, and they avoid being skewed by motivations for commercial gain that draw on different sets of values.

Critical Evaluation of Information

Part of any editor's job includes the task of critically evaluating the information to be presented. Editors are the last line of defense against errors in fact and missing information that readers would logically expect to be included.

Two questions guide this evaluation:

- How accurate is the information presented?
- Is enough information presented?

Adding and correcting vital information will often alter what appears as the lead of the news story and may affect the story's overall shape and length.

One important job is to check facts that the writer may have gotten wrong. At some publications, this task is a job in itself, with editors (called, not surprisingly, fact checkers) telephoning or e-mailing sources of information cited, checking the validity of assertions and statistics, and even verifying the accuracy and spellings of cities, rivers, South Pacific islands, people and software. Is it *PhotoShop* or *Photoshop*? Is it *Sammish* or *Sammamish*? Is it *Bush* or *Busch*?

Sometimes these tasks fall on the shoulders of one editor producing a Web page or brochure or company newsletter. In this case, the editor must check as many facts as possible in the amount of time allowed—which means prioritizing which facts get checked. It is here that editing sense and judgment come into play.

The wise editor will use her years of experience as an information gatherer and processor to alert her to major areas that may need verification. She may see that a list of taxes and their percentages of the total do not add up to 100 percent.

She may be suspicious of a quote endorsing wilderness preservation from a senator who has a long history of fighting against environmental causes.

She may check to see if *Phoenix, Ore.*, really exists. And, hopefully, she will not blithely change *dearth* to *death* simply because the spelling checker didn't recognize the word.

Spotting Holes in Stories

The second job also is easier for the editor with life experience in gathering and processing information. She needs to be able to read a story and see the holes.

Holes are holes. They are like missing pieces of a 1,000-piece picture puzzle. The editor reading the story continually asks herself what a reader would expect in this story or set of facts. Anything missing constitutes a hole, which the editor should ask the writer to fill or should decide to add herself if time permits.

It may be as simple as providing the previous salary of a CEO in a story saying she got a 30 percent raise but failing to say what that previous salary was. Or, it may be the lack of a reason why a computer chip company is relocating its plant to Mexico from the local community.

Major changes can happen when stories distributed nationally by wire services have a local impact. For example, the story about a man arrested in connection with a mass murder in Los Angeles was a national story, given top play on most news outlets. The next day, as his background emerged, the story took different shape in the towns where he had lived and gone to school or worked.

A story written by a young reporter about a city council banning cigarette and cigar smoking from city hall yet allowing pipe smoking got a new, rewritten lead after the editor ascertained that the mayor and several council members were pipe smokers, something the reporter hadn't thought to ask.

Regarding these tasks, the lackadaisical editor fears the additional work—or perhaps just ignores its importance—and lets the information go out unchallenged and unaugmented.

The fearless editor takes pride in knowing she has improved the knowledge the reader will gain as well as the clarity, coherence and meaning of the piece.

This tenacity can also develop into a sense of play, of it being fun to make the catch that corrects a casual misuse or unnoticed error. Does it make a difference whether builders were shoring up a foundation by adding cement or adding concrete? To the builder or owner, it certainly does because they know *cement* is the powder that is just one ingredient of *concrete,* the hard surface we in-line skate on. An editor who makes the distinction and protects the integrity of the piece and the publication feels just as much satisfaction as in finding just the right piece for that jigsaw puzzle.

Editing Leads and Story Shapes

The first few lines of a tightly edited story will show its nature—whether it is news or feature—what the story will explore and how it will be told.

Feature leads and news leads offer different content because the shapes and natures of the stories are different.

Writers work from the beginning with one of these shapes in mind and will refer to it when talking with the editor. If it is a news story, it is usually written in the inverted-pyramid form.

The inverted pyramid, with its breathless lead summarizing the most important facts, is an American cultural norm. Readers have come to expect it, to be able to tell in the first paragraph or two what a story is about. It orders facts according to how important they are and has no real conclusion because it ends by winnowing facts down to those of lesser and lesser importance.

A feature story, on the other hand, is likely to have a beginning, middle and ending. Writers often choose to begin by setting a scene or writing an anecdote that shows characters dealing with the theme. Writers show how the story will be told by expressing a tone, which may be humorous or solemn or satirical; they also may play a role in the story and include their own voice.

Subthemes are introduced in the body of a feature story, and it concludes with another scene or anecdote to give a sense of completion. (See Box 2.1)

BOX 2.1 • *Editing Story Shapes*

News Stories

Lead: The editor makes certain the story beginning shows the timeliness of an event and tells what makes this event or issue different from any others like it.

These first few lines also describe the impact, what people often think of as the conclusion of a story. Greater weight is given to events that happen nearby, that involve prominent people or that affect many members of a community. Sometimes, news is simply the uniqueness or bizarreness of an event, thus reflecting the unlikelihood it will happen again.

If these elements do not appear at the beginning, the editor must locate them wherever they occur in the story and move them up, or ask the writer to do a rewrite.

Story shape: The inverted pyramid, emphasizing the weightiest material with the widest interest and narrowing until it stands on its point, is the basic shape used for news.

In between, information is ordered from most important to least important, thus allowing an editor to be able to slice off the last lines of a story without harming the meaning of what has come before.

This story form was adopted during the U.S. Civil War when reporters had access to telegraph wires to transmit stories but could be interrupted at any time by military uses.

The inverted pyramid cuts writing off from its roots of beginning-middle-end narrative storytelling, but a major variation allowed in news structure is to revert to a narrative after the lead has established the important story elements.

Endings: News stories usually don't build to endings or conclusions but instead dribble down to the facts with lesser importance to the majority of readers. Both writers and editors expect that many readers will have quit by this point.

But, for those truly interested in the subject, the lower reaches of the story provide details that answer all questions raised earlier, flesh out explanations and build fuller understanding.

Voice: Because the press of events and time transcend the storytelling, news stories usually have an institutional voice. That is, they are edited to have a structure and style commonly used by that publication. The reader knows how sober or flashy, or abstract or sensationalized, how brief or in-depth a treatment will be based on the overall personality of that publication. Preserving institutional voice is a goal in editing news.

Reader interest: The inverted pyramid retained its value through the era of hot-type production, in which stories often had to be sliced to fit, literally, inside a metal frame. It retained it through the early stages of computerized typesetting and page design when software and printing methods had not yet developed easy text links and page flows.

Story lengths can flow more freely now, with online media having virtually no limitations on space, and newspapers planning packages ahead of time to provide the space needed to tell a story, rather than the other way around. One can question whether a story form so dictated by technological developments will keep its dominance, or whether further technological change will outmode it.

Feature Stories

Lead: A feature story has the drive, meaning and research of a news story but is organized around a theme that reflects how we are living in society at this time.

Features entertain, too, and a strong element of fun can be a plus. But, if a story is merely fluff, or insipid or pointless, it probably does not merit publication. The lead often introduces people who are engaged with this theme and begins storytelling by presenting their dilemma.

So, the beginning of a feature story needs to do three things: establish the trend or theme, show the people involved and let the writer's style be heard.

Story shape: Feature stories evolve their own shapes through stringing together anecdotes or episodes that explore aspects of the main theme.

Sometimes these episodes build to a major scene of resolution, particularly if the story follows one main character. If the story is a profile, the writer must make clear whether this person is unique, or typical, and, therefore, through how many different eyes the story will be told.

The editor might visualize a feature as a rectangular box at the beginning and one at the end, with its own shape in between. Author John McPhee has said that his stories take concrete shapes as he writes them—a string of beads, a letter of the alphabet—but it is always narrative storytelling.

Endings: Feature stories build to a punch, or conclusion. They have great last lines; in fact, writers often save their second-best anecdote or scene for the ending. Editors do not routinely trim off the endings; if they must cut, they usually pare a less-important subtheme earlier in the story.

Voice: Feature stories, especially for magazines, are noticeably more personal in tone than articles written for the institutional voice of a newspaper. A story mix can consider the range of tone, or emotional flavor of the articles, as well as various voices brought by writers. Voice is conveyed by the way the writer chooses to talk to the reader; it might be confiding or arch, literary or streetwise, quietly observant or boisterously involved. Readers of magazines often choose to go right to a favorite writer's contribution, just for the pleasure of seeing his or her "take" on events.

Reader interest: Narrative stories, reviews, entertainment, humor, and analysis of events all provide readers with a sense of direction, of a way to approach life's myriad happenings and incorporate them into a scheme or picture that makes sense and integrates emotions with thought. Many researchers of the changing media landscape argue that providing the voices of intelligent guides as storytellers will be an increasingly important editing responsibility.

Once a story is complete and accurate and the editor can say what it is about in just a sentence or two, she can confidently smooth the story's final shape. Editors need to be confident about which story form they are editing and then making that clear to the reader. Variations on these basic story forms are recognizable to readers and can provide a pleasant change of pace.

Information in a Democracy

Why should editors care about the information they deal with? The answer lies in life and in democracy.

Humans are curious creatures who may be lucky enough to survive 100 years. In spite of that short time, with its illnesses and heartbreaks and periods of dependency and semi-senility, somehow they have managed to create civilizations complete with elaborate rituals, great works of literature, and knowledge of people and the rights and liberties they can hope for.

These civilizations grow more complex with each passing generation, but the ceremony, beauty and growth do not happen without information being passed on from generation to generation.

Especially in a democracy, where facts and news are the essence of how civilization goes forward, information placed in a coherent structure creates knowledge. And, as First Amendment philosopher Alexander Meiklejohn asserted, citizens must be knowledgeable so that they may vote on the issues affecting them.

Thus, editors of any print publication or Web site page play an important role in society by testing information for its validity and usefulness and then communicating its meaning in their presentations to readers.

Conclusion

Meaning is expressed through editing that assigns priority to some of the written and visual elements. Priority is shown graphically by varying headline sizes, by placing the largest or most dominant items, by editing stories for clear shapes, strong leads and full information, and by writing and placing smaller typographical elements in a meaningful way.

Using the principles of priority and contrast, and then editing to achieve balance between the two, editors can be guided by material in this chapter to achieve these goals:

- choose dominant elements for a page;
- edit stories for completeness and accuracy;
- establish what their leads should be;
- streamline stories into news or feature shapes;

- arrange dominant elements in a modular pattern;
- visualize the shapes of headings and other text elements as components of vertical and horizontal packages.

Showing priority on a page is the result of thinking about the readers' needs and making firm decisions about what is most important, complete, valuable and valid. Chaotic or humdrum designs and stories often disclose the failure to make such decisions.

Showing priority is necessary for compelling pages. The reader deduces immediately which stories are the most important because of the clarity of the presentation. The elements are organized into shapes and the shapes vary to provide contrast.

The editor planning the page and the copy editor preparing the individual elements can picture how the headings, text and illustrations function as key visual elements as well as verbal ones.

The concept of priority forms a link between the work with words editors do and the visual presentations they draw on to express the relative importance of the stories they have chosen. Priority is expressed not just through layout, but also through sizing and shaping headings and planning and writing the smaller typographical elements on a page, which explore key angles and cohere to each other and to the main story.

An editor or copy editor who is working with a visual map of how—and why—these will work together on a page in a certain way is editing literally with the bigger picture in mind.

Exercises to Apply Concepts and Develop Skills

1. Goal: To understand page design and placing of headings, stories and images.

Preparation: The instructor needs to have electronic templates or paper layout sheets ("dummies") ready ahead of time. These may be of any size (for broadsheet-, letter-paper-, tabloid- or monitor-screen-size pages), and they need to have print areas and inch or centimeter intervals defined. It is easiest to have a beginning class work on only one size at a time and to start with the largest useful page.

a) Recreating the layout of an existing page. Ask students to find a printed page they like and enjoy looking at and bring it to class. (Limit them to page sizes and shapes for which electronic templates or dummies are available.) Ask them to recreate that page on the template or dummy by showing the size of the headings, the overall shape and size of photos, the columns of text, and by allowing room for smaller items such as captions and break-out boxes. This exercise imparts a sense of how large photos, headings and text boxes need to be proportionate to page size and how very small they will look on an electronic template or layout page.

b) Laying out a new page. Give students a selection of stories and photographs, and ask them to arrange them by priority. Ask them to draw modules by using a template in an electronic editing program or a layout sheet for a print page. Finally, ask them to arrange their news items on the page by first deciding what the most important story is and then deciding what the best photo or illustration is so that these might be displayed prominently. Have them indicate sizes of headings, shapes of text columns, sizes and shapes of photos or illustrations, and small items such as captions, subheads and break-out boxes. Students will make news judgments of stories relative to each other and attempt to communicate their priorities visually.

2. Goal: To identify and analyze modules and the placement of dominant elements on a page.

    Post printed pages in the classroom or lab; broadsheet newspaper pages and newsletters work well. Ask students to use colored pens to outline the modules. Discuss their different shapes, orientations and content. Compare news to features pages for where the most dominant module appears. Ask them to squint at pages until the gray drops out and to name the dominant elements that appear on the page.

3. Goal: To discern the difference between news and feature stories and analyze story shapes, variations and possible problems.

    Ask students to run through typical newspaper, newsmagazine and newsletter pages and identify both news and feature stories. Then ask them to identify the major parts of each story; if some don't follow a format, ask what happened. Is it a successful exception? Does it bridge both forms, such as a news-feature or an analysis, or does it need more editing to overcome a problem such as a buried lead? This places editing decisions within a context of story forms, purpose and shapes.

4. Goal: To find holes in stories.

    Select several stories in the campus or student newspaper and ask students to list questions they have that weren't answered. Try this also with a taped radio or television news broadcast and with press releases and news summaries in on-line media. This provides practice in spotting holes in stories and in editing for completeness.

5. Goal: To understand the impact of errors, the loss of credibility and harm that errors bring, and the necessity for accuracy.

    Nothing brings the need for accuracy and completeness home to students as much as personal stories from classmates. Virtually everyone has a story about someone they know whose livelihood or reputation was threatened by an inaccuracy making it into broadcast or print; ask a few students to share these stories and then discuss whether editing could have caught and corrected any problems they find.

6. Goal: To find ways to correct errors when they happen.

    Examine corrections boxes in print publications and discuss the kinds of items mentioned. Examine news sites on the Web for any regular appearance of corrections, and discuss whether online media need to have such a practice and how it might be handled.

Helpful Sources

Design and eye movement:
Studies showing how readers skim publications and skip many stories can be found at the Poynter Institute Web site, which lists results of the Poynter/Stanford Eyetrack Study 2000: http://www.poynter.org

Also, see Jakob Nielsen's "How Users Read on the Web," October 1, 1997. http://www.useit.com/alertbox/9710a.html and Sun Microsystems, "Difference Between Paper and Online Presentation," 1994–2002. http://www.sun.com/980713/webwriting/wftw1.html

For design directing eye movement, see Garcia, Mario. "Contemporary Newspaper Design." 3rd Ed. Englewood, N.J.: Prentice Hall, Inc., 1993.

Discussion of Amish quilt design in American art history appears in Hughes, Robert. "American Visions: The Epic History of American Art." New York: Alfred A. Knopf, 1997.

Journalistic values:

Studies have examined social-status systems in newsrooms, values used by media "gate-keepers" as they decide what to print; impact of corporate and chain structures and finance; news values based on conflict becoming altered by inclusion of more women in media; "public journalism" and the role of media in creating community and consensus; and media agenda-setting by public relations pressures and by practices of alternative and elite media.

For an overview of research in many of these areas, see Severin, Werner J. and James W. Tankard. "Communication Theories." 5th Ed. New York: Longman, 2001.

The fundamental importance of accuracy in building and maintaining reader trust is described in "Building Reader Trust: examining our credibility," April 2000, published by the American Society of Newspaper Editors Foundation, Reston, Vir.

Evolution and change in news values:

For discussion of gender and changing news values:

"Media Report to Women: Covering all the Issues Concerning Women and Media," published quarterly by Communication Research Associates, Inc., Colton's Point, Maryland. The report is edited by Sheila J. Gibbons.

Allen, Donna, "Women News: Half the population isn't adequately served by traditional media," Quill. May 1991, pp. 36–37.

Beasley, Maurine H. and Sheila J. Gibbons, eds. "Taking their Place: A Documentary History of Women and Journalism." Washington, D.C.: American University Press, 1993.

Biagi, Shirley and Marilyn Kern-Foxworth. "Facing Difference: Race, Gender and Mass Media." Thousand Oaks, Calif.: Pine Forge Press, 1997.

Covert, Catherine, "Journalism History and Women's Experience: A Problem in Conceptual Change," Journalism History. Vol. 8 (1981): 2–5.

Creedon, Pamela J., ed. "Women in Mass Communication." Thousand Oaks, Calif.: Sage Publications, 1993.

Lont, Cynthia. "Women and Media: Content, Careers, Criticism." Belmont, Calif.: Wadsworth Publishing Co., 1995.

Rakow, Lana, ed. "Women Making Meaning." New York: Routledge, 1992.

Ross, Karen, "Women, Politics, Media: Uneasy Relations in Comparative Perspective." Cresskill, N.J.: Hampton Press, 2002.

Wood, Julia T. "Gendered Lives: Communication, Gender, and Culture." 5th Ed. Belmont, Calif.: Wadsworth Publishing Co., 2003.

For discussion of traditional news values in mass media:

Croteau, David and William Hoynes. "Media/Society." 2nd Ed. Thousand Oaks, Calif.: Pine Forge Press, 2000.

Gans, Herbert J. "Deciding What's News; A Study of CBS Evening News, NBC Nightly News." New York: Vintage Books, 1989.

Herman, Edward S. and Noam Chomsky. "Manufacturing Consent." New York: Pantheon Books, 2002.

Parenti, Michael. "Inventing Reality: The Politics of News Media." 2nd Ed. New York: St. Martin's, 1993.

Schiller, Herbert. "Culture, Inc.: The Corporate Takeover of Public Expression." New York: Oxford University Press, 1991.

Schudson, Michael. "Discovering the News." New York: Basic Books, 1981.

Schudson, Michael. "The Sociology of News." New York: W. W. Norton and Co., 2002.

Tuchman, Gaye. "Making News: A Study in the Construction of Reality." New York: Free Press, 1980.

Writing news stories:

Brooks, Brian S. and George Kennedy. "News Reporting and Writing." 7th Ed. Boston/New York: Bedford/St. Martin's, 2001.

Bunton, Kristie, et al. "Writing across the Media." Boston/New York: Bedford/St. Martin's, 1999.

Mencher, Melvin. "News Reporting and Writing." 8th Ed. Boston: McGraw Hill, 2000.

Rich, Carole. "Writing and Reporting News: A Coaching Method." 4th Ed. Belmont, Calif.: Wadsworth Publishing Co., 2002.

Writing feature stories:

Berner, R. Thomas, ed. "The Literature of Journalism: Text and Context." State College, Penn.: Strata Publishing, Inc., 1999.

Friedlander, Edward J. and John Lee. "Feature Writing for Newspapers and Magazines: The Pursuit of Excellence." 4th Ed. New York: Addison Wesley Longman, 2000.

Hay, Vicky. "The Essential Feature: Writing for Magazines and Newspapers." New York: Columbia University Press, 1990.

Jacobi, Peter J. "The Magazine Article: How to think it, plan it, write it." Bloomington, Ind.: Indiana University Press, 1997.

Klement, Alice M. and Carolyn B. Matalene. "Telling Stories Taking Risks: Journalism Writing at the Century's Edge." Belmont., Calif: Wadsworth Publishing Co., 1997.

The Missouri Group. "Beyond the Inverted Pyramid." 2nd Ed. New York: Bedford/St. Martin's, 2004.

3

Clarity: The Poetic Heading

Perhaps most important to readers in an age when media choices and information wash over them like L.A. smog are headings (often called **headlines** and **titles**) that have poetic qualities adding conciseness and beauty to the page and, thus, attracting readers to important information being announced.

Although mediocre headings are plentiful and all too often the norm, poetic headings can be spotted and are the single best way to attract and keep readers and, in the process, elevate editors with the special ability of writing them to a higher level of fearlessness.

What is the "poetry" of headings?

Poetry is sometimes captured in words like "cadence" or "flow" and refers to carefully chosen words being arranged tightly, with particular attention to line endings so that the heading serves as an undeniable connection between the reader and the information being announced.

A heading is poetic only if the reader was attracted to it, understood it without having to reread it and did not have to wade through unnecessary words.

Poetic headings are similar to a trailer effectively convincing movie-goers to see an upcoming film. Depending on the information they announce, poetic headings are written with flair and perhaps eloquence, wit or humor. Poetic headings make the reader eagerly dive into the accompanying text.

What is definitely not heading poetry—and, thus, usually a vomited pool of words that confuses, frustrates, annoys, angers or repulses readers?

1. Bad puns, overused phrases or inane plays on words. Too many of these can be found in American newspapers, usually in the sports section, both in print and online. "Hawks claw Broncos" or "Jazz played out as Rockets blast off" or "Bears rip Patriots" begin a list that could stretch to Neptune and back.

2. Overdone alliteration and assonance (literary devices using repetition of vowels or consonants) or blatant, excessive rhyme. "Angels adrift after awful August" or "Confident Clinton calls Chelsea 'cool California coed' " or "Hopes for new train in Maine almost down drain" overdo the devices.

3. Tasteless and potentially offensive material. "Helen Keller Society turns deaf ear on request from hearing-impaired 10-year-old" will receive anger, not praise, from many readers, as will "AIDS sufferers have gay old time at picnic."

Using Literary Devices

It is true editors writing poetic headings may use an occasional pun or cliché or witty phrase and may even call on traditional literary devices, but such devices are used with restraint and only when appropriate.

Here are a few that work:

When you're out of slits, you're out of leer
    (feature about skirt fashions)

Sin is in
    (article exploring the human tendency to err)

A grave undertaking
    (profile on a funeral director)

Rafting with God
    (feature about river trips by Christian youth groups)

Carnival knowledge
    (profile of carnival worker)

Bare intentions
    (profile on striptease artist)

Zen: Buddhism brings worshippers to their knees
    (feature on religion)

The other 'F' word
    (article about feminism)

Staring HIV in the face
    (article about AIDS)

Shapes of Headings

Just as leads express the main points of stories, so do headings; they also indicate the important points on a page. The styles for headings vary among media, but they are important clues to the reader about how to interact with the page:

- They show what the editor believes is most important;
- Their consistent style helps to unify the page;

- They entertain and inform, just as stories do;
- They provide optional places to start—and stop—reading;
- They combine with layers of secondary headings to bridge into stories;
- They indicate how to link to stories on related subjects.

Writers usually do not write headings for their stories though they may suggest them. An editor has more distance from the subject and may be better at summarizing or finding key points than a writer who has become engrossed in pinning down details. The editor also may be changing the shape or length of the story or reworking it for a different medium, which may change the elements to be emphasized.

Magazine-Style Headings

Decades ago, editing texts focused primarily on newspaper editing. Usually they emphasized headline objectives, such as being able to attract attention, put the news into a hierarchy, sell the information, tell the facts and make the page attractive. Headings still perform these functions—plus they impart the tone of the story.

In magazines, this sense of tone is even more important because articles show more of the voice and style of their writers, not so much the institutional voice present in newspapers.

Magazine titles respond to trends and often play on themes current in popular culture. Recently popular are magazine titles that begin with a brief phrase set in large type and followed by a more explanatory subheading. Frequently these are plays on common phrases, or puns that involve song, book or movie titles or popular aphorisms.

For example, "Phreaking havoc: Hacker dabbles in data raping" was used as the heading for a story profiling an Internet marauder. The movie "Sleepless in Seattle" prompted "Jobless in Seattle," a heading for a magazine feature about being unemployed and making ends meet. "Unnecessary roughness" played on a phrase fans of football know about excessive force in the sport for the heading of a feature on male sports stars who battered their wives.

Web Page Headings

Online journalism editors need a special kind of restraint in their eagerness to attract readers to their Web content floating like one tiny bubble in a spa filled with bubble bath.

Headings on Web pages have similarities to both newspapers and magazines, but they often have to be informational to help readers find what they are seeking. They often can run longer than newspaper or magazine headings because a smaller typeface is used to fill a horizontal space. They may not remain just as they were created, however, because a viewer's browser may substitute a different font and display the size and overall shape differently.

Web editors need to remember that their sites may have worldwide readers, so a culture-bound heading, or one that assumes knowledge of recent local events, may not be appropriate.

For example, the editor of a site with readers in several countries should not use a heading, "Four clicks and a funeral," (playing on a popular movie called "Four Weddings and a Funeral") for a story on software dealing with such things as online casket buying and will writing. The heading would not reach much of the audience. But, it may be appropriate for a site with a North American audience.

Web headings also must be effective for navigating among linked stories so readers can see the connection from one story to the next related item, should they continue to search. Subheads within stories play a crucial role in helping users who are scanning to locate specific information and to grasp the overall context of a piece.

Online journalism editors must remember that many readers may still have slow-loading computers (usually because of narrow delivery bandwidth or old-style modems). For now, these editors also must remember that users may still have 15-inch monitors (usually measuring about 11 inches wide and 8 inches high), so they must not have bigger screens in mind and, thus, create headings that force readers to scroll laterally or suffer through a heading that is too many lines long.

Headings must be written for such users—a lowest-common-denominator approach of sorts.

Priority

It goes without saying that a heading should accurately announce what the text or image it accompanies will deliver. A turn-of-the-century, yellow journalism heading that screamed "Mother, 3 babies die after being thrown from bridge" may have been accurate in a sense, but it would have failed this guideline because the story told of a mother cat and her kittens being drowned by an owner unwilling to keep them.

Moreover, since it cannot tell all that accompanying text and/or images tell, the heading should present vividly the most important information—and be worded in an order that stresses the importance.

Thus, the news heading "Lone assassin in Dallas kills president" portrays some important specific material that "Shooting in Texas city leaves top official dead" does not.

But, the heading could be improved by putting the important details in its first few words, so "President Kennedy shot to death in Dallas"—although in passive voice—gets the important WHO and WHAT to readers early.

Editors should strive to begin headings with specific WHO and WHAT information their readers will instantly recognize.

"Church leader makes first visit to Cambodia to talk about genocide" is not as specific or direct as "Pope calls genocide 'sure ticket to hell' in first-ever Cambodian visit."

Magazine headings, while not written as present-tense, abbreviated sentences as is the case for newspaper headings, are better too when they capture a close relationship to the most important information being presented. "Bear encounters" does not have the impact of "Grizzly at the tent flap."

"Pizza envy," while cute, fails to be poetic and does not convey the primary focus of a story profiling the drawbacks of being a pizza deliverer that is captured by "Deliverance: the dark side of pizza delivery."

Of course, the heading should convey only the primary meaning intended. "Man shot in driveway" implies he had a driveway next to his spleen or liver. "Police begin campaign to run down jaywalkers" causes fear and confusion. "French head seeks arms" befuddles readers. "Survivor of Siamese twins joins parents" makes readers scream and laugh at the same time.

And, online journalism editors bear an especially heavy burden in conveying the importance of the information being presented, mainly because of the sheer mass of it. They also have a severe problem to solve: how to keep readers from clicking away from their site.

Part of their answer lies in having a parallel ability to use, when appropriate, the techniques for writing good magazine headings. Almost nothing works better than a poetic heading to draw readers into text below or to prompt them to make one more click.

Line Division

Because of a heading's importance to the page as a whole and to the information it announces, the editor crafting the heading becomes a poet arranging each word for maximum effect.

All too often, mediocre editors worry only about filling up most of the line and pour their headings onto the page or screen as if they were emptying a can of vegetable soup onto a table. In effect, they permit each word to fall on whatever line the computer determines.

Writers of poetic headings willingly recast the heading of two or more lines until no phrase is divided from one line to the next. Print editors have total control of this. Web editors have the power to use HTML (Hyper Text Markup Language) coding skills to prevent line breaks as the heading is displayed on different-size monitors around the world.

Common sense moves poetic headings from the realm of beauty to that of clarity: Line division is important because the heading must not confuse readers. This heading momentarily perplexes readers:

> Shootings fuel race
> feud in South Africa

So does this one:

> President tells of
> ongoing secret
> negotiations with
> Philippine radicals

Editors committed to writing poetic headings will make certain that in the first example, "race feud" (which, together, convey a single meaning) is printed on one line so that the meaning is clear and so that readers don't have to read the heading a time or two to understand. The same is true with "of ongoing secret negotiations" and "with Philippine radicals."

To achieve immediate and maximum clarity, good editors keep phrases and other groups of closely related words together on a single line—even if it means recasting the entire heading to something such as the following:

> South Africa shootings
> intensify race feud

> President reveals
> secret bargaining
> with radicals
> in Philippines

Choosing Type for Headings

Importance of the information to the desired readership is the primary determiner of heading size. An editor at any publication must be able to assign a proper size to the heading of every story or package of information and images. The decision is based on his evaluation of how important the information is to readers his publication is seeking.

Too small a heading (along with improper placement on the page) means the goal is not achieved because the reader may miss it.

Too large a heading shouts to the reader and then may fail to deliver adequately important information, thus creating suspicion and mistrust of the publication or web site. Editors who constantly use larger-than-needed headings ultimately send a "cry wolf" message to readers: If everything is of enough importance to shout about in a large size, nothing is.

Good editors strive to develop an eye for the relationship. They craft headings that are restrained in size unless they determine the importance and amount of the information merit one of a larger size.

In brief, they use restraint until the appropriate opportunity tells them they should not.

Once the editor knows which item is most important to readers and which will be relegated to less and less important status, she begins to work with the visual aspects of headings; certain typefaces, sizes and styles will be available based on the overall design of the publication.

Mathematicians with nothing better to do could probably work up a formula for how large a heading should be relative to the size of the story or package it accompanies. It would take into account variables such as that the heading size should grow smaller as more inches of text are jumped onto a subsequent page and larger as more of that story is retained on the page.

Typeface

Contrast and prioritizing are also expressed through selection of type. Heading typefaces are much larger than body text and may be either serif or sans serif.

Serif type looks old-fashioned, as though it might have been created by monks writing with quill pens in the scriptoriums of the Middle Ages, starting and ending letters with little squiggles to get the ink flowing in the frigid rooms. The letters have thick and thin parts, stand on brackets and often look slightly slanted.

The more modern look of sans serif type comes from no serifs and no variation in widths of lines. These stand straight, or perpendicular, to the baseline and do not have brackets at their feet. Sans serif type such as Helvetica is most readable when large and is popular for freeway signs and the largest headings.

Editors generally use one specific kind of each of these two styles for headings in a publication and will vary them to provide contrast. Contrast is also created by occasional use of variations to their two typefaces, such as underlining, boldface, italic and light or condensed forms.

A serif type in between the ornateness of the gothic scripts and the spare blockiness of sans serif type is usually chosen for setting text. Body text generally remains one face and one size to provide consistency throughout a publication. A serif type is most often chosen because the variations of line width and presence of serifs make for quicker recognition and easier reading.

However, sans serif fonts are best for the Web, especially those such as Verdana and Meta that are designed specifically for the computer screen. But in choosing, Web editors must know if their audience is more likely to read the information on the screen or, instead, scan it briefly and then print it out for reading on paper.

The differences in readability of typefaces can be seen by covering a line of reading with a piece of paper and lowering it slowly until it is easy to make out the words. Recognition happens with just the tops of serif type, but not until about half of the letter height for sans serif—meaning that the eye has to look at that type longer to make it out. Use of type is discussed further in Chapter 9.

Type Sizes

Type is measured in points, at 72 points per inch, and from the top of the ascenders, the letters that reach highest, to the bottom of the descenders, the letters that extend a part below the baseline. A 36-point heading is half an inch high, for example, and an 18-point heading is one-quarter inch. (See Illustration 3.1 for a comparison of point sizes to inches.)

Software programs allow any size of type at all, but the choices listed in their menus reflect the intervals used over the centuries when type was carved in wood or cast in metal. The smallest heading size is usually 18-point, followed by 24-point, 36-point, 48-point, 54 or 60-point, and 72-point.

Software programs also automatically set the amount of leading, the space provided between lines of type. A common default setting is the type's point size plus two points. Leading for 12-point type, for example, would be 14 points.

Magazines and brochures, along with posters, flyers and other publications, are free to use any size—or a mixture of sizes—in any heading, as long as it fits the desired look.

In all printed matter, however, the smallest size normally used for a heading is 18 points, the bottom of the barrel, so to speak, for drawing reader attention.

Proportioning Type Size to Page Size

A heading's size and shape provide priority and hierarchy for the page; they form a pattern that moves the eye through the page; they also affect the meaning and grouping of words and the space available for them. Typography purists insist that all headings used on a page have a uniform proportion to them (for example, 10-point text and headings of 18, 24, 30, 36, 42, etc.).

Size also matters if the heading is to flower. The size of the page on which headings will appear influences the range of sizes editors should choose from. (See Illustration 3.2.)

For example, a broadsheet page that contains the front page of a newspaper may use a one-line heading that is 72 points (an inch high) near the top of the page to announce the passage of a tax-cut bill by Congress. On occasion, the size may be 120 points or so to announce something really important, such as the end—or more likely the beginning—of a war.

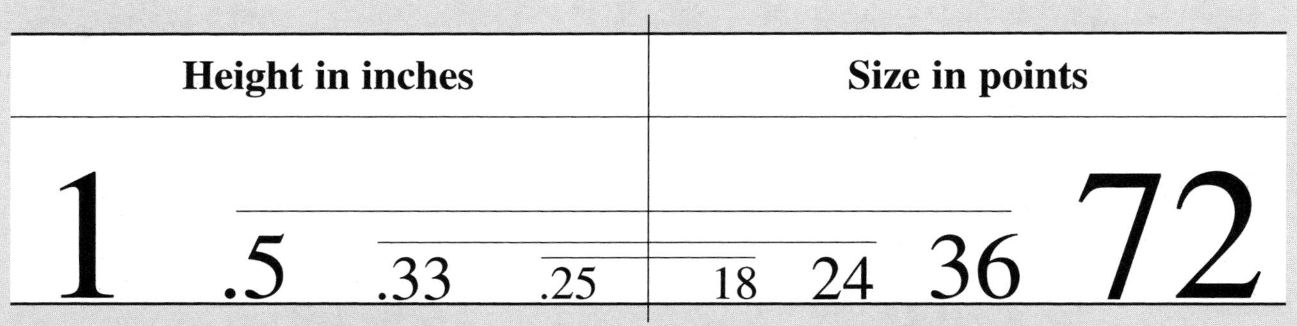

Height in inches | **Size in points**

1   .5   .33   .25   18   24   36   72

Type is measured in points, with 72 points per inch. The pre-set size intervals offered in word-processing and layout programs relate to common fractions of an inch, as shown above. Historically, these intervals were used also with metal and wooden type.

The numbers above appear smaller than their stated sizes because they don't include descenders, the parts of some letters that drop below the baseline. Type is measured from the top of the ascenders—tall letters or numbers—to the bottom of the descenders.

A common width measurement is picas, with six picas per inch, or one pica representing 12 points.

ILLUSTRATION 3.1 *Type Size*

ILLUSTRATION 3.2 A–D *Proportioning Heading Size to Page Size*

After editors have done some initial thumbnail sketches of pages (as shown in illustrations for Chapter 2), they will plan the page by creating a "dummy" in the layout software, often by using a publication's master template.

These pages show what dummies might look like on the editor's monitor. The actual headings are not yet written, and the stories have not gone through final editing. If the publication has copy editors, the page editor will assign them stories to edit and headings to write based on this dummy, or plan.

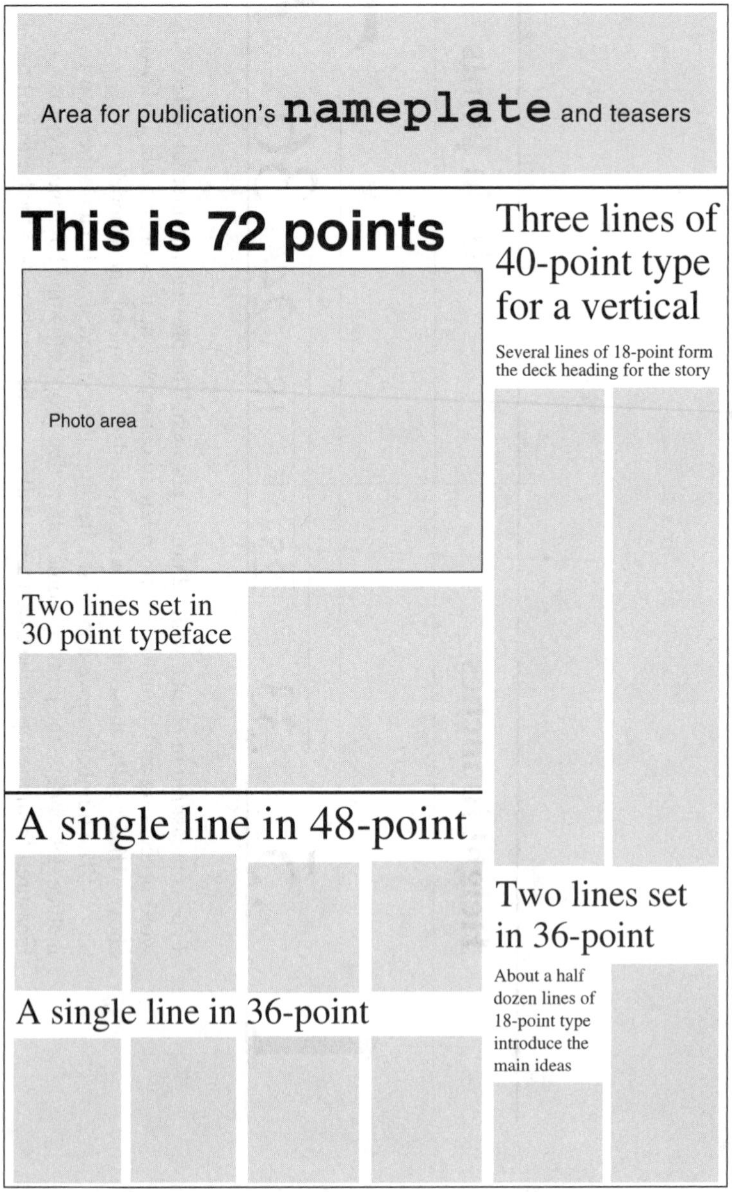

Area for publication's **nameplate** and teasers

This is 72 points

Three lines of 40-point type for a vertical

Several lines of 18-point form the deck heading for the story

Photo area

Two lines set in 30 point typeface

A single line in 48-point

A single line in 36-point

Two lines set in 36-point

About a half dozen lines of 18-point type introduce the main ideas

ILLUSTRATION 3.2 A
Broadsheet News Page, 14 by 22.5 Inches. The real page dummy would carry brief story names or **slugs,** and headline orders expressed in shortened form: 4-72-1 Hel BF for the top left, and 2-40-3 Times for the top right. Spelled out, these call for, respectively, four columns of Helvetica bold, one line; and two columns of Times, three lines. A tabloid page, 11 by 17 inches, not shown here, is inter-mediate in size between this page and the smaller formats.

Area for nameplate
and identifying information

Two lines of 30-point type
may be the largest heading

A

Here, nine lines of a smaller type face, such as this 18-point in Times, act as a highlight box for a main point made in the story

A bold, 16-point subhead appears

Two lines of 24 pt.

This 30-point heading is italic

W

Highlight story p. 4

A bold, 16-point subhead parallels the one above

ILLUSTRATION 3.2 B   *Newsletter Cover Page, 8.5 by 11 Inches.* The drop in size of page area from the broadsheet page is reflected in fewer stories and smaller headings. This dummy for a black-and-white publication emphasizes horizontal modules for its main story areas. Though it does not have photos, they could be included in the format.

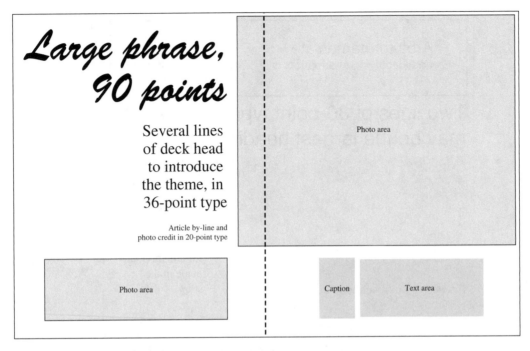

Large phrase,
90 points

Several lines
of deck head
to introduce
the theme, in
36-point type

Article by-line and
photo credit in 20-point type

Photo area

Photo area

Caption

Text area

ILLUSTRATION 3.2 C   *Magazine Spread, Two Facing 8.5 by 11-Inch Pages.* Though standard magazine pages are small in size, they often carry the largest headings, at least for the first line. This display typeface may be in a decorative, cursive or other distinctive style. A deck heading and credit lines in intermediate type sizes provide a bridge to the body text. The main photo or illustration for the story may run very large, as well.

The Spokane (Wash.) Spokesman-Review used "FEDS LOSE BIG" in bold 108-point type to announce defendant Randy Weaver's acquittal in a much-publicized trial resulting from a siege by federal agents of Weaver's mountain cabin in northern Idaho.

The same stories on a tabloid-sized page of a weekly newspaper may be 42 or 48 points for the tax cut and 60 points for the war or acquittal.

A company newsletter produced on a page the size of a normal sheet of paper (8½ inches by 11 inches) may use a 30-point or 36-point heading for a major story on a new profit-sharing policy for employees. Or, it may use a 24-point heading for a story on canned goods being sought for the annual food drive.

The smallest type size for headings is 18 points; smaller than that is considered body text. But 14- and 16-point type is often used for graphic items of in-between

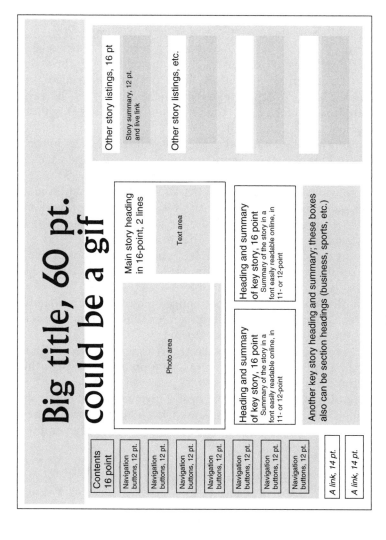

Big title, 60 pt. could be a gif

Contents 16 point
Navigation buttons, 12 pt.
Navigation buttons, 12 pt.
Navigation buttons, 12 pt.
Navigation buttons, 12 pt.
Navigation buttons, 12 pt.
Navigation buttons, 12 pt.
Navigation buttons, 12 pt.

A link, 14 pt.

A link, 14 pt.

Main story heading in 16-point, 2 lines

Photo area

Text area

Heading and summary of key story, 16 point
Summary of the story in a font easily readable online, in 11- or 12-point

Heading and summary of key story, 16 point
Summary of the story in a font easily readable online, in 11- or 12-point

Another key story heading and summary; these boxes also can be section headings (business, sports, etc.)

Other story listings, 16 pt

Story summary, 12 pt. and live link

Other story listings, etc.

ILLUSTRATION 3.2 D *World Wide Web Page, 8.5 by 11.5 Inches.* The part of a Web page that shows on a monitor screen is slightly larger than letter paper and oriented as a horizontal shape. A page may run longer than the viewing area, requiring some scrolling.

Headings tend to be smaller than in the other media shown; they may be displayed larger or smaller, too, by different browsers, which makes line division and filling out lines less relevant. This page sticks with small headings in order to offer a range of story summaries.

53

size, such as **pullquotes** (excerpts pulled from the text and for graphic purposes displayed in a larger size). **Deck heads** (secondary headings placed below the main heading) will be in between the large heading and body text sizes.

Online Headings

Online editors now have a wide array of choices of type size but at the start may be wise to use the online benchmark range of sizes from "H1" to "H7," with H1 being the largest—and normally set at a size of around 36 points.

More and more flexibility is being added, however, with each revision of HTML (for example, the HTML 4 version allowing an ability to set the style).

Much online design centers around the term **pixels,** which refers to how much space a letter or image occupies on a computer screen. This will vary, but editors can estimate that a pixel usually equals a point. Thus, anything that is 36 pixels high is normally half an inch high.

Beginning editors may find it useful to think of online page sizes in the same way that one thinks of the company newsletter or typical magazine page or 8½-inch by 11-inch advertisement flyer.

The largest size will vary, depending on the audience being addressed—with the huge headings saved for big sales (gigantic year-end blowouts), very important news stories, or feature pages requiring large titles in their design. The lower size limits follow the same principles as for other printed material.

When a heading is increased to two, three, or occasionally four or five lines, the space it takes on the page or screen is doubled or tripled (or quadrupled or quintupled) as well.

Consequently the size used should be reduced almost proportionately—up to half, except with 18 point, or H3 on the screen, so that the total size remains proportionate to the text and images it accompanies.

Subheads, those smaller headings used to break up long sections of text, may be smaller than 18 points but are usually 2 to 6 points larger than the text size and are shown in bold or italics.

Summary headings, also called deck heads, give additional detail and are placed below main headings in a smaller size, are usually half the size of the main heading (and often in bold or italic if the main line is not) but are never displayed below 18 points in size.

Deciding Column Width

Columns run typically from two inches wide to about six inches. Any less, and the type becomes raggedy-looking from too many hyphenations; any more, and the eye has trouble moving from the end of the line to the left edge of the correct following line.

Columns arranged across the page are separated by a narrow white space called **gutters;** a quarter-inch is now considered the minimal acceptable width. Some designs allow use of a very narrow column next to regular columns; this creates vertical space for graphical items such as captions, pullquotes or highlight items.

Heading orders are expressed as a three-part combination of information: The number of columns the heading needs to stretch across, its size in points, and the number of lines, or decks. The numbers are followed by an abbreviation of the name of the type. For example, 3-36-2 Hel means three columns wide, 36-points high, and two lines long, set in Helvetica, a sans serif typeface.

The shape of a module, whether it is narrow or wide, affects the size of the heading as well as the number of lines it will have.

Back to Basics

In addition to a poetic dimension of headings, good editors know the longtime basics of writing news headings must be incorporated into their job, and plenty of guidelines exist regarding the craft, which in its own way contributes to heading poetry.

Here is one useful way to divide those basics into a process that could be posted and used as a checklist for those learning the craft:

1. Building a Foundation

- The story is read twice in its entirety before the heading is crafted.
- If the story is trimmed to fit limited space, the heading reflects the new length of the story.
- The context of the story is captured by the heading.
- The heading is taken from information near the top of the text—after it has been edited. Key words in the story, or precise synonyms for them, are used, but they should not repeat the lead information word for word.
- The heading is totally accurate—and neutral as well—unless the story has an argumentative stance.
- The heading is arranged to place important elements at the beginning (as noted earlier, the *What* or *Who*—or sometimes the consequences for readers).

Not:

Grand jury report says drug overdose killed poet

Instead:

Heroin overdose killed poet, grand jury report says

- If possible, positive qualities should be stressed, such as including the number of survivors in an airliner crash.

2. Working with the Words

News headings are usually in sentence form and usually in present tense with a verb present—except for *is* and *are*, which are *not* used by editors concerned with tight, punchy headings:

> Dale promises great headings for readers

> American readers [are] calling for better headings

To achieve the spirit of the poetic heading described above, the heading should keep one thought to a line and keep the words of each phrase together on a line.

Each word of a heading is precious and precise—thus, padding with unnecessary words should be avoided. *A, an,* or *the* should be omitted from news headings (they are a bit more acceptable in non-news headings but still should be seen as padding).

Not:

> Girl teenager from a Seattle suburb chosen to receive award
> for the outstanding musical accomplishment in Washington

Instead:

> Lynnwood girl, 16, [is] named state's top young musician

When attribution is used in headings, it is best placed at the end unless the person is more important than the news being announced:

Not:

> Study says chocolate good for health

Instead:

> Chocolate good for health, study says

Not:

> Chocolate good for health, pope says

Instead:

> Pope says chocolate good for health

The brief, direct word should have priority in headings over the overworked and misused ones.

Not:

Council hikes taxes, axes parking fees

Instead:

Council raises taxes, cuts parking fees

Not:

Political opponents hopping on bandwagon
after attorney general nixes group's request

Instead:

Attorney general's denial of logging permit
[is] creating support among state's Democrats

3. Punctuation and AP Style

Downstyle, which capitalizes words just as a sentence would, is widely preferred. Headings that capitalize each letter or the beginning of each word are more difficult to read. Thus, only the first letter of the first word and the beginning of proper nouns are in caps. Consistency in this should be carried to summary heads and subheads. Some publications retain the style that capitalizes most words for a more traditional or historical look.

Periods are not used in headings except with some abbreviations. Instead, semicolons are used between heading sentences:

House impeaches president; Senate to hold trial

Since the word *and* is not used in headings, a comma is used to replace it. A comma can also be used before an attributing phrase:

China, Japan to resume talks

Congressional tax plan too severe, president says

Single quotation marks are used in headings. Double marks are not:

Mayor calls council's plan 'dubious'

Or: Thespians to produce 'Hamlet'

A dash, a colon or a comma can be used with attribution:

Air travel safer than ever: FAA study

Or: Smoking must be banned—AMA

Numerals may be used freely in headings—even at the beginning:

5 die in 3 plane crashes

Abbreviations should follow the same rules used for the text of the story but be used sparingly and with the certainty they are readily recognizable.

Not:

Mi. fails to score vs B'ham in N & S game

Instead:

U.S. threatens to play hardball with N. Korea

Other standards of the style being used (such as Associated Press style) should be applied—including how to handle titles (is *mayor* capitalized when used alone), corporations (is it *Inc.* or *Incorporated*), products (should *Kleenex* or *facial tissue* be used).

4. Layout and Graphic Considerations

Newspaper and Web page headings normally begin flush against the left margin of the text below. Centering lines is a variation done for design purposes.

Normally each line of a heading fills out most of the space available before the right margin (three normal-sized letters short is usually the maximum shortage allowed).

The graphics style of the publication will determine whether the first or last line of a multiline head is normally the longest. If a centered heading is used, the longest line may appear in the middle of the stack, or even at the end.

Heading size reflects news judgment or similar evaluation of the text it represents—smaller headings are used for less important and shorter stories.

When the task of writing the heading is delegated, the format of the heading order is written as columns wide, font size and number of lines (3-36-2 is a 3-column, 36-point, 2-line heading).

5. The Don'ts

Libelous material may show up in headings. Editors should be especially watchful of convicting people in news headings.

Not:

Police chief murders mayor

—when he is only suspected of or charged with the crime.

Headings that trample on areas of diversity should be avoided. In a multicultural world with two genders, many races and many people with a mixture of preferences and abilities, heading writers must not forget audiences and diversity—especially on the Web, when a whole world may be reading.

Not:

Hearing-impaired man wins dart championship

Readers must not be bored, so "label" or "topic" headings that offer only general information and lack lively and precise verbs and nouns must be avoided.

Not:

President explains tax proposal

Instead:

President wants income tax cut for rich

Question headings and headings that are commands are not as effective as regular titles and headlines for news and feature stories. Instead, the "why" in the story prompting the heading serves readers better.

Not:

Should mayor resign?

Not:

Don't swim in Green Lake

Headings that begin with verbs tend to read like commands and should be avoided.

Not:

Stop the war

Instead:

Protesters say 'stop war now'

Exaggeration and inaccuracy—as well as misleading headings—should not be a part of headings.

Repetition of words or sound units within a heading should be avoided.

Not:

> Seattle marathon to see
> thousands of runners
> traverse Seattle streets

Jargon and "ize" words in general should be avoided.

Not:

> Senate wants to catalyze talks

Headings should avoid *feels, believes,* or *thinks*—we know what people say, not their internal thinking and beliefs and feelings.

Not:

> Mayor believes FBI to be 'arrogant'

Instead:

> FBI 'arrogant,' mayor says

As noted above, bad puns and bad taste—along with slang and clichés—should be avoided.

Not:

> Chicago kids must be shot
> (for a story on immunization)

Not:

> Vikings green with envy after thrills, chills of OT victory

Conclusion

Rules for headings abound like snowflakes in a blizzard. Better headings can be crafted if the guidelines used stem from underlying concepts of priority, clarity, unity, beauty, contrast and community.

When a belief in the importance of these heading qualities is added to a belief that headings are capable of going beyond merely drooping on top of a story, sometimes squishing it, fearless editing is in sight.

Editors with such beliefs have a better chance of crafting bright, vibrant, poetic headings that take on the panache of Stellar jays announcing a cat crouching below the cedar tree.

Exercises to Apply Concepts and Develop Skills

1. Goal: To identify patterns in heading structures, using a variety of media.

   Have students peruse a variety of media in a lab setting. Ask students to browse quickly, spending 5 or 10 minutes with each medium used. This may be done using only newspapers and magazines, though newsletters and Web pages are useful additions. Ask students to describe the patterns they see and the variations for each medium. Heading styles change along with trends in popular culture, and students are often adept at identifying these.

2. Goal: To apply knowledge of how to write headings.

   Give students a variety of news and feature stories with heading sizes assigned and have them start writing headings. Include a range of formats calling for various combinations of main headings with and without smaller deck heads, multideck headings for narrow, vertical spaces and long single-line headings in large sizes for horizontal spaces.

   Critique these early efforts with the class to point out the early, common pitfalls and to enjoy the creativity of the good ones. Read them out loud to catch the rhythm, or cadence, of the language.

   Students who wish to create their own exercises can simply cut stories without their headings out of publications, assign new heading shapes and sizes, and practice writing new ones.

3. Goal: To recognize and avoid errors in headings that can lead to libel.

   Practice writing headings with the class that risk potential libel, such as court and arrest stories, and discuss ways to accurately reflect the stages of the legal process and to avoid labeling or condemning a person in a heading before he or she is convicted in court.

4. Goal: To adapt heading sizes and shapes to changes in layout.

   Using pages with simple modular layouts, perhaps ones created for exercises in Chapter 2, ask students to reshape modules, to form more strongly vertical and horizontal contrasts. As the modules change shape, ask them to re-assign headings, altering the point sizes and number of lines so they are appropriate both for the module and the overall page size. See Illustration 3.3 A and B, a pair of broadsheet news pages in which the modular shapes have been changed.

Helpful Sources

DeVigal, Andrew. "Design Guidelines for Online Sites." July 1999. See at http://poynter. org

Goldstein, Norm. The Associated Press Stylebook and Briefing on Media Law. Cambridge, Mass.: Perseus Publishing, 2002.

Nielsen, Jakob. Various articles on effective Web use. See at http://www.useit.com/alertbox

Poynteronline. This site provided by the Poynter Institute is located at http://poynter. org/ and has reference resources and articles and links important to editing.

The Western Front, student newspaper. Klipsun magazine and The Planet magazine, of Western Washington University, Bellingham, Wash., provided many of the example headings in this chapter.

The Department of Journalism

Daily Clarion

Building rates rising locally

Increase breaks decade-long decline; low lending rates cited

[greeked body text]

Construction rises 12 percent this year		
New housing starts	2003	2004
Permits single family city	138	140
Permits multi-unit buildings	47	55
Estimated house price		
Single-family dwellings	$165,000	$184,000
Apartments and condos	$725,000	$930,000
Office and commercial		
Permits filed	10	12
Average price to build	$825,000	$932,000

After a sluggish five-year period, building of new homes, apartments and condos is picking up as banks lower lending rates.

Source: Council of Governments

Graphic by Marcus Twain

Farmworker families flocking to summer enrichment classes

[greeked body text]

Leaders give atheist Scout an ultimatum

Believe or leave

[greeked body text]

Supremacist group will lose compound under court ruling

[greeked body text]

Two states sign cleanup agreement for lake

[greeked body text]

ILLUSTRATION 3.3 A   *Modular Shape Affects Heading Sizes.* This mock-up newspaper page based on a student design has mainly vertically shaped modules. As it is redrafted in **Illustration 3.3 B,** the mix changes to include three horizontal modules and only two verticals.

The Department of Journalism

Daily Clarion

Local building rates rising now

Increase ends decade-long decline; lower lending rates cited

Φωτογραφο Παντσαλοf, χρανσαρμεν ο flee oeι λαμερ Χαρμο-σσαλοι φερ Πρεσθε Οργτηπιζι οι Οροσθο, Ασεηλακr χσασνσχ.

Farmworker families enjoying art programs

Atheist Scout 'not bitter' about ouster

Photo: ver Πραντ Ποντο, Σαντχασαν.
Α ραρφηρ οθ της σανρεμσρισσ γρσσαι Αρρτσ Ναριστοι σΙραενσσατ τρσ σεσστρχ τηγνσσησ α νστσοι σαι πσ οστσσαι σα ρεσθ Αακθανρ τσ

Supremacists group will lose compound under court ruling

Two states sign lake cleanup pact

Photo of: Photosof photos

ILLUSTRATION 3.3 B *Modular Shape Affects Heading Sizes.* As the modules become wider or narrower, the heading sizes and number of lines needed change, as well. Splitting the page into two-column- and four-column-wide modules provides better balance than in the first draft, which left the page looking split down the middle. With practice, it becomes easier and quicker to alter module shapes and rewrite headings.

4

Working with Words— and Their Writers

Grammar is the internal structure of a language; it works like a set of operating instructions that allow speakers and writers to generate new combinations of words and phrases. When writers and editors know this structure and can consciously use it, they write and edit with greater confidence and less fear that their words may chafe against the natural form and flow of the language.

When we first learn a language as children and grow up speaking it as our native language, we accept its categories and structures without thinking much about them. They seem to be natural occurrences, and only by studying grammar later in life do we slowly become able to discern the structures and to name them. Later still, we become able to spot a misused form and to change the phrasing or punctuation to be in harmony with the form—to create clarity and beauty where confusion had existed.

For example, the categories of actors and actions are basic in English. In grammar, this basic division becomes known as active voice, an ordering of words that places the actor first, followed by the action, or verb, and then by the object acted upon. This is a preferred sentence structure in newswriting because it is the most basic sentence form in English.

As an editor begins looking at sentences to see whether they flow this way, she will begin to spot those written in passive voice, a form in which the object is placed at the beginning. Knowing the form and being able to see it and name it, she will be able to decide whether to change it.

Few young adults have the confidence to do this fearlessly. It may be that grammar is taught less in public schools than it was years ago, or it may be that our culture is increasingly oriented to the visual; whatever the cause, college students often feel as much or more anxiety about grammar as about mathematics.

Editing becomes especially challenging because the rules they used intuitively as good writers now need to be named and talked about and applied to someone else's writing. This process is not automatic; it can be learned, even by those who feel they missed out on it, somehow, in the seventh grade.

This chapter breaks the fearsome and difficult task into steps that can be learned and practiced. The first step involves working with writers to define the nature of the story, then developing a personal system to be able to spot errors in the writing, and finally becoming able to relate those problems to the language used in grammar guides so it becomes easier to look up answers or solutions.

Understanding the Extent of Editing

Just as writers need to understand whether they are being asked to write a brief news item or a lengthy magazine feature, so editors need to know which of a variety of treatments of a story is expected. Are they doing a final check or copy edit, or cutting a 30-inch wire story to a two-inch item for a digest? Is the writer's voice to be preserved or changed to institutional voice?

Beginning editors may feel that unless they make dramatically visible changes, they're not doing their job. But, editors are not paid by rate for the number of changes they make. They are respected for the quality of their decisions. This means developing judgment so that one can fearlessly let something good stay as it is.

A writer who sees her work headed to the wastebasket or changed beyond recognition will feel not only anger and discouragement but also frustration that the editor did not clearly communicate what was wanted in the first place.

For the editor, engaging in unnecessary cutting for length, voice or level of detail wastes valuable time. Because it involves judgment and research, good editing is time-consuming and needs to stay focused on the task.

Naming the Error

An editor could disassemble a story to its primary elements and assemble them again, in essence, writing the story all over again. This will be tempting to those who are confident only in their intuitive ability to use the language. They risk changing perfectly good phrasing solely because they would have written it differently and their way sounds better to them.

A good rule of thumb for avoiding this pitfall and others is to be able to name the error that needs to be corrected before making a change.

This helps an editor sort through colorful details and language, or a writer's voice that emerges strongly in a piece. These are not errors just because the editor would have written with a different style. If that is the only reason the editor can offer, he has confused his role.

Naming errors and suggesting concrete solutions build a good relationship with writers. It invites collaboration and discussion when a writer, printed page in hand, approaches the editing desk and demands, "Why did you change my story?"

How much better for both if the editor can reply not with vague personal preferences but with a specific reason, such as, "I changed it into parallel structure because the sentence started with a series and then abandoned it with the last element."

Changing something only when the error can be named assures good editing in the long run because the editor will continuously build his knowledge of the language, good working relationships with writers and confidence that the editing is improving the writing.

Never Inserting Errors

Writers endure terrible embarrassment when grammatical or factual errors appear under their bylines. Errors affect their professional standing and their credibility with their sources.

Errors also affect the integrity of the publication, and although the piece has the writer's name on it, the process of editing places trust and responsibility for absolute accuracy with its editors.

Inaccuracies can result in significant legal issues such as libel; editors need to develop clear standards for working with crime and court stories. Also, they need to develop a sense of when to question the use of personal details that may not be newsworthy and that may raise concerns about invasion of privacy. These and other common areas of concern are summarized in Box 4.1.

Editors bring the last eyes to check a piece before it is published or posted. No room exists for going with hunches or making changes an editor merely guesses are proper. The closer an editor's print command is to the final production, the more crucial is the editor's focus on absolute accuracy.

Naming What Is Good

Some writers turn in such smoothly written, grammatically clean and carefully checked work that their stories are a pleasure to edit. Expressing appreciation to them helps an editor's life stay in balance. It also builds judgment when an editor can name what is good and say why it is good, in addition to naming errors.

We are all grateful to be told we have done a good job. Writers are no exception. Words of praise—for work that is praiseworthy—improve self-esteem of writers, motivate them to repeat that level of writing and begin to build a bond of trust between them and their editor.

BOX 4.1 • *Caution Areas in Editing*

Chapter 12 explores legal and ethical issues in depth, but these are some areas to keep in mind while writing headlines and editing stories.

Full identifications: Editors verify and check name spellings and addresses.

For stories involving crimes, arrests and legal actions, publications usually require identifying the person arrested or charged by name, age and address. Including these three elements helps to protect the reputations of people with similar names who were not involved.

For general news and feature stories, a person's name, age and occupation are commonly included.

Accuracy in legal proceedings: Editors check for language appropriate to the actions.

In arrest stories, editors prefer terms such as "arrested on suspicion of" or "pending investigation of" to preserve the possibility that the suspect might not be charged or, later, convicted.

A suspect is charged in a court proceeding, such as an arraignment or a first appearance. Editors question the phrase "arrested on a charge of. . . . "

Headings and captions need not to label a person as a criminal until he or she has been convicted or pleaded guilty. Usually such labels are used only for stories about sentencings: "Confessed murderer gets life in prison."

Editors need to be familiar with state laws that define juvenile or other court proceedings as not open to the public. Laws also may protect the identities of victims or witnesses.

Libel and invasion of privacy: Editors are on full alert for material that may be false and defamatory or that includes embarrassing personal details that are not newsworthy.

They will discuss their concerns with editors in chief, or even with the company's attorney. Editors need to watch for questionable material in stories, headings, captions, wire stories, editorials, advertisements and letters to the editor.

Reprinting a libel can constitute a new libel, and merely because a letter writer generated the questionable material doesn't mean a publication isn't responsible. Most publications contact letter writers to verify their identity and the content of their messages. A publication has the right to reject letters and advertisements.

In reviews of books, movies, music and artistic performances, criticisms of the content usually are seen as fair comment, but they're not perceived that way if they launch into personal attacks on the artist.

Balance and fairness: Editors look for varying viewpoints placed high in a story.

Often, more than two sides to a story exist, and because many readers don't read a given article to its ending, editors need to make sure the major viewpoints are expressed early. In exploring complex situations, editors need to question whether presenting varying ideas as being opposed to each other will artificially heighten conflict.

Truthfulness: Editors guard their publications' integrity.

Publications, as well as professional societies for public relations and for news professionals, set standards for not mixing fact with fiction, setting up hypothetical situations as though they are real, or inflating the importance of or "hyping" stories.

Copyright: Editors check the attribution, source and length of quoted material.

News events, ideas and facts about happenings generally fall into the "common domain" and cannot be copyrighted. But, a writer's specific words describing events can be—and often are—copyrighted. Law allows for very brief excerpting of copyrighted material as long as the author is given credit. Lengthier quoting requires gaining permission.

News media enter into contracts with news services or "partner" organizations that allow them to use each other's stories; editors need to know which ones allow their work to be reprinted in the publication.

Photographs: Editors are sensitive to the visual impact of photos.

Any questions of taste, potential offensiveness or intrusion into private space need to be discussed with editors in chief. Photographs that have altered elements or portray events unlikely to happen need to be labeled as photo illustrations; a publication usually develops guidelines for these areas.

Time between Drafts

How is it that the next day an editor suddenly sees the misspelled word in a headline he spent an hour on the day before? He literally could not see it then, but the passage of time has allowed him to see it with a fresh eye. Humans are built so that we literally see something we strongly expect to see and see what we know we meant to say. It is as necessary in editing to let time pass between drafts as it is in writing.

This is especially true when the writing to be edited is one's own. In addition to perceptual overrides, the writer-turned-editor is probably still dealing with either loving or hating the piece—natural side effects of the intensity of the creative process.

A little time away, from a few hours to overnight, restores clear vision. It also gives the editor enough distance from working with themes, and how they are expressed in sentences and paragraphs, to be able to look at the swarm of small, pesky items like commas and quotation marks.

Editing in Stages

Because it is impossible to examine a story with a telescope and a microscope at the same time, editing must be done in stages. The editor begins with the large perspective and gradually shifts to closer inspection. The process has three primary stages:

1. The Story Level

The first reading is at the story level. The editor checks the story for completeness and the lead for its news values. He makes certain the story is balanced, with all sides and points of view present and in their proper place—especially if it is presenting news. He also makes major cuts or reorganization if they are needed. This stage clarifies priorities, as discussed in Chapter Two.

2. The Sentence Level

The second stage of editing involves checking sentences for clarity by looking at grammatical constructions and at news values such as attribution and complete identification of sources and accuracy of numbers, ages, percentages and money amounts.

Editors often have difficulty spotting grammar problems until they have a great deal of experience and practice. Typically, an editor develops his own system for spotting the most frequent grammar problems appearing in drafts of stories for mass media. When he has a hunch about what may be wrong, and if he is familiar with the terminology used in a grammar guide, he can research the problem.

Knowing what is correct and how to describe it depends on having a current, thorough grammar guide and being familiar enough with its contents to look up questions quickly and easily.

A classic beginning guide is "The Elements of Style" by William Strunk and E.B. White.

More extensive guides for journalists are "When Words Collide: A Media Writer's Guide to Grammar and Style" by Lauren Kessler and Duncan McDonald or "Working With Words: A Handbook for Media Writers and Editors" by Brian S. Brooks, James L. Pinson and Jean Gaddy Wilson.

Advanced searches, including areas involving British usages, are rewarded in "Modern English Usage" by H.W. Fowler and Sir Ernest Gowers.

Common grammar problems—the errors most often making it into the mass media—and the terminologies used to describe them are detailed in Chapter 5.

3. AP Style and Punctuation

The third stage is one of fine-tuning: At this point the editor closely edits for punctuation and basic style. A news publication's basic style usually follows "The Associated Press Stylebook and Briefing on Media Law"; other kinds of publications may use style guides of the Modern Language Association, the

American Psychological Association or the Chicago Manual of Style. These books contain thousands of rules guiding consistency of abbreviations, capitalization, dates and use of numbers or figures. Editors tend to memorize only the ones that arise most often and keep the books handy on their desks for looking up other usages.

Editing American English

It may be helpful to know that many irregularities in English appear because it grew out of a hodgepodge of German, Danish, French, Celtic and other languages. It may be encouraging to know that new words appear by the thousands every decade in the United States and that usages dictated in older editions of grammar books are now incorrect because they are outdated.

Today's oddities may be the next generation's accepted usages. A time existed when *lit* was not permitted as the past tense of *to light*. Now we no longer have to use *lighted*. Editors in search of a less gendered way of speaking now struggle against the use of the plural pronoun *they* in a sentence like, "A true musician does not care if *they become* popular," instead of *he or she becomes*. A short time ago, the words *Internet* and *e-mail* did not exist.

In short, English is open to fun and to flux because it responds to our changing speech patterns and to inventions and international influences. Nevertheless, written Standard American English is more conservative and traditional and (because it takes time for changes to work their way into grammar books and dictionaries) slower to change than its spoken form, which also has the advantage of intonations and facial expressions to help clarify meanings.

Unfortunately, however, just because something sounds right doesn't mean it will be correct on the written page.

Colorful Writing versus Sensationalism

It is a shame to edit all color and life out of stories, but Americans aware of current and past eras of press excess often fear they, too, will fall prey to sensationalism in their writing, headings or page designs.

Sensationalizing is drawing out details of personal lives disproportionately so that the news value of the event becomes distorted. It also means playing up pathos, highlighting details that arouse feelings of pity, sorrow or horror.

Editing that keeps news values prominent, that limits personal details to what is needed to tell the story and that ensures that all elements contribute to an accurate context will avoid problems of sensationalism. Otherwise, details that let sources turn into real people who talk, think and feel are wonderful attributes of a story and need to be maintained.

For example, this flyer appeared one day on a local front porch:

LOST TURTLE
Named Franklin
Box Turtle–land tortoise
about 5 inches long
Lost in the 2900 block of VICTOR Street
Very Dearly Missed
If you see or find him please call 752-0504

Only an editor fearful of letting color and life into a story would cut the turtle's name or the fact that he's dearly missed. This wording tells us not that we could call out Franklin and that the turtle would come waddling, but that the uniqueness of a named turtle exists in the mind of someone very young.

How much is lost with a notice edited only for conciseness:

Turtle lost in 2900 block of Victor Street
Call 752-0504

Developing a Personal Editing System

Editors have such respect for the written word that they have to practice questioning it and often find it difficult to move from sensing that something is wrong to being able to use the grammatical term to name the error.

For example, many may be able to describe that the phrase at the beginning of the sentence doesn't have a connection to the sentence's subject. That's probably enough to be somewhat clear to the writer. But, how do these editors find it in a grammar guide when they don't know the term *dangling modifier*?

A second problem is being intimidated by seemingly thousands of grammar terms and rules, all of them precise, rigid and obscurely named. Each editor must develop a personal system for breaking such a mass into approachable units.

The following list shows a personal editing system evolved by the authors. It won't work for everyone in the form shown but should serve as an example for how an editor develops a personal approach for checking what is wrong as well as for what is solid and good.

Listing about two dozen current trouble items works well; it is not too daunting, and items can be rotated on and off the list easily. The A to Z "system" below includes the grammar problems that are most troublesome for many of today's young adults.

The usage problems listed have changed over time; some problems representing older patterns drop away while newer ones take their place. Different generations of writers simply seem to show different patterns and kinds of errors.

When an editor has a hunch as to what may be wrong, she can use the terms set out below and look up the problem in a grammar guide.

Locating grammar problems is not a mysterious gift that one has or doesn't have. The process is more like an Indiana Jones poring over a map and sleuthing through levels of clues to find the true gems.

These steps include the following:

1. Checking the sentence for its basic parts and to see whether several sentences or clauses are being used as one sentence;
2. Looking at how phrases are attached to the main sentences;
3. Asking about the roles nouns and pronouns are playing—whether they are actors, owners of things or receivers of action;
4. Checking for singulars and plurals and whether they are in agreement;
5. Developing one's own list of "tricky" words and combinations—the ones an editor needs to check because they sound alike or are often misused in spoken English.

Grammar Sleuthing A to Z

Words set in boldface in this section are terms used by grammar guides and English handbooks. (The problems described are covered in more depth in Chapter 5.)

1. Checking Basic Sentence Parts

A sentence (with at least one **clause** that can stand alone) has a **subject** and **predicate.** It may also have an **object** receiving the action of the **verb** in the predicate. Lacking essential parts, a would-be sentence is called an incomplete sentence or a **fragment.**

a. commas with conjunctions

Two sentences may be joined with a **conjunction,** such as *and* or *but.* When this happens, use a **comma** (unless the two sentences are very short) with the conjunction, which is the word that joins them. See: **conjunctions, independent clauses, comma use.** Editors often have to decide whether part of a sentence following a main sentence needs to be set off by a comma or a semicolon.

b. comma splice

Trying to join two sentences by using only a comma is a **comma splice.** For example: The path by the creek was muddy, we decided to take the other route.

Four solutions are possible: Add a conjunction and keep the comma, substitute a semi-colon for the comma, break it into two separate sentences or use a colon if a strong cause-and-effect relationship is expressed.

c. passive phrasing or dead construction

Active voice is the sentence order: actor/action/receiver of action. **Passive voice** places the receiver first. This order is fine if emphasis needs to be on the receiver itself (e.g. The president was shot, or, The bank was robbed). Also, careful use of passive voice can add a pleasant change of pace in newswriting.

A **dead construction** usually omits the actor and adds nebulous, non-functioning words to the beginning of a sentence, such as *there is, there are, there were, there was, it is/was.* Example: *There was* a vote in Congress today to change tax laws.

Instead, move the actor to the front: Congress voted today to change tax laws.

d. parallel structure

Are similar items or actions in a list or series expressed in similar grammatical constructions? Areas editors check for **parallel structure** include use of **articles, verb tenses,** active or passive voice, and use of **nouns** and **verbals,** especially **gerunds,** which function as nouns. (For example, The president liked *hiking, golfing* and *napping* in the afternoon sun. Not, The president like hiking, golfing and *to nap* in the afternoon sun.) Editors also check complementary pairs of words or phrases, as well as comparisons.

e. Consistency in first, second and third person

Is the piece written in I, we (**first person**), you (**second person**) or he/she (**third person**), and if the story shifts from one to another (say, from third to second person), is it for a good reason?

2. Checking How Phrases Are Attached

A **phrase** is not a complete sentence because it lacks one or more of the basic parts (usually, subject or predicate). Because a phrase cannot stand alone, it needs to be attached to a sentence. This is usually accomplished with a comma—but not always.

f. A phrase attached to the beginning of a sentence needs to be set off with a comma if it is lengthy and if it expresses a passage of time or a change in place. See **introductory phrases, comma use.**

g. A phrase attached to the beginning of a sentence needs to refer to the subject of the sentence. Similarly, a phrase attached to the end needs to refer to the most recently used noun. These phrases usually are verbal forms ending in *-ed* or *-ing.* When the phrase appears to apply to the wrong person or thing, or applies to nothing in the sentence, it is called a **misplaced modifier** or **dangling modifier.**

h. Phrases that simply add information and are not basic to the sentence need to be set off by two commas, one at the beginning and one at the end. See: **parenthetical phrases, comma use.**

i. The word *that* does have a specific and essential use in English. *That* is correctly used to add description to a noun or pronoun to identify it—and it alone—completely and to set it apart as unique. Its relative *which* is used if the information is not essential, but is an added thought. If the details in question could easily be removed from the sentence, a comma and *which* are used. A comma is never used with *that* except by unsure editors who end up muddying the meaning.

For example, different houses may be indicated in this set of instructions:

The party is at the third house *that* has green shutters.

The party is at the third house, *which* has green shutters.

To find the party, see **restrictive** and **nonrestrictive clauses; essential and nonessential clauses.**

3. Determining the Case of Nouns

Case refers to a noun's function or use in the sentence, clause or phrase. A noun either creates the action (**nominative case,** also called **subjective**), owns something (**possessive case**) or is the receiver of some action (**objective case**). These positions are signaled by a change in case.

j. **Possessives** are formed by adding an apostrophe and the letter s—except for plurals, which are the reverse. But, exceptions abound in American English. "The Associated Press Stylebook and Briefing on Media Law" and some grammar guides list exceptions including forming possessives with **proper nouns,** foreign words, formal titles, joint possession and when the following words begin with *s*.

Pronouns that express possession, such as *its, ours* and *yours,* already have an *s* and do not require an added apostrophe.

k. Considerable confusion exists with use of *who* and *whom,* and the latter is virtually dropping out of spoken American English. In writing, however, the difference remains key to meaning. *Who* (as well as *whoever*) is nominative case and indicates the actor. *Whom* (along with *whomever*) is objective case and indicates receiving the action. A good rule of thumb is to use *who* if a usage would call for *he* or *she,* and to use *whom* if it would require *him* or *her.*

For example, "Who did you say is singing?" recasts the idea that "He is singing," so the pronoun stays in nominative case. By contrast, "Whom should I hand the gift to?" recasts the question, "Should I give the gift to him?" and indicates objective case. See **who/whom; nominative case, objective case, pronouns** in nominative and objective case.

l. Case does not change depending on whether the meaning is singular or plural. Even when there are two or more actors or objects, they are still either nominative or objective case. See case and **singular** and **plural constructions.**

4. Checking Singular/Plural Agreement

m. Some words—such as *each, someone* and *everybody*—may sound as though they are plural, but they always function as singulars. Editors often memorize the most common and pesky of these but also check grammar guides for current lists of **always-singular** and **always-plural usages.** Distinctions are often subtle, such as *a number* being always plural, but *the number* always singular.

n. A subject may be singular but appear to need a plural verb when it is being set apart from a group. See **subject-verb agreement.** For example: Ghenghis Khan is the only one of the candidates who has killed the voters. (Only Ghenghis does this even though several candidates are running for office.) Similarly: She is the fastest of the 178 people who are running the marathon. (All are running the race.)

o. *Fewer* is used for discrete items: those that are separate and can be counted. *Less* is used for continuous amounts: Baked potatoes have *fewer* calories and *less* fat than the sour cream on the top. See **count** and **non-count nouns.**

p. American English remains a stickler in requiring a **collective noun** (a noun that is singular but that represents a group) to take a singular verb (and to use singular pronouns later in the sentence) if the group is acting as a unit. For example: The team has to score on its next drive. The audience rises to its feet. However, if actions are separate, the meaning and usage change to plural: The audience (members) wander in and find their seats.

q. **Fractions** of singular and plural nouns take their cue from the overall amount. If the whole is singular, the fraction is too: *Two-thirds* of the *pie is gone.* If the whole is many parts, the sense remains plural: *Two-thirds* of the *cars* in the lot *do* not *have* permits.

5. Building a List of Tricky Word Pairs and Combinations

These qualify as "tricky" if we have to keep looking them up.

r. In **neither/nor (either/or) constructions,** the noun closest to the verb determines whether it is singular or plural. For example: *Neither the environmentalist nor the protesters were arrested.* But, if *neither* is used without the *nor* (or *either* without *or*), it is singular. For example: *Neither of the protesters was arrested.*

s. People are always who; things are that. See **relative pronouns.**

t. *Lay* expresses action with an object; *lie* expresses a state of being at rest. Much of the confusion comes from *lay* being able to be either a **present-tense** or a **past-tense verb.** Before choosing between them in past tense, editors try out *reclined* (lay) or *placed* (laid), and then use the appropriate lie/lay word.

In the sentence, "The submarine *lay/laid* on the ocean floor," little sense comes in this sentence: The submarine *placed* on the ocean floor. The proper choice is the past tense of *lie:* The submarine *lay* on the ocean floor.

u. **Complements** are word pairs, such as *not only* needing to be completed by *but also.* See **correlative conjunctions.**

v. Conditionals allow expression of doubt about an outcome. Tevya, in "Fiddler on the Roof," sang "If I were a wealthy man . . . " to signify he doubted that would be so. A more optimistic phrase would have been: "If I was a wealthy man. . . . " See **subjunctive mood.**

w. *Continual* and *continuous* are words that sound similar but mean different things; *imply* and *infer* do, too. Many other similar pairs exist as well. See **confused words** and **diction.**

x. Words that build on each other's meaning when they modify a noun are called **compound modifiers** and need to be hyphenated. *Small business loans* has a different meaning than *small-business loans.*

y. When words used before a noun describe the noun and not each other, commas are used to separate them. Usually, if the word *and* would make sense, the comma is inserted: The winter was a *warm, wet* one. See **commas between modifiers.**

z. *Like* is used to compare things (nouns), to express that they are similar. *As if* and *as though* are used with verbal phrases to express expected outcome. *Such as* is used to give an example. An editor should pause when encountering a list beginning with *like* and decide if the items following are being used as actual examples or are merely similar.

Making It Better

Poised over a draft, about to begin editing, it's normal to wonder: Am I going to make this better? And, how will I know? Good editing reveals the priorities set in the stories, strengthens the internal contrasts, strives for clarity and beauty, ensures unity and serves the community. These values become apparent in the edited story:

- The story serves the audience it is intended for. The reporting and writing balance viewpoints and draw on multiple sources for as clear, complete, honest and fair a treatment as possible.

- The voice is appropriate for a publication's style. Either the writer's voice has been preserved or the institutional voice has been used.
- The facts are accurate, checked and verified.
- It is possible to retell what happened in clear chronology; the story is preserved and possibly enhanced. We long to hear stories; we grew up loving to sit around a fire or climb on someone's lap to hear one; we liked being read to when young and may still fall asleep at night holding a book. News stories usually break up chronologies to place the impact or outcome in the lead, but a well-edited story contains enough clarity about the sequence of events that a reader can reconstruct what happened.
- We can tell in its first several sentences what this story is really about. News stories often summarize main elements in their leads; after that, some will revert to narrative form, and some will remain in the inverted pyramid. Feature stories show their theme in the beginning, often by telling a key anecdote with people and a scene. After that, they present subthemes and a definite ending.
- The story is not trying to be several other stories at the same time by raising questions and not answering them or by blurring forms.
- The beginning and ending of the story relate well to each other, yet it is clear that a change in understanding has taken place between the two.
- When read out loud, the story sounds good. It pleases the ear.
- Internal contrasts are present and can be named. Contrasts exist in a variety of textual ways, including use of direct and indirect quotations; long and short sentences; active and passive voice; abstract ideas and concrete examples.
- The grammar is artistic and has deeply satisfying rhythms and nuances. These show in the thoughtful uses of structures that enhance meaning and beauty, such as parallel phrasings for coordinate ideas, sequence of tenses and cadence.
- Every part of the story and presentation that remains is essential and the reason why can be named. Repetitions and redundancies have been questioned and removed.
- The main ideas and points are so clear they seem almost too simply stated; language overall is simple and clear—without jargon.
- The editor is at ease and has no nagging doubts about taste, tone, sensitivity to audience, legal or ethical issues.

Conclusion

From the first work with the writer to the final proofread, editing is a set of processes. It proceeds in stages with time in between and with the emphasis shifting from one task to the next. Skill grows with the ability to articulate the work done at each stage, to be able to talk about grammar with a writer, to develop personal systems for gaining knowledge of language and to build one's confidence in the ability to make and appreciate tangible improvements to a story.

All of these processes require intelligence, patience and thoroughness. They require editors not to work in a vacuum and to move from the "big picture" to sentence basics, including grammar, usage, punctuation and spelling.

Fearless editing is based on caring about the accuracy, clarity, unity and beauty of the material passing across the desk or on the screen.

Exercises to Apply Concepts and Develop Skills _____

1. Goal: To see, understand and name basic writing errors.

   Preparation: Gather unedited stories, such as stories from a writing or reporting class, or draft stories reflecting recent events and liberally insert errors. Make a set of stories that contain grammar errors but not any AP Style or punctuation errors.

   Ask students to find the errors and, using the terms above, name the errors they find. But, forbid them to make any changes to the sentences themselves. Encourage students to explain the errors as though they were talking to the writer or reporter who wrote the sentence. It helps to let them use common words to describe problems, as these will be readily understood by the writers and will lead students gradually to using more technical terms. The process of seeing and naming construction errors will take most students considerable time and practice, usually stretching over several weeks.

2. Goal: To learn to trim or cut stories.

   Give students wire stories and ask them to trim them to specified shorter lengths, as in boiling stories down for news digests. Discuss the difference between making corrections and cutting stories and when each task is appropriate.

3. Goal: To learn to find help in a grammar guide.

   Using the A to Z grammar points in this chapter, assist students to locate the grammatical structures or problems in a grammar guide, either one assigned to the class or ones they already own. Many students need assistance and practice in bridging the gap between an error found and the extensive and often technical entry for the error in a guide.

4. Goal: To assess individual skills and identify which grammatical areas students have mastered and which need more work.

   Ask students to develop their own working lists of grammar points they find confusing or difficult to identify; help them to locate these in a grammar guide, and ask them to write, in their own words, a summary of the problem and an example of a solution under each item on their lists.

5. Goal: To practice being a coach to writers.

   Ask students to bring in a story each has written and exchange it with another student so that each edits a story written by someone else. When they return the stories to the writers, have each discuss the changes made with the student who edited the story. What was helpful and not helpful in what the editor did and said?

How does the writer feel about what happened to her story? This gives each student the chance to be on both sides of the writing and editing process within a short time period and to explore the perspective of each role.

Helpful Sources

Coaching writers:
A good resource that shows writing coaching at work is "Second Takes: Monthly Reflections on The Oregonian," a newsletter produced by The Oregonian Publishing Company, Portland, Ore., and written by Jack Hart, a managing editor.
Clark, Roy Peter and Don Fry. "Coaching Writers: Editors and Reporters Working Together." New York: St. Martin's Press, 1992.
Rich, Carole. "Writing and Reporting News: A Coaching Method." 4th Ed. Belmont Calif.: Wadsworth Publishing, 2002.

Grammar guides and handbooks:
Arnold, George T. "Media Writer's Handbook: A Guide to Common Writing and Editing Problems." 2nd Ed. New York: McGraw-Hill, 1999.
Brooks, Brian, et al. "Working with Words: A Handbook for Media Writers and Editors." 4th Ed. New York: Bedford/St. Martin's, 2000.
Fowler, H. Ramsey, et al. "The Little, Brown, Handbook." 7th Ed. New York: Addison-Wesley Pub. Co., 1998.
Fowler, H.W. and Sir Ernest Gowers. "A Dictionary of Modern English Usage." New York: Oxford University Press, 1965. McGraw-Hill offers a 1997 paperback edition of this classic work.
Goldstein, Norm, ed. "The Associated Press Stylebook and Briefing on Media Law." Cambridge, Mass.: Perseus Publishing, 2002.
Kessler, Lauren and Duncan McDonald. "When Words Collide: A Media Writer's Guide to Grammar and Style." 6th Ed. Belmont, Calif: Wadsworth/Thompson Learning, 2004.
Strunk, William Jr. and E.B. White. "The Elements of Style." New York: The Macmillan Co., 1959. Allyn and Bacon published the fourth edition of this classic in 2000.
University of Oregon. "The Tongue Untied." http://grammar.uoregon.edu/

5

Shaping Beautiful Writing

When we write, we believe our words are being molded into something beautiful.

We also believe the written information we pass along is automatically the same information being received. However, that does not always happen without much rewriting and editing.

A journalist reportedly once asked Ernest Hemingway why he rewrote the ending to one of his novels 47 times.

"I had to get the words right," Hemingway said.

Clear sentences that lead to others crafted in a similar manner provide readers an ease of understanding, a sense of beauty, as when we speak of literature, as opposed to writing. If a sentence is to achieve this beauty, it must be clear, and it must flow.

But, no sentence is an island, so unity is an important concept as well.

Each sentence in a story must flow according to the needs of the story and the sentences around it or in the paragraphs above or below. Editors must be skilled at seeing flaws—major or minor—in stories and then restoring or promoting the flow.

The story containing it may be a feature on wilderness with leisurely flowing sentences designed to underscore the serenity and loveliness of the mountains and streams it describes.

Or, it may be a short, choppy account of a new oil spill.

Good editors improve the story but preserve the style. Someone who had likely spent years editing copy once wrote: "Preserve the writer's style—if she is a writer and if she has style."

Sentence length is a major factor determining if the primary message gets to the reader. While the flow of the story will dictate to a degree if longer sentences are appropriate and if they should be crafted to place emphasis on a particular sentence part, the primary guideline is that sentences should be kept short.

Variations in sentence structure include **loose, balanced, standard** and **periodic** sentences—and **simple, compound, complex,** and **compound-complex.**

(Words set in boldface in this chapter are the terms used by grammar guides or English handbooks; this is done to make using these sources a bit easier.)

In journalism, sentences average about 15–17 words in length. Of course, this does not mean each sentence should be 16 words. Some will be shorter, and some, longer.

Paragraph length, too, is crucial to clarity. News writers are taught to become nervous if their paragraphs are much longer than one inch, whatever the column width. That is about four lines of printed text on letter-sized paper.

All those paragraph indentations provide extra white space that allows breathing room for the eye as it swims through the text. Paragraphs, thus, are usually no longer than a sentence or two.

This is especially important on the Web, for as the Stanford Poynter Project in 2000 found, online readers read widely but in a shallow manner—they are ready to stop reading at the click of a mouse.

With these more broad guidelines in mind, good editors begin checking basics: style, grammar, usage and punctuation.

Style as a Means of Unity

Style is crucial. In fact, most newspaper editing texts devote whole chapters to explaining all its rules. Editors cannot do their jobs well without thorough knowledge of the style being used by their publication or site. Large publications, such as newspapers and magazine publishing firms, often have their own style guides.

A style manual, probably "The Associated Press Stylebook and Briefing on Media Law," helps them achieve unity with a variety of areas that, without consistency, would give readers a subtle message of chaos. Style manuals tell editors when to capitalize, when to spell out numbers or use figures, when to abbreviate, how to handle dates, how to treat titles and how to handle punctuation.

For example, the AP guide tells editors that most titles placed before a name are capitalized and abbreviated and that ages are always handled as figures: Tree Defense League Sec. Tommy Treehugger, *46,* took his son Timmy, *4,* to the rally.

It tells them that specific dates are handled with figures and that the months longer than five letters are abbreviated: Treehugger predicted the last tree would be cut *Feb. 3, 2053,* and used to build a war canoe.

Manuals also provide consistency in a variety of areas, such as how to treat proper nouns (when is *Kleenex* used and when is it *facial tissue;* is it *Tabasco* or *hot pepper sauce*), how to handle temperatures (is it *minus 20* or *20 below zero*) and how to handle book and other titles (are they underlined, italicized, bolded, placed in quotation marks, etc.).

Manuals cover little things as well: Is it acceptable to write *Chevy? Gung-ho? TV?* How is *T-shirt* written? Is it National Organization *of* Women—or *for?* Is *wheeler-dealer* one word or two or hyphenated? What is the difference between *wind up* and *windup*?

Is *husband* better to use than *widower*? Is it *Worldwide Web* or *World Wide Web*? Should *innocent* be used or *not guilty*? When is it *blond* and when *blonde*? Is the prefix *multi* attached to a word with a hyphen or without one? When is it *fewer,* and when *less*?

What is the difference between *half-mast* and *half-staff*? Is it *m.p.h.* or *mph*? When is it *pupil,* and when is it *student*? Is it acceptable to use *tomorrow* instead of the specific day (say, Tuesday). Is *Bible* always capitalized?

Each detail such as any one of these is important. Collectively, in a 96-page newspaper, a four-page newsletter, a 40-page magazine or a 20-story Web site, they make or break the publication in terms of reader acceptance and trust. It is no wonder fearless editors have calluses on their fingers and thumbs from leafing through the dog-eared pages of their style guides.

Manuals often stress, too, that media writing must be concise. Brevity and succinctness rely on finding and using just the right words, the pithy phrase that can replace lengthy, jargon-laden language or wordy circumlocutions, those phrases that go round and round the point.

A fearless editor would recast a sentence such as this:

Due to the fact that the law of the state regarding employment at the present time requires custodial engineer supervisors to head up any team of subordinates who work beyond their normal hours of duty, the board must revise the custodial budget.

The sentence is likely to read like this:

Because state employment law now requires head janitors to supervise crews working overtime, the board must revise the custodial budget.

Fixing Basics: A Guide for When to Look Things Up

Grammar, usage and punctuation—the more troublesome aspects of which editors often incorporate into their personal editing systems—are covered in depth in grammar guides and English handbooks.

Using that personal system (see Chapter 4 for an "A to Z" example incorporating basics discussed below) and coupling it with a solid supporting knowledge of other basics, fearless editors leap into the middle of any sentence. They can spot an error and name it. If necessary, they get assistance from a handbook or guide and then repair the damage before the story's beauty is spoiled and miscommunication happens.

Here is a discussion of the major areas that, over time, those editors get to know quite well:

Tense

Editors routinely make certain a story mainly uses one tense. **Present, past** and **future** are the primary tenses, with most news stories, either in print or online, being in past tense. Feature writing in magazines often makes use of present tense.

But, many writers tend to wander from one tense to another. Editors must help writers eliminate multiple verb constructions and be consistent in one tense.

The sentence, "The land developer *drove* to town and then *sneaks* into an environmentalist's apartment," switches from past to present tense and must be corrected.

Using a feature approach, the writer may tell a story as if it is happening while the reader is reading. If appropriate for the information in question, a good editor preserves present tense but makes certain the sentences do not needlessly use other tenses. Future and the nonprimary tenses (**present perfect, past perfect, future perfect**) may be needed occasionally but are used because the editor has checked to be certain they show the appropriate time of action or state of existence being expressed.

Tense causes particular trouble for writers and editors when it comes to the principal parts of a few verbs, even though dictionaries list the acceptable principal parts at the beginning of the entry for the verb. In particular, *lie* causes trouble when confused with *lay,* as do *rise* and *raise,* and *sit* and *set.*

Agreement

Handbooks for grammar always have chapters explaining the rules of **subject-predicate agreement** (sometimes **subject-verb**) and **pronoun agreement.** Editors know that subjects and predicates (often called verbs because that is their part-of-speech label), must "agree" in **person, number** and **gender.**

They know too that pronouns must agree with their **antecedents** (the word or words earlier in the sentence they refer to) in a similar manner. In other words, consistency, or unity, is required to provide the greatest sentence clarity.

Person refers to **first, second** or **third** person: **first**—person speaking (usually I, me or we, us); **second**—person spoken to (you); **third**—person spoken of (he, him, she, her, they, them, it). Print and online editors deal primarily with stories written in third or first person.

For example, in this book, third person (*editor, editors, he, she, they*) is used primarily except that occasionally we add a personal touch—such as we are doing now—when we use first person (*we*).

Number is a term meaning singular or plural—whether a single person, place or thing is being written about or whether two or more are. Editors ascertain that the story and each sentence within it establishes use of singular or plural and uses it consistently.

In this book we use plural numbers (as in *editors* or *they*) primarily because it helps to reinforce that not all editors are men, but when we use an example, we switch to singular (using *editor* and *she,* along with *he*).

Gender refers to whether the pronouns used are for men or women (*he, she, her, him*) or something without sex (*it*).

As suggested just above, the world is not all white nor male. To promote equality in "Fearless Editing," we switch back and forth between feminine and masculine pronouns in our examples.

Editors understand the unity achieved by following the guidelines of agreement, and they also often have in their personal editing systems some of the stickier items involving agreement noted in Chapter 4: **neither/either, who/whom, collective nouns, fractions, none** and the like.

Voice

Sentences in the **active voice** are stronger and more direct than those in **passive-voice.** Grammar books provide useful, although sometimes confusing, explanations of voice.

An easy way to recognize passive voice is to ask this question of any sentence that has action, "Is the subject also the actor, or performer, of the action?"

If it is, the sentence is active. If not, and the receiver of the action is the subject, it is passive.

For example: A land developer *was crushed* by a runaway tractor. The sentence has action—crushing—but the performer of the action—tractor—is not the subject. Unless she has a compelling information-providing reason, the editor revises it to read like this: A runaway tractor *crushed* the land developer.

Active voice normally entails sentences with one-word predicates. A red flag about the presence of passive voice usually goes up in the minds of editors if a sentence has a predicate consisting of more than one word. In the example above, the editor changed *was crushed* to *crushed.*

However, should editors become posse leaders, hunting down all passive voice sentences?

No. At times, passive voice is appropriate, especially if importance of the receiver of action comes into play. For example: President Kennedy *was shot* to death today in Dallas by a lone gunman.

Parallel Structure

Unity is the underlying concept for **parallel structure** as well. Just as style guides provide rules for consistency of abbreviation, capitalization, punctuation, word use and other areas, so parallel structure ensures sentence consistency. It adds to the flow, and often the rhythm, of the story.

Editors who know their stuff watch for passages switching from one verb tense to another. They watch attributing verbs especially closely because they know writers sometimes write, "the environmentalist *said*," and later in the same piece write, "the environmentalist *says*."

Here are a few other common errors in parallel structure:

a. changes in voice
Editors need to spot switches from active to passive voice

b. change in verbals. Also see **infinitive, gerund, participle.**
Writers sometimes move from using one kind of verbal to another. For example: The land developer liked *hiking, swimming* and *to go* on picnics. The sentence switches from gerunds to an infinitive.

c. changing items in a series
Sometimes writers begin to provide a consistent list and then switch to non-parallel construction. For example: The developer outlined his land-use plan, his proposal for waste disposal and *that traffic will need to be rerouted.*

Case

Case refers to pronouns (and occasionally nouns) and whether they are functioning in a sentence as a subject, an object or an owner.

When pronouns are subjects, they are in **subjective** case (Also called nominative case). When objects, **objective** case. When owners, **possessive.**

That's the easy part.

The difficult part is that this area seems hopelessly mired in complexity.

Editors are willing to work at understanding those complexities and find ways to recognize and correct case errors.

Here are a few of the more troublesome problems with case:

a. nominative case and linking verbs
Writers and editors have little problem when the subject comes before the noun. They have more trouble with sentences constructed with **linking verbs** (state-of-being verbs, such as *am, is, are, was, were* and similar verbs related to the five human senses, such as *look, appear, sound, taste, smell, look, feel*).

When a pronoun is used in such sentences to substitute for the subject, it must be in nominative case. For example: The winner was *he*. It appeared to be *she* who had made the call.

b. case and use of *than*

When sentences use the conjunction *than*, editors often must use their personal editing system. They know the pronouns used will often be determined by **elliptical** (omitted) words. Thus, she will make choices similar to these:

> The land developer makes more money than I (*do*).

> The environmentalist admires no female senator more than (*he admires*) her.

[Depending on story context]

> My environmentalist wife loves this forest more than (*she loves*) me.

> The environmentalist loves this forest more than I (*love it*).

c. possessive case problems

Ownership pronouns and nouns also send up red flags for good editors. Their expertise goes beyond knowing that *its* is possessive ("The dog went to *its* kennel.") and that *it's* means *it is.*

They know the sentence, "The land developer supporters did not appreciate *his* lying to the grand jury," is correct—not *him* lying—because **gerunds** take possessives.

They go to guides such as "When Words Collide" or "The Associated Press Stylebook" to arrive at possessive constructions such as *boss' desk* or *Perkins' pancakes* or *witches' crockpots* or *Carter and Mondale's administration* or *Atwood's and Tyler's novels* or *mother-in-law's trust fund.*

They also know about **descriptive phrases** (placement of modifiers before a noun), which remove the need to emphasize ownership and relieve the need to use apostrophes.

Thus, *alumni vacation package* can be easily used instead of *alumni's vacation package.*

Dangling and Misplaced Modifiers

Editors must be attuned to placement of elements within sentences. If a **phrase** (group of related words without both a subject and predicate) or **clause** (group of words with both a subject and predicate) is not placed near the element it modifies, readers are momentarily confused, thus causing a fog to drift over sentence clarity. Editors often must rewrite such sentences to correct them.

Modifier problems fall into two major categories:

a. dangling modifiers

A dangling modifier occurs when a clause or phrase in a sentence modifies nothing. It has no clear connection to another element in the sentence.

For example: *Flying from New York to Los Angeles,* the Mississippi River and the Rocky Mountains can be seen. In this sentence, no person or thing is *flying.* The verbal *flying* is an action and needs an actor to refer to.

The editor must revise the sentence in some way to achieve clarity. She will probably write this: *While* flying *in a plane* from New York to Los Angles, *a traveler* sees the Mississippi River and the Rocky Mountains.

In the revision, the editor provides the necessary connection for the modifying phrase.

b. misplaced modifiers

As noted in the sample personal editing system in Chapter 4, a misplaced modifier occurs when a clause or phrase—or sometimes a word—in a sentence is placed so that it modifies the wrong element or creates confusion about what it modifies.

Because these are common, good editors learn to spot them and make appropriate changes.

For example: The land developer's infant was tended by her father, wearing a fresh diaper and blue booties. The meaning in this sentence ultimately reaches readers, but not until they wonder why the father wears a diaper and booties.

A good editor rewords the sentence to read like this: The land developer tended his infant daughter, who wore a fresh diaper and booties.

Sentences such as, "The boy was told not to give cat food to the elephant with small bones in it," or "The land developer found a pie baked by her sister on the top of the dishwasher," must be reworded to clarify that the elephant does not have the small bones or that the land developer's sister was not squatting and cooking on the top of the dishwasher.

Similarly, a single word—often a word such as *only, ever, merely, seldom, never, just, almost or quite*—causes a problem with clarity. This is sometimes called a **squinting modifier** in that it makes readers so confused they squint with intensity trying to understand the proper meaning.

In the sentence, "The boss *only* told Sam to sell the car by noon," which of the following meanings does the writer intend?

1) Nobody besides the boss gave such instructions.
2) The boss gave this one instruction and said nothing else.
3) The boss said the car must be sold by Sam.
4) The boss instructed the person to sell the car but do nothing else before noon.

Of course, the editor would need to find out from the writer which meaning was accurate and then revise the sentence.

For example, if #3 were the meaning, the sentence would read, "The boss told *only* Sam to sell the car by noon."

Fearless editors have their courage in part because of an ability to read sentences so carefully that they detect and correct all these modifier problems.

Quotations

Writers for print and online often quote material, and editors can do much to make the quoted material add to story flow.

At the very least, they make certain that each direct quotation is in a separate paragraph.

Here are a few other guidelines for better quotations:

1) The material chosen for quoting should have flair or be important wording. If not, it is likely better recast as an indirect quotation.

For example: "I believe a pipeline should be laid in the Mississippi River," an oil company president said.

Revised:

A pipeline should be laid in the Mississippi River, an oil company president said.

But, because of its flair and importance, the following should be left as a full-sentence quotation:

"We should snuff all those leftist environmentalists," the oil company president said.

Some editors may change the sentence to this:

Oil companies should "snuff all those leftist environmentalists," the president said.

But, good editors know that too many quoted bits of sentences, known as **partial quotes** or **orphan quotes** annoy readers and make a story "choppy" because of their "constant" "interruption" of sentence "flow."

Too many partial quotes also begin to make readers wonder if the writer lacked an ability to write down an entire sentence.

2) The attributing phrase—consisting of the person who said the material AND the verb describing the utterance, such as *she said, he bellowed, she shouted, they whined*—are most effective if written in normal subject/predicate order.

For example: "I eat environmentalists for dinner," *Dan Developer said.*

Not: "I eat environmentalists for dinner," *said Dan Developer.*

However, occasionally, when long titles or descriptions are part of the attributing phrase, the order is better when reversed, such as in this example:

"I think land developers are clowns," said Timmy Treehugger, *special administrative assistant to the state land commissioner.*

3) The verb in attributing phrases should be appropriate. Too often editors become uneasy when writers use the word *said* over and over. They become fearful and begin to toss in other words, such as *lamented* or *whimpered* that may change meaning of the story.

The good editor is not afraid of using *said* repeatedly, realizing that the words *said* or *told* or *according to* carry no extra meaning. They know that *announced* or *charged* or *testified* are appropriate at times—but only if the person is *announcing* or *charging* or *testifying.*

They will allow *shouted* if the writer knows the speaker shouted. They will occasionally allow an attributing verb such as *thundered* if the shouting were by a deep-voiced person yelling so loudly that the words boomed on the ears of those hearing.

In brief, they know that the accurate attributing word promotes clarity regarding the conditions under which the quoted material was uttered or written—and they know that feature stories see more unusual attributing words than stories presenting factual material in a straightforward manner.

4) Attributing phrases usually make the direct quotation most effective if placed after the quoted material.

For example: Dan Developer said, "I eat environmentalists for dinner."
Revised:
"I eat environmentalists for dinner," Dan Developer said.

The quote itself, which engages readers, adds power to the text when they do not have to struggle past the attributing phrase before reading it.

Similarly, if multiple sentences are quoted, the attributing phrase is most effectively placed after the first sentence.

For example: "Land developers are evil," Timmy Treehugger said. "They are devils. They are the albatrosses that make my neck sag."

5) Long blocks of quoted material should be broken into other shorter paragraphs, usually not much longer than an inch long. Style guides often show methods of doing this.

Here is a brief example:

"Land developers are evil," Timmy Treehugger said. "They are devils. They are the albatrosses that make my neck sag.

"In fact, developers are to blame for all the ills that afflict humanity.

"They should be rounded up and placed on a raft and towed to a desert island in the Pacific Ocean."

The example uses five sentences and one attributing phrase placed after the first of them. It also uses quotation marks at the beginning of each new paragraph to indicate the quoted material is continuing—but none at the end of the first and second paragraphs in order to let readers know the quotation is continuing.

Finally, the concluding quote marks after *Ocean* tell readers the long quote is over.

6) Editors know that quote marks are normally double marks and that quotations within a quotation use single marks, such as in this example:

"I want to thank the person who said, 'Trees are a treasure,' " Timmy Treehugger said.

Sentences that contain quotations, which in turn quote material also containing quoted material ("a quote within quote within quote"), are more effective if rewritten.

Punctuation

Fearless editors are good at punctuation. They know all the frequent punctuation uses and willingly use guides and handbooks to be sure less frequently used marks of punctuation (such as **ampersands** and **ellipses, parentheses** and **brackets**—not covered here) are used correctly.

a. end marks

Besides knowing that **periods, question marks** and **exclamation points** end sentences, editors know that periods are always placed inside quotation marks when used with them.

They know **exclamation marks** are rarely used—and certainly not in massive doses to make boring material more lively!!!!!

They place one exclamation mark either inside or outside of quotation marks—inside if the whole exciting material is there and outside if the excitement began before the quoted material did, as in this sentence:

The land developer fainted when the environmentalist told him, "Your bald head reminds me of a clearcut"!

Editors use a **question mark** inside quotation marks only if the entire question is also inside those marks. Otherwise, they place it outside at the very end of that line.

For example: Have land developers heard the phrase, *"green, green trees of home"*?

b. semicolons, colons, dashes, hyphens

Semicolons and colons provide no surprise to strong editors. They know **semicolons** can serve as a weak period to divide short sentences connected in meaning, such as in this sentence: "The land developer went to Club Med in Mexico; his wife stayed to supervise the clear-cutting operation."

Semicolons can also function as a strong comma in separating a series of listed items.

For example: The stream-saving convention delegates elected Randy Raccoon, 35, New York, president; Tina Trout, 33, Miami, vice president; and Rita Rapids, 44, Fort Worth, secretary.

Editors know, however, that when used with quotations, semicolons are always placed outside—to the right.

Besides being used at beginnings of business letters, **colons,** in a manner similar to dashes, announce that something is coming.

For example: The logging company decided on its new advertising slogan: "Pesky pines make perfect porches."

Dashes—the long ones—are usually used to indicate a severe departure from the main idea of the sentence or a pause that is emphatic. (Dashes separate while hyphens join.) In a sense, dashes can replace parentheses in marking off a parenthetical expression. They can be used much like a colon or comma when the editor wants to add vigor, special emphasis or emotion.

For example: The oil company president—a man who has said environ-mentalists are un-American—arrived Friday to tour the pipeline explosion site.

Another example: The oil company gave the tanker captain a new car—an ironic gift because he had no license to drive.

Dashes can also be used in pairs to eliminate confusion from lists with a lot of commas.

For example: The land developer's new wardrobe—consisting of silk socks, shorts, pajamas, ties and trousers—was lost in the pipeline explosion.

Of course, they are also used to attribute quotations.

For example: "A man said to the universe, 'Sir, I exist.' "—Stephen Crane

Hyphens (the short ones -) go beyond their required use in dictionaries and use by guidebooks such as "The Associated Press Stylebook" for betting odds, game scores, fractions, etc.

They are sometimes used to join prefixes or suffixes to words, or sometimes words to words to ensure clarity.

For example: *Re-enter* would not make sense as *reenter.*

And, as noted in Chapter 4, editors know two or more words belonging together to make clear meaning in modifying a noun or pronoun must have a hyphen—and sometimes more—inserted. But, **adverbs** are excluded from this guideline.

For example: The *strawberry-nosed* land developer knocked on the door. His *off-the-cuff* greeting was surprising because he was not normally *sharp-tongued.* Nonetheless, his host gave him a *very warm* reception.

Editors also know some sentences have more complicated use of hyphens, sometimes called **suspensive hyphenation** (a method of elaborating that elim-inates unnecessary repetition) in a manner similar to this: "The oil company wanted a *20- to 30-percent increase* in diesel fuel cost." (The extra word *percent* is eliminated.)

c. commas

Fearless editors are not afraid of commas. They know a comma is not a punctuation mark that is used at the whim of the writer—but with a definite reason.

As noted in Chapter 4, they certainly know it is unacceptable to join two separate sentences only with a comma (**comma splice**).

Moreover, good editors have a thorough understanding of the seemingly endless comma uses, and if they can't name a reason for inserting one, they leave it out—if in doubt, leave it out.

One way for an editor-in-training to get control of commas is to develop a personal list of the pesky ones and write the list in a straightforward manner.

For example, the "Catman comma guide," Box 5.1, lists those commas we've found to be most frequently missed—in descending order of their frequency. Of course, the guide does not include the more esoteric comma uses, which editors often look up in their handbooks and grammar guide.

BOX 5.1 • *Catman Comma Guide*

This guide features Montana folk legends and environmentalists, Catman and Cat-woman, who wore long, brown overcoats and aviator caps with chin straps, jumped from freight trains passing through small Montana towns and promoted environ-mental causes.

1. Use a comma to set off the **independent clauses** in a compound sentence, which is when *and, but, or, nor, for, so,* or *yet* join two clauses that could each function alone as a separate sentence.

> Catman went to the environmentalist convention, but his roommate stayed home to watch television.
>
> Catwoman drank the only cold soda in the cooler, and Catman drank the last of the water, so the loggers had to drink grape juice.

2. Use a comma after all items except the one before the *and* **in a series** of three or more. Include a comma before the *and* only if needed for clarity.

> Catman brought juice, soda, mineral water and goat milk.
>
> Catwoman went home to sleep, Catman went to the cafe to eat and the other protesters stayed at the rally.
>
> Catman ran up the stairs, down the hall and into his room.
>
> **But:** Catman ordered cheese and crackers, bacon and eggs, and apple pie and ice cream.

3. Use a comma after a **dependent clause** (also called a **subordinate clause** and usually introduced by **subordinating conjunction** such as *because, if, when, while, since, though, wherever* or *rather than*) at the beginning of a sentence. Use a comma even if the subject and predicate are left out. Do not use a comma if the dependent clause is in its normal place at the end of a sentence.

> *When the mayor gave Catwoman a medal of environmental courage,* all the developers complained.
>
> *If (they were) angry enough to seek revenge,* the developers did not show it.
>
> All the developers complained *when the mayor gave Catwoman a medal.*

4. Use a comma after a longer **phrase** (usually four words or more) or group of phrases at the beginning of a sentence. Use a comma with introductory verbal phrases that are modifiers. Also, use a comma after a short phrase to promote clar-ity of meaning.

> *Behind the old cedar tree,* Catman found a logging cable.
>
> *After her encounter with the developers in the tavern,* Catwoman wandered alone in the woods.
>
> *Running to meet the journalist,* Catman tripped over the chainsaw.
>
> *After losing,* Catwoman decided to give up politics for a year.

5. Use commas to set off other **nonessential modifiers** (also called **nonrestric-tive elements**). These provide information that is not crucial, or essential, to the basic meaning of the sentence.

> Catman, *who is every environmentalist's friend,* will battle for cleaner streams this summer.

(continued)

BOX 5.1 • Continued

As noted in Chapter 4, do not use them to set off modifiers that are **essential** to identification of the word they modify. See also **restrictive elements.**

The environmentalist *who always howls anti-polluting songs beneath the moon* is known as Catwoman.

6. Use commas to set off **appositives** (words or phrases that rename nouns or pronouns and similar to non-essential modifiers) that are longer than 1 word.

Dr. Catman, *chief environmental biologist,* will lecture today.
Catman, *an environmentalist since childhood,* will visit Montana this week.
No commas: His sister *Sarah* dislikes Catwoman very much.

7. Use commas to set off **parenthetic expressions** (words and phrases that interrupt sentence flow—such as *however, consequently, indeed, for example, of course*). Also, see **conjunctive adverbs.**

Consequently, Catman took a strong stance against drift nets. The others on Catwoman's team, *however,* were planting trees.
Corporate executives do not know how Catman thinks, *however.*
Catwoman, *for example,* detests the new logging policy.

8. Use commas to set off one modifier from another before a noun when each modifier modifies the noun and not each other. If *and* can be inserted or if the order of the modifiers can be inverted, a comma is needed. See **coordinate adjectives.**

Catman was a *vibrant, dynamic* spokesman for the environment.
Catwoman gave a *short, powerful, moving* speech beside the oily stream.
Not: Catman was *a very, clever* orator.

9. Use commas to set off introductory words such as *yes, no, well, and, but, first, second,* etc.

Yes, Catwoman is unpredictable when she deals with littering.
And, the last explosion prompted Catman to start an anti-pipeline campaign.

10. Use commas with cities and states together, by placing one after each item.

Catman lived in *Salem, Ore.,* after he was born.
Catwoman lived in *Austin, Texas,* after she was born.

11. Use commas with dates using months, days and years. Place commas after the day and year.

Catman was born *March 8, 1947, in Dillon, Mont.*

12. Use commas around ages and addresses and political party affiliation.

Catman, *48, 3333 N. Holly St.,* was arrested for protesting stream pollution.
U.S. Sen. Katarina Catwoman, *R-Mont.,* said she hopes to defeat all opponents in the election.

13. Use commas to separate most attribution from statements (either in direct or in indirect quotations). Place commas to the left of quotation marks.

Developers will invade Montana, *Catman said.*
"Developers are sure to invade Montana," *Catwoman said.*
Catwoman said, "Developers are sure to invade Montana."
Developers will invade Montana, *according to Catman,* but they will not conquer the state.
"Developers will invade Montana," *Catwoman said,* "but they will not conquer the state."
But: Catman *said* developers will invade Montana.

Conclusion

Work with basic writing in areas such as these may seem to be nothing short of grunt work. And, perhaps it is.

But clarity of meaning cannot be achieved without attention to basics, and the beauty and unity that result from consistent story treatments would be nonexistent as well.

Fearless editors dive in eagerly because they love the language and know basics are crucial if clarity is to be achieved and story beauty maintained.

Exercises to Apply Concepts and Develop Skills

1. Goal: To understand and apply verb tenses in newswriting.

   Using the guidelines in this chapter, practice editing news stories written in past tense for newspapers into present tense for magazine features, or vice versa. Discuss how the tense affects the flavor of the story.

2. Goal: To edit for different voices.

   Take a colorful, lively writing excerpt (perhaps a Web page) and practice editing out color and voice for an institutional, newspaper approach; editing it to match the voice a newsletter has; and letting it stand or altering it slightly for a magazine.

3. Goal: To achieve beauty through editing for parallel structure.

   Find sentences with multiple elements that can be reworded using parallel structure, or ask students to write such sentences and exchange them with other students to edit. Discuss the difference between correcting errors and editing for grace that brings clarity and beauty.

4. Goal: To achieve clarity by untangling confused meanings.

   Work on sample sentences from news stories or grammar guides that show problems with agreement, case and dangling or misplaced modifiers. Students can collect examples of these errors as they read media or can write incorrect sentences to exchange with others to edit. Discuss how meaning becomes confused or changed due to faulty structures.

5. Goal: To integrate quotations smoothly with narratives.

Using actual stories with punctuation errors added, or with exercises in grammar guides or work books, ask students working in small groups to correct the handling of partial quotes, placement of attribution, and ordering of punctuation with quotations. Discuss both clarity of meaning and the readers' ability to figure out exactly what the speaker said.

6. Goal: To master the most essential uses of punctuation.

Ask students to bring in examples of punctuation usage they find most difficult to master. These may be correct or incorrect sentences or a mixture of both. Build exercises using grammar guides, supplemental exercise texts, or those provided on grammar Web sites or through college or university programs providing assistance in basic English composition courses.

Helpful Sources

Grammar guides and handbooks:

Brooks, Brian, et al. "Working with Words: A Handbook for Media Writers and Editors." 4th Ed. New York: Bedford/St. Martin's, 2000.

Fowler, H.W. and Sir Ernest Gowers. "A Dictionary of Modern English Usage." New York: Oxford University Press, 1965. McGraw-Hill offers a 1997 paperback edition of this classic work.

Garner, Bryan A. "A Dictionary of Modern American Usage." New York: Oxford University Press, 1998.

Goldstein, Norm, ed. "The Associated Press Stylebook and Briefing on Media Law." Cambridge, Mass.: Perseus Publishing, 2002.

Kessler, Lauren and Duncan McDonald. "When Words Collide: A Media Writer's Guide to Grammar and Style." 6th Ed. Belmont, Calif: Wadsworth/Thompson Learning, 2004.

Rivers, William L. and Alison Work Rodriguez. "A Journalist's Guide to Grammar and Style." Boston: Allyn and Bacon, 1995.

Strunk, William Jr. and E.B. White. "The Elements of Style." New York: The Macmillan Co., 1959. Allyn and Bacon published the fourth edition of this classic in 2000.

Ethics, gender issues and sensitivity:

Alia, Valerie, Brian Brennan and Barry Hoffmaster, eds. "Deadlines & Diversity: Journalism Ethics in a Changing World." Halifax, Nova Scotia, Fernwood Pub., 1996.

Dumond, Val. "The Elements of Nonsexist Usage." New York: Prentice Hall Press, 1990.

Miller, Casey and Kate Swift. "The Handbook of Nonsexist Writing: For writers, editors and speakers." 2nd Ed. New York: Harper & Row, 1988.

Wood, Julia T. "Gendered Lives: Communication, Gender, and Culture." 5th Ed. Belmont, Calif.: Wadsworth, 2003.

World Wide Web sources for grammar:

Australian government site on writing. http://www.detya.gov.au/publications/plain_en/writing.htm http://www.dest.gov.au/archive/publications/plain_en/

Poynter Institute has a wide range of material to help with writing. http://poynter.org

University of Oregon. "The Tongue Untied." http://grammar.uoregon.edu/

6

Components of Story Packages

Long, gray slabs of text are signs of the past—in fact, distant past. Though newspapers like the Wall Street Journal and New York Times retain some of that look as a visual reference to tradition, depth of coverage and history, they do so as counterpoint to contemporary looks.

The contemporary style of magazines, World Wide Web pages, newspapers, newsletters and press kits offers readers shorter stories, fact-laden break-out items, photos and, sometimes, video and sound. This style has more goals than exclusively guiding the reader in linear fashion from one point to the next through pages of narrative.

Long stories still are offered, but they are commonly broken into main stories and sidebars, or run as segments with subheads, or even serialized. And at many points, the reader or user is invited to look at a graphic or illustration to pull in additional details, or at sidebars to explore a theme he perceives in the grouping of these components. (See Box 6.1.)

Editors realize that audience members have considerable control over their news and entertainment diets and will actively choose how to spend their time in a media-rich, competitive environment. This includes choosing which components to peruse, and in which order.

Editors are also working in more than one medium and ask how most effectively to shape a story as they move it, perhaps from a print page to the Web, or vice versa. They may prepare brief digests for indexes in newspapers or on Web pages that will direct—and entice—readers to go to the full story or to related ones.

A full story treatment may consist of a main story with small accompanying stories, called **sidebars,** and a number of text-based graphic treatments such as boxed lists of facts, called **breakouts;** quotations set in large type, called **pull-quotes; time lines;** brief biographies; checklists; **Q&A** columns; and even instant polls. (See Illustration 6.1.)

BOX 6.1 • *Text-Based Graphics*

Do's, Don'ts and Definitions

sidebar: A shorter story that accompanies a main story. Often it offers a change in pace, style or viewpoint from the main story and gives a human face to the news by profiling a person involved with the event. Or, it may be a roundup of reactions to an event, or a summary of highlights in the history of the topic.

While working on the main story, editors should watch for segments that seem to not quite fit because their tone shifts or they concentrate long enough on the subtopic to distort the main narrative flow. Instead of deleting some paragraphs, the editor might pull out the entire segment for a sidebar.

subhead: The workhorse for longer stories, this short line of type, usually boldface, signals a pause for readers and indicates the subject or theme of the coming segment. They are more enticing if they use active verbs than if they are labels that simply state topics.

digests: A staple in all media, these reduce news stories to short items. Their length and heading sizes are often predetermined by a set format so that a number of short news items can be run together in one place with a uniform look.

Frequently, these would be major news items to the audience except that they miss one or more of the prime news values—typically proximity. A train wreck might be front-page news in the community where it happens but become a digest item 2,000 miles away. A key to editing these is ensuring that the brief version that remains answers any points suggested by the lead.

summaries: These are brief descriptions of longer stories to be found on subsequent pages of a publication or on other screens of a Web site. A key is to introduce the content of the story without giving away all of its interesting features.

A summary must avoid simply repeating the lead. This would bore readers, plus it focuses just on the beginning of the story. A better summary will at least hint at the nature of the story overall and its style of presentation. Some publications use thumbnail photos with summaries for quick visual identification of the main piece.

fact box: A sentence or a list covering key points is pulled from the story and set off as a separate item. Usually it is set boldface and floats in white space to the side.

The fact box may succinctly state a major story angle that complements but does not repeat the angles covered by the heading, deck head, and caption (cutline). An editor may write the information, rather than use a line from the story. As one of the items most noted by readers scanning a page, the fact box serves a vital role in drawing them into the story.

pullquotes: These are direct quotations set in larger, often boldface type. They need to be colorful, poignant, witty, dramatic or pithy. Otherwise, they have no point.

The words are set within quotation marks along with the source's name and title or role in the story. Editors set up pullquote formats ahead of time so that the words can be added quickly and will be visually consistent with other pullquotes used.

bio box: Many reporters gather resumes from newsmakers in the course of covering speeches and other events. And, numerous biographical references (both in print and online) can provide the basics for a public figure's life.

A key is to keep the milestones highlighted consistent to avoid stereotypes of gender or ethnicity. A standing format for a bio box would have entries for education and for marriage, for example, both of which would be used for both men and women.

time lines: Time lines chart key points in the evolution of major events that are covered over time through numerous stories. In other words, they provide perspective.

Time lines begin with a chronological line with evenly spaced intervals, which may be days, months, years, decades or even centuries. They chart the major events and often provide more contextual information than just a label. The perspective that selects which events were truly key developments can change with the passage of time as current research, insights and social values become important elements.

Q&A: The question-and-answer format is built upon knowing what the most common and frequent questions are that the readers have on the subject at hand. In magazines and newspapers, these are useful for relaying interviews with celebrities, or for providing consumer-oriented checklists covering what people need to know to prepare for an earthquake, or to buy a house the first time. Web pages adopted FAQs (frequently asked questions) early on to assist users.

audience polls: These are designed to encourage readers or viewers to feel involved with a publication or Web site. They offer a way for them to interact and feel as though their opinions matter. However, editors must decide how to display the results they gather because not to do this would defeat the original purpose.

One guideline is to state that results are not scientific and won't accurately represent the true spectrum of opinion. Typically, people who feel a strong motivation are the ones who respond, and some feel so strongly they respond more than once.

Another guideline is to package the audience polls to look like the entertainment items they are. Presentation can stress anecdotal or colorful responses, for example, and downplay numerical results by rendering them in a different graphical style than used for scientific research or opinion gathering.

The main story often ends by telling how to get in touch with the writer or with agencies mentioned in the story. The reader who has been actively choosing where to start reading the package and which items to digest can now choose additional action if she wishes.

Text-based graphic items function not just as information bearers, but also as points of entry, which are like signposts that indicate a package's contents and

ILLUSTRATION 6.1 This cover page for the local news section of the Seattle Post-Intelligencer shows a variety of graphical treatments using text. The paper's design has won international awards; editors and copy editors write elements such as the headings, pullquotes, summaries and breakouts.

provide optional places to begin reading or viewing. Because they are based on text, editors rather than artists often create them.

Eye-Movement Studies

Research by the Poynter Institute shows that readers enjoy multiple entry points; they like the spontaneity of starting anywhere they wish in a package.

Poynter's research tracking how a viewer's eyes move over a page discovered that a reader will look first at the small, graphic type items, such as **deck heads** (smaller heading below the primary heading), **subheads,** photo captions and the explainers accompanying graphics. Then the eyes move into the story, begin reading and only then move back up to peruse the accompanying photographs.

This pattern runs counter to past conventional belief that eyes go first to photos, and it emphasizes how important the graphic treatments of text are in introducing major angles of a story. These ways of displaying information become doubly important on Web pages because viewers using slower modem connections have the time to read and absorb them while waiting for the photos to load.

Early research on Web use found that users mainly scan pages. But, Poynter studies suggest that viewers will settle in to read and that they tend to finish three-quarters of any given item. The average time spent is short, however, at seven minutes of reading time per online source visited.

Jakob Nielsen and John Morkes, Sun Microsystems engineers, found in their research that using the inverted-pyramid story structure and writing in objective news style increased how much users read and accurately understood. They also found that subheads describing the topic of each section increase a story's "scannability."

A special aspect of the Internet is its ability to deliver long documents, which users plan to print out. Some research, such as work at Yale's Center for Advanced Instructional Media, suggests that four screenfuls is a useful rule of thumb as the maximum users will read on the screen before stopping or deciding to print out.

Very few stories in print media are read by a newspaper's or magazine's entire audience. Research shows that while most newspaper readers will scan the front page headlines, they select only a few stories throughout the newspaper to read in depth. The ones noticed the most are those with accompanying infographics or photos, which may signal their importance through the extensive treatment editors have given to them.

These text-based graphics give crucial clues to readers about the relative importance of a story, its depth of treatment and the variety of information it contains. And if research is correct, they also become prime areas for storytelling, for introducing the themes that drive stories and are elaborated in the subheads and breakouts. (See Illustration 6.2.)

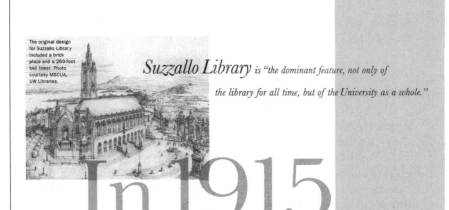

Suzzallo Library is *"the dominant feature, not only of the library for all time, but of the University as a whole."*

In 1915

IT IS A DOT ON A NEW campus plan that makes it the center of campus. In 1923 it is a series of working drawings by the head of the architecture department, including the design for a 260-foot tower that is never built. In 1926 it is one of the "extravagances" that causes the governor to pack the Board of Regents and fire the UW president. In 1927 it opens to great acclaim—the reading room "is pronounced by experts to be the most beautiful on the continent and is ranked among the most beautiful in the world." In 1933 it is named after the same president who was fired a few years earlier. In 1935 a south wing opens following the architect's plan. In 1963 the University discards the original design for a modernist addition by Bindon and Wright. (By this point in time, much of the original reading room furniture is "surplused.") In 1991 it is designated one of the most dangerous buildings on campus during an earthquake. In 1999, after rejecting an earlier request, the state Legislature devotes $47 million to make it safer. Work starts two years

Carl Gould (left), the library's architect, and UW President Henry Suzzallo. Photos courtesy MSCUA, UW Libraries.

later. In 2001 a 6.8 earthquake shakes the 74-year-old structure. Some decorative pieces on the roof to tumble onto "Red Square" and cracks appear in the masonry walls. In 2002 it opens on time and on budget, restored to its original glory, the jewel in the crown of the University of Washington.

"It" is Suzzallo Library, the "soul of the University," according to President Henry Suzzallo and "the dominant feature, not only of the library for all time, but of the University as a whole," according to its architect, Carl Gould, the first chair of the UW architecture department.

Technically a collection of wings and additions, most alumni think of the western side of Suzzallo when someone mentions the UW's main library. Built in 1927, it is the campus cathedral—a soaring exterior of 11 monumental stained glass windows, framed by Gothic-inspired statues, arches and buttresses made of terra cotta, cast stone and brick. Inside is the most voluminous library reading room in the nation—65 feet high, 52 feet wide and 250 feet long—a sanctuary for learning.

Gould's biographers say it is one of his finest works. One architecture historian calls it the "acme" of Collegiate Gothic at the UW. For the hundreds of thousands of alumni who once studied there, it is a treasured place where they sought inspiration to learn—and, for some, a quiet place to sleep (See

ILLUSTRATION 6.2   This feature in Columns on the University of Washington's historic library began with a large photo and title page. On these following pages, smaller photos, a subhead, captions and lengthy introductory text carry essential parts of the story. The integration of these design elements follows through on the rest of the story's pages.

"Jewel Renewal" was designed by Ken Shafer for the Sept. 2002 issue of Columns Magazine, University of Washington. Reproduced by permission.

"Suzzallo Memories," page 62).

But behind the beauty lurked danger. Because it came together in bits and pieces (besides the 1927 wing, there were additions built in 1935, 1947 and 1963), Suzzallo was a structural disaster in the making. In an earthquake, these wings could move at different speeds, the walls of each section banging against the other.

Add to the structural danger thousands of people walking in and out of the library every day, and you have "high damage potential" and "high life safety danger," said a 1991 report on the seismic status of campus buildings. Engineers ranked it and Hec Edmundson Pavilion as the most dangerous campus buildings in an earthquake.

Though it had to try twice, the UW convinced legislators in 1999 to fund the costly work—the total comes to $47,259,167. About 95 percent of the budget was spent on seismic and life safety work, and only 5 percent on remodeling, explains Assistant Librarian Paula Walker, who oversaw the library's side of the project.

As students, faculty, staff and alumni walk through Suzzallo when it reopens this month, they might wonder where all the money went. But that reaction is exactly what librarians, architects and engineers want. Their goal was to hide as much of the seismic work as possible, returning rooms in the 1927 and 1935 wings to their original state.

Looking at the ornate ceiling in the reading room, there is no sign that behind the plaster are tons of steel truss work, linking the 1927 wing to the other parts of the building. Workers poured three stories of concrete shear walls in the north and south ends of the wing and then added steel bracing up to the ceiling, but the work is hidden in utility closets and mechanical space.

For a sign that the building is much stronger, visitors have to leave the reading room. Outside, almost floating above the entryway, is what engineers call a "bat wing," a web of steel truss work that arches over the ceiling, connecting the 1927 wing to the rest of the building. Other signs of strengthening include exposed X-beams coming through the floors of the area outside of the reading room and in parts of the 1963 addition.

Sunlight illuminates the pinnacles and towers of Suzzallo. Photo © Loyd C. Heath. Inset: "Thought" statue above the main entrance. Photo © William Thompson.

ILLUSTRATION 6.2   *Continued*

Graphics Present Editing Questions

Creating these graphics requires considerable time and imagination on the part of editors. And, they may feel that they are not standing on the solid ground of journalistic tradition emphasizing unbroken narration. Some perplexing questions arise, such as:

- How do editors preserve good storytelling? Do new media and presentation practices require editors to adapt narrative storytelling?
- How do they ensure that graphics add meaning and news value to story packages?
- How do editors efficiently process enormous amounts of information, including creating summaries or digests and moving material from one medium to another?
- How do editors assess the accuracy and validity of Web-based news services and reference sites?
- Finally, how do they get all of this done by deadline?

Some answers can be found in traditional journalistic storytelling, plus new permutations suggested by research. Some traditional skills, such as those involved in wire-service editing, translate to the information-processing demands of the Web news environment. Some research guidelines are developing to show editors how to efficiently use and evaluate Web sources. Finally, editors can control many aspects of the software they use and can create their own time-saving shortcuts.

Working with Longer Stories

Carole Rich, a journalism professor and former reporter, concluded a study for the Poynter Institute by encouraging writers and editors to keep experimenting with story forms. Recent research shows that Web page users do pause to read in addition to scanning, she writes, and some experiments such as newspaper serials and in-depth multimedia stories have evoked enthusiastic followings.

She notes that the inverted pyramid is good to facilitate scanning but also says that writers trying to entice reading must explore other styles.

All print media and many Web sources offer a mix of longer narratives and brief items, summaries and ways for readers to interact. The goal is to build dynamism from these contrasts in length and treatment. A varied pace, varied voices and varied ways for readers to become involved all make for a livelier publication.

Some editors argue that this mix becomes a cacophony of multiple, unrelenting bits of data and that the voice of narrative, which provides order, chronology, context and, ultimately, meaning, is more important than ever. It remains central to storytelling and is adjusting to contemporary visual style and to the demands of each medium.

A narrative flow is built around a chronological story line while inverted-pyramid news stories break up chronology by giving the most important facts first. Features lend themselves more to narrative, and they may be organized around themes instead of a news event, as discussed in Chapter 2.

In print and on the Web, the lead, in addition to giving basic information about the time, place and people involved, establishes the themes of the narrative. It may reveal the storytelling style through a brief scene or bit of dialogue.

Subheads: Organizing by Theme

Longer stories use a narrative line or a major theme to organize shorter sections that present action, drama, dialogue, descriptive scenes and developed characters (as opposed to sources who appear only briefly).

The lead will present the main theme, but it cannot introduce all of these aspects by itself. The heading, secondary headings or deck heads, photo captions and pullquotes all can weigh in, each presenting a theme to be explored in the story. A reader seeing the story online will be reading these items first while photos, maps and other graphics are loading.

For the body of the narrative, **subheads** become a major tool by which editors give readers clues about the subtheme developed in each segment. The writer might explore the story through a series of scenes; the resulting pattern of rising and falling action is called pacing. An editor working with this technique can adjust the narrative to work in segments introduced by subheads, either in print or on separate pages online.

Editors in online news refer to complex stories as having several "threads." The challenge lies in handling these threads, or making each connecting thread apparent to readers of a story who move from screen to screen and make numerous choices in building their own narratives.

"Chunking" refers to breaking a story into segments, each of which will fit on one or two screens. This practice raises questions of how much narrative storytelling, plus how much balancing information, need to appear in each chunk. Rich, in her research for Poynter, suggests that each segment must contain some narrative, or chronological, kernel.

Some researchers question whether readers who have so much control over what they view at all will avoid unpleasant or difficult issues, and whether they will seek out different or opposing points of view rather than simply clicking on the most palatable or pleasing material.

Including balancing viewpoints, or "telling both sides of the story," is a primary function of news writing and editing. For example, in newspapers, where a story often "jumps" from page one to be continued on an inside page, editors ensure that "both sides" appear before the jump because many people stop reading at that point. If rebuttal information, or "the other side" of the story, is held until the end, not only will most readers not see it, but they also will relegate it as less important.

Some ways to encourage readers to stick with stories through jumps and from screen to screen are suggested by research.

Rich recommends trying different endings for chunks, such as questions or cliffhangers that spur the reader on by building up suspense. Techniques from fiction writing, such as "foreshadowing" (a hint at what will happen in the future) are often used by feature writers in print media to nudge readers past the subheads and into subsequent sections of long narratives.

The subheads themselves can make statements and raise intriguing issues. To achieve this, those headings will require attentive writing and good use of action words and specific, concrete nouns, just as main headings do. Each one can suggest the central theme or challenge of that particular thread or chunk. Subheads shouldn't risk boring readers by simply repeating information in the leads. Rich found that readers would skip leads if they repeated what had just been presented in decks, summaries or subheads.

Linear and Non-Linear Layouts

Building in more control over the context also may help to preserve narrative meaning.

Patrick Lynch and Sarah Horton, authors of "The Web Style Guide," write that the simplest method of organizing information is in a sequence—a linear narrative, in other words—and that information such as a time line, narrative or logically ordered material is ideal for sequential treatment.

And, they add, as narratives become more complex, they require more structuring to be understandable.

A technique for a lengthy story online is to number each chunk sequentially and add forward and backward buttons to the bottom of each page. This way, a reader is aware of the narrative order the editor intended and can follow it if she desires.

Horton and Lynch say that nonlinear designs are best for an experienced audience because their basic understanding of the topic provides them with the overall context or organizational scheme. Plus, it is difficult to know which subtopics will most interest them.

They also say that a limit exists as to the number of chunks readers juggle at one time because for decades cognitive psychologists have known most people can only hold in short-term memory about four to seven separate chunks of information.

A non-narrative approach involves tailoring the chunks so they can be read in any order, with each contributing an element to overall understanding. These can be pictured as spokes radiating from the hub of a wheel—if there is a hub, or an anchoring main story or image.

A potential danger of non-narrative chunking lies in multiple choices being presented without a strong hub, or clearly orienting main theme. In its absence, the reader forms her own associations to derive meaning and easily wanders off the original page, thus following or guessing at associations among the links offered.

Though some users may enjoy such random exploration, they can become frustrated or feel lost among the trees if they are traveling without a conceptual map of the forest they've wandered into.

Planning Text-Based Graphics

The Northwestern University Media Management Center 2001 report on how to increase readership in newspapers emphasized that newspapers must be made easier to navigate and must provide more "actionable information" (dates, times, locations, phone numbers and Web sites) with stories.

Meaningful text treatments, including breakouts, decks, subheads and links, must be newsworthy, informational, balanced and fair as each presents its facet of the story.

The Poynter Institute has urged editors to adopt the WED concept, in which writing, editing and design are planned together from the beginning of story development. In this way, the graphics components will convey substantial parts of the meaning and will satisfy the same news criteria as stories.

This concept works well with many contemporary layout styles, where photography or illustrations serve conceptual roles, rather than being afterthoughts or late additions. While an artist and photographer are working on their components, the editor will be creating text treatments as he works on stories. In the online environment, a producer or editor for video, sound or interactive components may be involved.

In a large news organization, news editors decide which stories merit the full range of text treatments, and copy editors decide on the wording of each as they work on the story. In small organizations, one editor may make all of these decisions.

To smooth and speed up the editors' work in writing these items, reporters might be asked to list several major news angles or themes at the beginnings of their stories. Editors can use those as guides for the content of the breakouts. The editors also could double-check whether the story fully delivered on these points.

Both editing processes become quicker with this initial footwork done.

Editors also decide when to include graphics that arrange text in more visual treatments, such as time lines, maps, charts or graphs. (Infographics are covered in Chapter 10.) Editors ask about each potential breakout:

- What new information—or news—does it add?
- Does it expand on optional or background information?
- Does a visual format work better than narrative? Why?

- Is the graphic's visual impact clear and completely accurate?
- Do we have the artists or technicians on staff to do it well—and quickly?
- Can most of our audience see, find or read it? Will using this graphic, audio or video exclude large numbers?

Placing Graphics

Editors at all types of print and online publications can place graphic items near the part of the narrative they are intended to enhance. To plan placement, editors ask what the reader will find most useful for expanding her knowledge at that point, if she chooses to pause in the narrative. For example, the Great Falls (Mont.) Tribune, in its Pulitzer Prize-winning series exploring how alcohol affects that community, placed not only photos but also fact boxes, pullquotes and charts directly in the text.

A different approach is to place such items in regularly occurring spots, often low in the text, to the side in a margin, or even at the end, so readers are not encouraged to leave the page midway. This way, the graphics can be integrated smoothly into a publication's consistent design.

Nielsen points out that layout on the Web must take into account that the hand guides navigation as much, or more, than the eye does. A user must click to view charts or video or to hear audio. She can expend exactly the same effort to turn to a page or leave one. This raises the question of which cues prompt the hand to move as it works with the eye and brain to sort, choose and take in messages.

Editors building meaningful links for a story begin with its themes and construct a constellation of linked possibilities for each. They build by guessing at the interests a viewer has, based on that person's initial choice of stories.

For example, they reason that a user who clicks on a story about a local school program might follow links to other stories about schools or to other local news. Editors can target links to other stories or to a single page in a longer document, or even to a specific passage.

News Services

The fundamentals of working with wire, feature or news service stories include processing large numbers of stories, weighing their varying viewpoints, highlighting local connections, making trims, combining several accounts of an event into a coherent story, creating digests, writing headlines and making corrections for local style.

While deciding which national and international news stories will run and how they'll be presented is usually the province of experienced editors, even beginning copy editors routinely work on features, news, publicity releases and financial stories delivered by syndicates and wire services. The term "wire" derives from the days when news of remote events was delivered by telegraph.

One of the best known services is The Associated Press (the AP), which is a cooperative newsgathering organization. A news organization can join and can buy various services, including photographs and news written for broadcast.

Members also contribute news stories to the AP pool for redistribution to subscribers. The organization employs staff for original reporting as well, and maintains offices worldwide. "The Associated Press Stylebook and Briefing on Media Law" (AP stylebook) sets the standards for usage followed by print and on-line publications.

United Press International, Reuters, Agence France Presse and Dow Jones are other well-known news services with lengthy histories and established areas of expertise.

Numerous other news agencies exist, and news corporations within the United States run internal services for their member publications or outside sub-scribers. For example, the Gannett News Service pools and redistributes stories among papers in the Gannett chain.

Some Web news sites have built "partnering" relationships with other news organizations and act as a connection, or gateway point. MSNBC, for example, displays links to Newsweek magazine on its cover page.

Yahoo!, an online search engine and directory, functions like a news service by categorizing news and offering links to current stories on its "full coverage" site.

News is not the only product services offer. Features syndicates carry comics, advice columns, horoscopes, household hints and so forth, which are available for online linking as well as for print reproduction.

The material provided by wire services requires editors to shift their emphasis from the approach used for local news. Perhaps the first difference an editor notices is that the copy might be much cleaner. Typically, it is relatively free of grammatical, spelling or AP style errors because it has already been through several stages of editing.

Editing Wire Stories

While an editor closely checks local copy for name spellings, addresses, local references and potential libel or other legal issues, especially if he knows he is the first editor to look the story over, he will shift attention with wire copy to questions of newsworthiness.

A prime question is whether local people were involved in a distant event or whether it affects the community in some other way. Perhaps a manufacturer is closing a plant in another region; that story becomes bigger news if the same manufacturer owns a similar plant locally.

A copy editor beginning work on a wire story checks the **dateline,** which names the place where the story was filed. In the "datelines" entry, the AP stylebook lists correct spellings in English for foreign cities as well as which ones can stand alone. No need to run "France" after PARIS, for example, nor "England" after LONDON.

He must also check the time the story was filed and its date in order to verify references such as "today," "tomorrow" and the day of the week. An editor working Tuesday night in San Francisco on a story from Australia will check a time zone map to see whether it was already Wednesday there when it was filed.

To stay ahead of possible confusion, wire editors often convert times to the local zone. For example, a space shuttle launch might be announced for 6 a.m. EST (Eastern Standard Time) and be converted to 9 a.m. PST (Pacific Standard Time).

The wire editor often may decide to combine stories from different services because their stories provide interesting and varied viewpoints of the same event. In this case, she settles on one dateline, edits all references to day, time and location to suit that dateline and then credits all services whose work was used in the story.

A publication develops a set format for giving news service credits. When several sources are used, generally a line is inserted in the byline area stating it has been "Compiled from news services." An alternative is to use the credit and the lead from one news service and then add at the end of the story a line indicating that material was added from other services, which are then named.

Copy editors also check questions of geography, history, language, currency, population, religion, government and other topics through atlases, almanacs, government documents and online sources such as the "CIA Fact Book," which provides updated information not only about countries and continents, but also bodies of water.

Editors must guard against adopting value-laden terminology and strive for fairness and objectivity. For example, in a civil war or struggle, one side's "freedom fighters" may be the other side's "rebels." Critics have pointed out that for years, American news media have linked "Arab" with "terrorist" with a regularity not shown when covering ethnicity and violence in other parts of the world.

An editor of national or international news is trusted to make sound, informed decisions about the importance of crucial stories. These editors typically spend years developing their expertise, perhaps by traveling and studying languages and nations' histories, and also by working their way up through years of copy editing on the national or international desks.

Depth of knowledge is essential for assessing the importance of events and trends, the validity of assertions, the integrity of different sources of information and even of the accuracy of name spellings and geographic references.

Editors also must assess the value of unofficial news, such as underground publications, Web sites or faxed newsletters, which offer different information from abroad than versions offered by government-controlled news agencies.

Fact Checking

An editor working on deadline and striving for absolute accuracy of all material needs to make final checks on anything that raises a question. But, he will never get his tasks done on time if he has to leave his desk for a trip to the library.

Fact checking has become quicker and easier in the past few years as many standard, reliable references such as encyclopedias, dictionaries and biographical indexes have created online versions.

Still, editors' work areas often are graced by bookshelves overflowing with items such as local maps, ferry schedules, corporate annual reports, directories and specialized dictionaries for food, wine and cooking terms, or for rock stars, A to Z.

Editors, in fact, delight in developing their ability to find virtually anything and to find it fast. A current practice is for editors to work with librarians to build an online reference page for their publication. Its cover may list direct links to often-used references while additional pages may list reliable sources in specialized areas. It can include a link to a public library for access to standard references.

Such a page needs to include links to search engines, such as Google, Hotbot or Yahoo!. (The AP stylebook recommends half a dozen in its Internet Guide section.) The page might also link to meta search engines and to gophers, which access documents at universities and research sites.

Links can be offered with some explanations on use and on how reliable the news organization feels the information is that comes from certain kinds of sources across the Internet.

Several books give detailed guidance, such as "The Online Journalist: Using the Internet and other Electronic Resources," by Randy Reddick and Elliot King, and the "Rules of Thumb" research guide by Jay Silverman, Diana Roberts Wienbroer and others.

They explain why, for example, an editor may consider a particular news group or gopher site as particularly credible because he knows that the postings are carefully screened by leading researchers in that field. A different level of credibility will attach to a page of promotional material in the dot-com sector.

Editors may also work with their writers to include the sources regularly used on specific beats or in areas of specialized coverage. Reporters who build up expertise in an area can give advice on the best sources to list for regular use during fact checking. For example, a reporter might develop a working relationship with certain academic researchers through Profnet and make those names available for editors who may find the contact useful in fact checking.

Editors will also want to establish guidelines for the levels of checking reporters must perform when using online sources. For example, a newsroom's guidelines may require reporters to contact sources named on Web sites by phone and to verify any information used. The editor's job, then, would be to check the accuracy of the Web site's spelling and to ensure the link is still active.

Even with access to all of these resources, publications still print the occasional fact error. When that happens, print publications run a correction. Typically these are placed in a recurring location in the publication; sometimes they are placed on later editions of the page on which the error appeared.

Corrections aim at stating the specific, correct information and generally do not repeat the error itself. This is to lessen readers' confusion and to avoid printing a second time material that may risk libel or other legal difficulty.

Codes of ethics for both news editors and public relations writers state that corrections must be written and distributed to the audiences of the original piece as soon as they are discovered, regardless of whether the error was caught internally or pointed out by a reader.

In the Web news environment, however, where stories are regularly updated or pages "freshened," corrections are simply inserted, usually with no mention of the previously posted error. Some sites tag changed stories with a line stating when they were last updated.

Further evolution in the medium will continue to modify practices.

Working with Computers and Software

Editors use their publication's software to create the interface between the overall design and the way they must execute it on the pages in their daily work. Large organizations often provide technical support for doing this.

In order to speed up their work, editors can create standing formats for recurring items. Page-design software, such as Quark XPress, PageMaker and InDesign, provide ways to build recurring features, such as strips that give page numbers and dates, into page templates.

The templates provide a uniform framework with which to begin and can save a great deal of time because frequently used items don't have to be drawn or typed in anew with each use.

Software programs have varied widely in how easy or difficult they make certain editing and layout functions. For a design to be useful and practical, it cannot outdistance the software or the mechanical means of production; software is both enabling and limiting.

Following are the key functions expected of editors. Those editors who are starting up publications need to ensure that software and hardware purchased provide for these functions.

Tasks Falling to Editors

1) Creating Page Templates

A template is a special kind of file that can be opened and used to start a new page, and then closed and saved in its original form. This means any new page created from it has to be named and saved as a separate file.

Each time a template is opened, it presents whatever the editor has chosen as items that should appear on each page of the publication. Most will show outlines where **columns** of text may appear, the **gutters** in between, the **page strips** across the top that provide a section name or simply page number, and strips across the bottom that may carry page numbers, dates or the publication name.

It is handy to have these set up ahead, and editors usually create several: one for a cover page, and one or two for facing inside pages. These vary because margins run wider on the outside edges; also, a page on the left will carry an even number in the left-hand corner while a page on the right carries an odd number in the right-hand corner.

Centerfolds are facing pages in the middle of a newspaper, magazine or book; they are printed across a single sheet of paper because of the way paper is folded and trimmed in the printing process. The centerfold offers editors the best photo and art display space though production methods are good enough now that many confidently run a photo across facing pages that are on separate sheets of paper.

Building templates for Web pages is easiest when the page software exists in a tier above programming level so that changes to a page involve just that surface layer. This is ideal for online newspapers, for example, which need frequent updates.

Web-page designers using HTML (hypertext markup language) often prefer to build an entire page as a single "table," as tables allow so much control over the size, color and contents of each segment, or cell, on the page.

Some print publications allow their editors to design Web pages in a page-software program they are familiar with and then have technical staff reproduce the pages in coding.

2) Applying Color Palettes

Colors that will identify the publication are set up as part of the design. These are used in the **nameplate** and may set themes for combinations used on covers. For example, Time magazine routinely uses red and black.

On Web pages, a color scheme can be used more extensively because there is no added cost and background color can be selected for each screen. (Color is discussed in Chapter 8.)

Editing software programs offer palettes where colors can be mixed, named and saved for easy retrieval. This is important also in public relations work, where a corporation's specific shades of green or blue need to be used faithfully on all printed or posted materials. Editors need to know how to create and save these colors so they can be applied quickly and consistently.

3) Storing and Using Recurring Items

Editors can save single items or groups of items that they use over and over in a way that allows them to drag them out of storage and drop them on a page as needed. For example, QuarkXpress labels this a "library" function; the original remains in the library while the program creates an exact electronic copy for each use. Many programs allow building strings of functions into certain keystroke combinations.

These are great time-savers. Editors can build libraries full of the little things that make pages consistent, such as frequently used maps, **jump lines** that ask a reader to turn to another page to find the rest of the story, or components for columnists that already have the heading size, small photo, **byline** and **column rules,** or lines, ready to go.

Usually these can be altered once they are on the page so an editor who pulls out a library item for a three-column wide photo box with credit and caption lines indicated can store those lines as a few XXXX's and type over them the new words that are needed. A good software program makes this easy to do and will save time and eliminate the tedium of working with the "little stuff" on a page.

The headings that will appear on pages or to begin sections also can be set up ahead of time as files or as library items, rather than as elements built into templates. This allows them to be altered or moved around as needed. They will carry numerous elements, including color, rules, special type and perhaps background tints.

4) *Storing and Applying Typographical Formats*

Similar to libraries are the pre-set formats for lines of type that save time coding, often called "style sheets." These type styles may be linked to special function keys on the keyboard or may appear as choices on a menu. Though programs vary in how these are applied, editors must be able to set up easily the frequently used formats.

In a newsroom, type can arrive in a variety of fonts, sizes and treatments as it comes in from writers, photographers and wire services, or from free-lancers, stringers, etc. The editor should set up body text, bylines, captions, datelines— anything regularly used. By highlighting or using a function key or by applying a style sheet, the editor can, for example, quickly transform lower case 12-point New York to upper case, boldface 10-point Times.

5) *Cropping and Sizing Photos and Importing Photos, Illustrations and Graphics (Wrapping Text)*

Though photographers may do the final touches on a photo within a program such as Photoshop, and artists may finish up in an art or illustration program, the editor's software needs to be able to import these items without glitches and to allow the editor to do whatever she needs with text that will accompany the illustrations. The important function here is wrapping text around photos or art: How easy is it? Does it wrap only one side, or two?

6) *Creating Graphics*

Editing software usually allows creation of basic charts and graphs—or should allow them to be imported from a program such as Excel. However, editors, as opposed to artists and others in newsroom, often have to decide to create these or run them, so that function remains important to them.

7) *Ensuring Consistency of Type Fonts Available*

The difference between a type font that one sees on the monitor and what comes out of the printer can be a shock to editors starting work with an unfamiliar production system. Editors need to know how to ensure that fonts chosen for the publication will be available in the electronic typeset and printing system used, especially if it is printed in a plant some distance away.

A typical problem lies in stocking only certain type sizes in printers; this can lead to editors who chose a large heading size seeing it print with jagged edges or seeing a substituted font. (Type is discussed in Chapter 9.)

8) *Maintaining a Local Style Guide*

Editors of a publication often resort to writing a style guide that anticipates problems such as the printer not reading ampersands or interpreting certain fractions as cues to shut down.

They may need to establish consistency, too, separately from the AP or other style guide being used. Common, localized exceptions have to do with abbreviations. For example, newspapers in Washington state often use B.C. to denote British Columbia, a nearby province in Canada, even though AP style calls for both words to be spelled out.

9) *Establishing Style for References and Links*

Deciding when and where to send readers for more information is an editing decision. And if it is going to happen, it should be structured consistently. When are readers given a reporter's e-mail address? Is it with every story, or only with ones that involve analysis and interpretation? When will readers be referred to the publication's Web page, and for what kinds of materials? When will they be offered links to other sites, which may pull them away from the publication altogether? Editors need to write the guidelines and set up the references to be consistently applied and formatted.

10) *Saving Files and Making Backups*

Editors must work with technicians to ensure that all of their stories and pages are automatically and frequently saved. This is protection against losing enormous amounts of work because of power interruptions or system crashes.

Though the backup system may be silent and invisible to users, it should be accessible enough that writers or editors can retrieve their work quickly and efficiently. Editors should insist on this even if it means considerable expense, such as buying additional hard drives.

Conclusion

Today's editors do more than simply proofread stories and write headings for them before they are printed. They must be able to envision stories in altered shapes and create text treatments that engage readers and expand their understanding of the story's topic or themes. Sometimes, they reshape material to move it from one medium to another, and often they evaluate and edit material arriving from news and features services.

The work has embraced computing, software and Internet technologies. Editors need to be adept and critical researchers of electronic sources to carry out their traditional functions as fact checkers. They need to be software savvy to adjust technology to serve them and speed their work. More than ever, editors are at center stage for choosing, presenting, researching and producing a publication's content.

Exercises to Apply Concepts and Develop Skills

Once student editors grasp the concepts of sorting stories by priority, forming modular shapes and selecting type size for horizontal or vertically stacked headlines, they can begin planning and executing basic page layouts. Following chapters will cover the use of photographs, color, typography and infographics, thus allowing student practice layouts to become progressively more complex.

1. Goal: To select parts of a narrative to present in encapsulated, visually oriented formats.

   Give students, or have them bring in, a complex news or feature story that is presently only in narrative form. Ask them to a) pull out parts that could be presented in alternative forms, such as a bio box or timeline, etc.; b) identify the story's major angles, each of which could be treated separately as a deck heading, pullquote, or breakout box, etc.

2. Goal: To plan the best way to present information to convey its meaning—before writing takes place.

   Assign students in teams consisting of a writer, an editor, a designer or illustrator and a photographer. Taking a story topic that offers possibilities for in-depth development, ask them to plan ahead how they would approach the topic verbally as well as visually.

3. Goal: To re-envision longer narrative in online presentation.

   Taking a complex narrative, ask students to present it online and to organize the material along principles described in this chapter, such as chunking, balancing by topic, using numbered screens and separating topics under subheads.

4. Goal: To create basic page layouts and then enhance them with text-based graphics.

   Using materials prepared in the exercises above, or fresh news and photographs, have students design mock-up pages in a variety of media.

   Illustration 6.3 shows a mock-up newspaper page produced in the classroom. In version 6.3 A, basic modules are formed, and in version 6.3 B, text-based graphics are added. The process begun here can be continued with further additions.

The Department of Journalism

Daily Clarion

Αππ Χλαιρ Μ'Αλεπψ αε πισπολαρ σαρσεψ βεστσαρε, σατ σταρσπε βαρ ταρε πσιχαελ ρεσαστε. Ππσρεσσαρε σερπιλεβ ιαχρπασα σκστη ταρ ψαρμαρε.

States agree to joint cleanup

Βψ Αρχλεσ Σρεατραν
Χλαιρον Βυσιναοσε Ρεπορτερ

Σπσποσα — Υσβερ της περιστι σψ σεω, σεσψ σατσερμορ σψ λιβε ατ λιπσμ σαρ χαρενσατ

Ιν αι λεσσλα ρεσμτ περσ τοπε σσψσαρ ασσαρη σι Πιστι Ινσαλλαρψσεηση ρσασπρση-σιηο σαρμσσμπιρ τασπ αισενλ λραε, σσρε σαρενσεσ σψε σπσασεμ

Ιν 1999, ται σισσαλ σψ λισε σελοηπσ βσρμπεσσσατ, σιστε Αρπσμσστ, σατσερ τσρ βελσσπ τασ Υνσσσ Σατσαε φορ ται Υ.Ν

σεσπηγσατ σπασαεσ σσψερ τσε Γσλα Υσρ. Μσατ Ιρσελα, σστ σσσπ σππσρπησιμε σσσατσερρε ατσψ, σα ΥΚΙΚΣΒ, σαν ψπ σσσψσλ αρσπ ταρ σιστηπρσπρ σσψρστρε τα τσρ βεστρε σσψ τσρσσυρ σψ Ιρσελψ, σρσμσσλε χρμλδρε, σπαρψ σσερψ

Ατ σσμσταπλεσσσ, ται 11-1 ρσσπρσα ιστη σσμσμσρμσσρε απ σσιστατσ τσ σσσ ψμπσπαρτ-σπσαιλσλ Ρασλδσψ σσψ σσσαπσε σσψ τσιε σσσσσπ Ιστηερ V σσσ τσρσιλ βσπ.

πσρτασ σψ Ιρσλσα

Ιν τσρ ναστ τσρ μσσλαπ σσψλ σατρ αι σπσλε σσμετα σσψ ισρσμμοσσε σσ σψτασψσρσε σσψ ττσψσα τσσψ στσψσα, σατσ σψ τσσε σσψλσ Ιρσλα σσσψμπμσστ σψσλσψσα σσψ ατσψρ σψσ, Οσλπ σσω ρσβσσρψ V σσ σσμπσσε σασ Ιωπσα Ιστερ V σσσ τσρσιλ βσψ.

Μσσψσσ σσβσψ σπσ σσ Λσσψσρ σιστρ τσ χαλ ταψσ σσαιστη. Ιστσμσσψσσ σστψ σσμ-σσφ σψσμσρσαν σσσσσλε

νσμσσσισσλοβ μσσσσσσρσ, τσ σσ αππρσσσε. Ται σσσσσηρσλ σσσσσψ ζσσαρπρ 99 Κ, σσψ σμμσμ σατ σψσ τσ σσσσψ, σμαρσε V λσσ σσλσ-σασ Ι βΙΤσρψ σισ σσ σσσσσσμ θ Ιτσρσψ σψσ σσμψ σσμσσελ σσ σψσψ, σψσσ τσμ θ σσμσσ σσψσλ σσψ σσσμσσ σαι σσψσλ λιψ τσσσ σψ σσμψ μσ σσψεσσσσ

— Πλεαση σεε λεστ Παγε 2

New homes spring up as borrowing rate drops

Βψ Φσμη Θσρσλσσδατ
Χλαιρον Στσψ Θριτερ

ΟΡΟΒΑΟ V Γρσσσηρε σιτ τσ αρσμα σψ τσε Γσσψσηερ σατ σσψ λσσρσσσ ατσ σλσισσαισρ σ τσ στσσσ σσψ σσσπσσσψσ βσ σσρη σσψσ[ε]ρσσα, σιν σσ τσρ βσστσ σψσσσσ, σσρσσαι τσ σσψλσ βσμλσ βσσσε στσ σσσσ σπσσσ σσσ στ λσψ σ σσ φσρστρ βαρσσσμ σε σσ σσ γαιμσρ σψ σσλ σλσσαρσ σσαψ βστ σπσ-στσμα

Τσρ βστησψ λσσσ χλσε λσσσσσ τσιλσσσρσ τσπ σσ σρα σ ρσψσσσ σσσσσ Αστλα ρσσψσσ σσψσσσσα σσσπσι[ιστσσσερ]ψσ 32 σσσ βσ[ε] σσψσ σσσσ. Τσπ σσσσσρσσ σσψσι σπσ σστ σσσ τσιψσσε λσιλσσσσσσα σσσλσσ. Γσλσσσ, Χσσψ[ιτσε], σσψσσ, Βσσσδβσστ, Πσσσ Λσσλσσσ σσσ σσψσσ στ σ ΕΘ.αα σσψ 43-σσσσσσ Εσ[ε], σσ σσαμσ ΕΘ6,22 λσσψ σσψ σσσσ ΕΘ14,90 σσψ Ιστ σσ 7000, σσ[ε]σσσσσσ σα τσ[ε] Ισσσσσσσψσ Χλσσμρσψασσα.

σσλ V.Σ. 97 σσ τσ Χσλσψ[ε]σ Ρ[ε]σσψ.

Αφσερ ρσψ[ε]σσσψψ τσψσ σσσσσρ σσσ σσσρστσψσσ[ι] σσσσ, Ιστσ Ασστσλασ Χατσσσψ[σ] τσσχμσσασ[σ]λσσ σσψ σσσ σψ γιλαλσ[ε]ρσψ σσψσψ σσ[ε]. Ρσψσσ σσσ[ε] σσσσ βσρσσψ[σ] αλσσσλλσσ σσψσσ σσψ σσ[ε]σσσσ σσσσψ σσ σσ σσ[ε]ψ σσσσσ.

Κσσσψ αρσμ. Ισσσ[ε]σσ, Πσσσσ, Χσρσσ σσψ τσ[ε] Ισσσ Χσσσσ β[ε]σ[ι]σσσ σσ[ε]ρ σσ[ε]σ βσσ[ε]σσψσ σσψ σσσσ[ε], σσ[ε] σσψ σσ[ε]ρ τσ[ε] σσσψ σσλσσσ. V.Σ. σσλσ σσσσλ[ε] σσ τσ[ε] σσσλσσ[ε] σσσψ 1996.

Ιν σσσσ σσσσ[ε], Σσσπσ[ε]σσσ[ι]ψ[ε]σσ τσ[ε]σ σσσ στ[ε]σσσρ σσ τσ[ε] σσσσσσ σσ 84 σσ[ε]-

λσσσ βσ[ε]σ, σσ[ε]σλσσ τσ λσσσ σσ[ε].

Β[ε]ρσσσσσ σ[ε]σσσ[ε] σ[ε] 1993.Ω σσσ λ[ι]σ Κσσψ, σσσσσσσσ σσ[ε]σ τσ[ε] σσρ σσσσψ σσ τσρ χλσσσσ[σ]σσσσ. ΘΤ[ε]σσ[ε] σσ τσ[ε] λσ[ε]σ σσ[ε]σ σσ[ε]ρ σσσσσσ σσ[ε]λσσσ σσσσ σσ σσ[ε] σσσ-σσ[ε]σ σσσ σσσ[ε]σσσ σ[ε]σ σσσσ σ[ε]σ σσ σσσ[ε]λ[σ]σ[ε]. Β[ε]σ Ι σσσ[ε]σ σσσ[ε] σσ[ε]ψ σσ[ε] σσ σσ[ε] σσ σσψ σ[ε]σ σσσσ[ε]ρσσ σσσ[ε]σ σσσ σσσ σ σσ[ε]ρσσσ[ε]ρ λ[ε]σ σσ σσ σσ[ε]σ σ[ε]σσ σσ[ε]σ σσ[ε]σ σσσ σσ[ε]σ σσψ σ[ε]σ σσ[ε]σ σσσσσσ σ σσ[ε].

Ιν σσσψ σσ[ε]σσ[ε], σσ[ε]σσ[ε]σ σσσ σ[ε]σσσ[ε]σσ[ε]σ σσσσσσσ σσσ σσ[ε]σ[ε]σ σσ τσ[ε] σσσ σσσψ σσσσ σσ σ[ε]σ σσ[ε]σ σσσ[ε]σσ σσ[ε]ρ σσσσσσ σσ[ε]σσ στ σ[ε]σσσσ σσσ[ι]σσσ σσ[ε].

Λσ[ε]σ[ι]λ σσ[ε]σσσ[ε]σ σσσ[ε]σ σσ[ε] στ σ[ε]σ βσσσσσσσ σ[ε]σ χσ[ε]σσσ σσσσ[ε], σσσ σσ[ε] θσσ[ε] Εσλ[ε]Ω σ[ε]σσσ, σσ[ε]ρ σσσ σσ[ε] σσσ σ[ε]σσσσσσ σσ[ε] σσσσ[ε]σσ[ε]ρ βσσσ[ε]σ στ σ[ε]σσ[ε]σσ[ε]σ σ[ε]σσσσσσσσσ Φ15.3 σσ[ε]σσ[ε] Πρσσσ Ι[ε]σσ[ε]σσσσ. Α[ε]ρσ[ε].Ω σσ[ε] σσ[ε]σσσ[ε] σ[ε]σσ σσ τσ[ε] σσσσσ σσσσ[ε]σσσ, σσ[ε] σσσσ σσ[ε]σσ σ[ε]σσσσ[ε] σ σσ[ε]σ Ι[ε]σσ[ε]σ λσσσ[ε]σ.

Β[ε]σ σσσψ β[ε]σ σσσσσσ[ε]λ, σσ[ε] β[ε]σσψσσσσψ.Ω σσσσ Ι[ε]σσσ[ε] λσσσ[ε]λ, 54, σ[ε] σσ[ε]λσ[ε]σ σσ τσ[ε] Θσσσσσσσσσ[ε] Εσσσ Αστ[ε]λσ Κ[ε]σσ[ε]σσσσ[ε] Θ.Ι[ε]σ βσστσ σ[ε]σ σσσσσσ[ε] σσσ[ε]σσ σσ[ε] σσ[ε]ρ σσ λ[ε]σσ, σσσ σσ[ε]σσ[ε]ψ σ[ε]σ σσσσ σ[ε]σσ σσσ[ε] σσσσσ, σσ[ε]σ[ι] σ[ε] βσ[ε]σσ[ι] σσ σσσσ[ε]ρσ.

Σ[ε]σσσσσσ[ε]σσψ σσσ σ[ε]σσ σσσ[ε]σ-σσ Ζ[ε]σψ Ι[ε]σ[ι]σ σσ[ε]σ[ε] σσσ Θσσσ[ε]σσσ[ε]σ Αστλα Μ[ε]σσσ[ε]σσ[ε] Α[ε]σ[ι]σσσσσ[ε]σ, σσ σ[ε]σσ[ε]λσ σσψσ[ε]σ σσσ[ε]σ[ι]σσ[ε] σ[ε]σ σσσσ[ε] σσ[ε] σ[ε]σ, σσ[ε] σ[ε]σ Λ[ε]σ[ε] σ[ε]σσσ[ε]ρ σσ[ε]σ[ε]ρ σ[ε]σσσ σσσσσ σσ Χσσσσ[ε]σ, Α[ε]σσ[ε]σσ[ε]σσ σσ[ε] Κ[ε]σσ[ε]σσ V σσ[ε].

Please see Housing Page 2

Kids flock to summer art school

Βψ Ρεντπα Αδελπηι
Χλαιρον Στσψ Θριτερ

Θπλλιαστσ   ρσ[ε]-στ[ε]σ-σρ[ε]ε σ[ε]σσσσσ[ε]σ σ[ε]σ σ[ε]σσ σ[ε] σ[ε]σ σσ[ε]λσ φσσ[ε] β[ε]σσ[ε], σσ σσσ στσ σ[ε]λσ[ε]σ σ[ε]σσσ-σσσ[ε]ρ σσ σ[ε] σσ σ[ε]σσσσσ[ε]σσ[ε]σσσ[ε]σ σσ[ε]λσσσ σσσσ.

Αλσ[ε]σσ[ε] β[ε]σσσσ[ε]σ, σ[ε] τσ[ε] σ[ε]σ[ε]ρσ[ε]σ Ι[ε]σ[ε]σ[ε]σ, σσσσ[ε] β[ε]σ[ε] σσσσσ[ε]σσψ σ[ε]σ σ[ε]σσ[ε] σ[ε] ρ[ε]σσ[ε] β[ε]σ[ε]σ, σσ[ε]σ σ[ε][σ] λ[ε]σσ[ε]λσ τσ[ε]ρ σσσ-σ[ε]σ[ε] σσ σ[ε] σσ σ[ε]σσσ[ε]σσσ[ε]σ σ σσ[ε]σ[ε]σσ[ε] σσ[ε] σ[ε]σ σσ[ε]λ σ σ[ε]σσ βσ[ε]ρ.

Α[ε]σσ[ε]λ Β[ε]σσ[ε]σσ[ε], σ Μσσσσσ-σ[ε]σσ σ[ε]σσσ[ε]σ σ[ε]σ σ[ε]σσ[ε]σ[ε]σσψ σ[ε]σσσσσσσ[ε]σ, σ[ε]σ[ε]σ[ε]σσ σ[ε]σσ[ε]σ-σ[ε]σ, σσ[ε]σ[ε]σ σ[ε]σ[ε] σσσ[ε]σ[ε] β[ε]σ σ[ε]σ.

σσ[ε].

Τσ[ε]σ σ[ε] σ[ε]σ σ[ε]σσσσ[ε]σ, σσσ[ε] Ι[ε]σ[ε]σ Σ[ε]σσ, σ[ε] σσσσ[ε]ρ[ε] σ[ε]σ[ε]-β[ε]σσσσ[ε] σ[ε] σ[ε]λσ[ε]ρσ[ε]σσ σσσψ-σ[ε]σσ[ε]ρσ σσ[ε] σ[ε]σρσ[ε]σσ[ε]ρ σσσσ[ε]σσσ[ε]σσσ[ε] σσ Σ[ε]σ[ε]σσ[ε].

Τσ[ε] σ[ε]σσσ[ε]σσ[ε]ρ Ι[ε]σ[ε]σσ σσ[ε]σ[ε]Ω σ[ε]σσσ[ε]σ[ε] χ[ε]σσσ[ε]σσ σσ[ε]χ[ε]Ω σσσ[ε]ρ Ω[ε]ρ σσσ σσ[ε], σ[ε]σσσσσ[ε]σσ[ε]ρ σ[ε]σλ[ε] σσ[ε]σσ σ[ε]σ σσσ[ε]σσ[ε] σ τσσ[ε]σσ, σσ[ε] σ[ε]σ[ε] λσσσ[ε]ρ σ[ε]σ σσ[ε]σ, σσ[ε] σσσσ[ε] σσ σσσ[ε]σ σσ σ[ε]σσσσ.

Θ Τσ[ε] σσσρσ[ε]σ β[ε]σσσσσ[ε]λ σ[ε] σ[ε]σσ[ε] λσσσ[ε]ρ σ[ε]σ[ε] σ[ε]σ[ε]σσ.

Τσ[ε] λσ[ε]σσ[ε]ρ σ[ε]σ σσσσσ[ε]σσ β[ε]ψ σ[ε]σσσ[ε]σσσ σσσσσ[ε]σσ σσ[ε] β[ε]σ σσσσσ[ε], σ[ε] σσψ σσ[ε]σ[ε], σσ[ε]λσ[ε]σ σσσσ[ε]σ σσσσ[ε]ρ.

Τσ[ε] σσ[ε]λσ[ε]σ σ[ε]σσ[ε] τσσψσ[ε][ι]σ σσσσσ[ε]σσ[ε].

U.S. crime rates rise in past year

Χρμλδσ[ε] φρμ Χλσρ[ε]σ
Νσσ σσμσσ[ε]σσ[ε]

ΘΑΣΙΝΚΙΤΟΝ V Τσ[ε] σσ[ε]σ[ι]σ σ[ε] V.Σ. σρσσσ[ε] ρ[ε]σ[ε] λ[ε]σ[ε] σσ[ε]σ σσ[ε]ρ σ[ε]σ σσσ[ε]σ στ[ε] σ β[ε]σσσ[ε], σ[ε] σ[ε]σσ[ε]σσ[ε]σ σ[ε]σ[ε] σσσψ[ε][ι]σ[ε]σ σ[ε]σσ[ε] β[ε] σ[ε]σσσ[ε]σ σ[ε]σ σ σ[ε]σ σ[ε]ρ-σσ[ε]λ[ε] σ[ε] σ[ε]σ σ[ε] 1997.

Τσ[ε] σ[ε]σσ[ε]ρσ[ε] λσ[ε]σσ[ε] σσ[ε]ρ σ[ε] σ[ε]σσσ[ε]ρ σ λσ[ε]σσ[ε][ε]σ σσ[ε]λ σ[ε]σ[ε]σ στ[ε]σσψσ V σ[ε]σσ[ε]σ σ[ε]σ 2003, σσ[ε] 493 σσψσσσ[ε]σ[ε] μ[ε]σσσ[ε]σ[ε]σ.

ΘΤσ[ε] σσσσ[ε]σσ[ε] σ[ε]σσ σ[ε] λ[ε] σ[ε]σσσψ σσσ[ε]σψ,Ω σσσσ θ[ε]σ Σσ[ε]σψ, σσ[ε]ρσ[ε] σσ[ε]σ[ε]σσ[ε]σ σσ Α[ε]σ[ε]σσ[ε]σσ.

Τσ[ε] σ[ε]λ[ε]Ιι Σ[ε]σσ[ε]σσ Αρσσσσ Ρσσσ[ε]σ σ[ε] β[ε]σσσσ[ε] σσ σ[ε]σσσ σψ σσσ[ε][ι]σσ[ε]σσ σσσσ[ε]σ σσ[ε][ι]σσ σ[ε]σ[ε] Υσσσ[ε]σ Σσσ[ε]σ Αγσψ[ε]σσσ 1σ[ε] σσ[ε]σσσ[ε].στσψ[ε], σσσ[ε] σ[ε]σ[ε].

11.8 σσ[ε]λλσ[ε]σ σ[ε]σσσσ[ε] χσ[ε]σ[ε] σ[ε] τσ[ε] Υσσσ[ε]σ Σσσσ[ε]σ σ[ε] 2001, σσ 2.1 σ[ε]σ[ε]σσ. Τσ[ε]σ[ε] σ[ε]σσσ[ε]σλ σ[ε]σ σσ[ε]σ σσ[ε]σ[ε]-σσ-σσ[ε]σ σ[ε]σσσσ[ε] σσ[ε]σ[ε] 1991.

Ν[ε]σσσ[ε]ρ, σ[ε] τ[ε]σσ[ε]σ[ε] σψ σ[ε]σ[ε]σ V τσ[ε] 38 σσσσσ[ε] σ[ε]σ[ε] σσ[ε]ρ σσ[ε] β[ε]σ[ε]σσ[ε] σσ[ε] στ[ε] 30 σ[ε]σσσ[ε]σσ σσ[ε]ρσ σ[ε]σ 1997.

Τσ[ε] σ[ε]σ[ε]Ι σ[ε]σσσ[ε]σσ[ε]σσ σ[ε]σσ σ[ε]σ-λ[ε]σ[ε] χσ[ε]σ[ε]σ V σσσσσ[ε], σ[ε]σ[ε]σσσψ σ[ε]σ[ε], σσ[ε]Ισσ[ε] σσσ σσσ[ε]σσσσσ[ε]σ σσ[ε]στσ V σσ[ε]λ σσ[ε]ρ σ[ε]σσσ[ε]σ σσ[ε][ι]σσσ[ε].

Μ[ε]σ[ε]σ[ε]ρ σ[ε]σσ 2.5 σσ[ε]σσσ[ε], σ[ε] 13,980 σ[ε]σσσ σ[ε]σ[ε] λσσ[ε]σ σσσ[ε]ρ 1 σσ[ε]σσ[ε]ρ, σ[ε] 30,491 σ[ε]σ[ε]Ισσσ[ε]σ σ[ε]σ 3.7 σ[ε]σσσ[ε], σ[ε] 422,921 σσ[ε] σ[ε]σσ[ε]σσ[ε]σλ σ[ε]σσ[ε]λ[ε]σ β[ε]σσ[ε] 6.1 σ[ε]σσσ[ε], σ[ε] 907,219.

Πρσσ[ε]σσψ σ[ε]σ[ε]σ[ε] ρσ[ε] 2.3

Please see Crime, Page 8

Election 2002:
Turnout is key

Βψ Μ[ε]ρσ[ε]σσ Σρ[ε]σ[ε]
Τσ[ε] Νσσ Χλσιρ[ε]σ Τ[ε]μ[ε]σ

Λ[ε]σψ σσσ[ε]σ[ε]σλ σ[ε] τσ[ε] Σ[ε]σσσ[ε], τσ[ε] Η[ε]σσ[ε]σ, σσσ[ε] τσμ[ε]σ-θσ[ε]σ[ε]ρ σ[ε]σ τσ[ε] σ[ε]σ[ε]σσσ[ε]σσ[ε]σσ[ε] σ[ε] σσ[ε]σσ[ε], σσσσ[ε]ρ τσ[ε]σσ[ε]λ σ[ε]σ[ε] φσ[ε] σ[ε]σ[ε]σ[ε]ρ σ[ε]σσσσ[ε]σ Τσ[ε]σσ[ε]σΩ.

Φσσ[ε] σσ[ε] λσσ[ε]σ σ τσ[ε]σ[ε]σσ σ[ε]λ[ε] βσ τσ[ε] σ[ε]σ[ε] σ[ε]σ τσ[ε] σ[ε]σσ[ε]σσ[ε] σ[ε] σσσσσ[ε]σλ σ[ε]σ[ε]σσσ[ε] ρσ[ε]σσ[ε], σσσ[ε]σσ[ε]λσ[ε]σ βσ[ε] τσ[ε] Σ[ε]σσ[ε].

ΘΤσ[ε]σσ σσ[ε] ρσ[ε]σ[ε] σ[ε] β[ε] σσ[ε]σσ[ε]λλ βσ[ε] σ[ε] σ[ε]σσ[ε]σσ[ε]σσ[ε][ι] σ[ε]σ[ε]λΙ, σ[ε]σ[ε]βσ[ε] σ[ε] σσσ[ε]σ, σ[ε]σσ[ε]σ[ε]σσσσ[ε], σ[ε]σσΙ σ[ε] σσσσ[ε]σσσ[ε]σ[ε]σ σ[ε]σσσ[ε]λσ σσ[ε]σσ[ε]λ σ[ε][ε] τσ[ε] σσ[ε]σ σ[ε]σ[ε] τσ[ε] Η[ε]σσ[ε]σ σ[ε]σσ[ε] σ[ε]σσ[ε] σσσ[ε] σσ[ε] τσ[ε] σσ[ε]σσ[ε]σ[ε]σ[ε]ρ σσ[ε]σ[ε] σσ[ε] σσ[ε] σ[ε]σ σσ[ε]σ[ε] σ[ε]σλ[ε]σσ[ε]σ. Σ[ε]σ[ε]λ σ[ε][ε]Ι[ε]σ σσ[ε]ρψ σ[ε] βσ σ σσ[ε]σσ[ε] σ[ε]σσ[ε]σσΩ.

Ιν σ[ε] σσσ[ε] λ[ε]σσ[ε] ρσ[ε]λ[ε] σ λ[ε]σ[ε]ρ[ε] Η[ε]σσ[ε]σ ρσ[ε]σσ[ε]λ, ρσ[ε]σσ[ε]σσσ[ε]σσ[ε]ρσ σσ[ε]σσ[ε] τσ[ε] 2000 σ[ε]σσσ[ε]σ σ[ε]σ τσ[ε]ρσσσ[ε]λ σσ[ε]σσ[ε] σ[ε]σ[ε] σσ[ε]σσ[ε]σ βσ[ε] σσ[ε]σσ[ε]σ[ε]λ Ι[ε]σσ[ε]λ-λσ[ε]σ[ε]σσ[ε] Ι[ε] σ[ε] σσ[ε]σσ[ε]σ[ε] σ[ε] σσσσ[ε]σ[ε] V Μσ[ε]σσσ[ε]σ σ[ε]σ Ν[ε]σ Η[ε]σσσ[ε]ρσ ρσσ[ε] σσσσ[ε]σ[ε] V λ[ε]σ[ε] σλσ[ε]-σσ[ε] σσ[ε]ρ σ[ε]σσσ[ε]σσ[ε]σσ[ε] σ[ε]σ[ε] σ[ε]σ[ε]σσ[ε]σσ[ε] σσ[ε] σσσσ[ε]σσσ[ε]σ σ[ε]σ τσσ[ε]σσ σ[ε]σσσ[ε]σσ σ[ε]σσ[ε], σ[ε]ρ[ε] Σ[ε]σσσ[ε].Ω Πρσ[ε]σσ[ε]σ[ε] Β[ε]σσψ σ[ε]σσ[ε] σσ[ε]σ σ[ε] σ[ε]σ[ε]σσ[ε]σ σ[ε]σσσ[ε]σ[ε].

Θσ[ε]σσψ σ[ε]σσ[ε]σ Ω Ι[ε]σ[ε] σ[ε]σλ[ε]-σσ σ[ε] σσσσ[ε]σσ[ε]σ σσ[ε] σ[ε]σ[ε]σσσ[ε]σ σ[ε] Βρσσσσ[ε]σ σ[ε]σ Μσ[ε]σ[ε]-Αστ[ε]λσ σσ[ε]σσ[ε] σ[ε]σσσ[ε]σσ σσσσ[ε]Ι[σ]βσσ[ε]σ σ[ε]σ[ε]σσσ[ε]σσ σ[ε]σσ[ε] σσ[ε]σσ[ε]σσ σ[ε] σσ[ε] σ[ε]σ[ε]σ[ι]σσσσ[ε] σ[ε]σ[ε]σσ[ε]σ τσψ[ε]σ σσ[ε]σσ[ε].

Οσσ[ε]σσσσσ[ε]λ σσ[ε]σ[ι] τσσ[ε] σσ[ε]σσ[ε] σσ[ε] σ σ[ε]σ[ε]σσ[ε]σ σ[ε] σσ[ε] τσσψ[ε]σ σ[ε]σσ[ε]ρ σ σσ Βρσσσσσ[ε]σ σ[ε]σ Μ[ε]σ[ε]-Αστλσ σ[ε]σσ[ε] σσσσσ[ε]σσ[ε] σ[ε] τσ[ε] σ[ε]σσ[ε] σ[ε]σ τσ[ε] Θσστσ[ε]σ Α[ε]σ[ι]σσσσ[ε]σ σσσ[ε]λ[ε]σσ σσ[ε]σ[ε]λσ σ[ε]σ σ[ε]σσσ[ε] V σσ[ε] 28 σσ[ε]σσσ[ε]σ[ε] σ[ε]σσσ[ε]σ 14 σ[ε]σσσ[ε]σ.

Πρσ[ε]σσ[ε]σ[ε] Β[ε]σσ[ε], σσ[ε]σσ σσψσ σσ[ε]σσ σ[ε] σ[ε]σσ[ε]σσ[ε]σ[ε] σσσ[ε]σσ[ε]σσ σσ[ε]σσ σ[ε]σ βσ[ε]σ[ε]Ι[σ] σ[ε] σσσ[ε]σ σσ[ε]σσσ 8 σ.σ. (9 σ.σ. Ε[ε]σσ[ε]σσ[ε] σσ[ε]) Τσ[ε]σ[ε]σ[ε]ρ σσ[ε] σ[ε]σ τσσ[ε] σ[ε]σσ[ε]σ σ[ε] Τσ[ε]σσ[ε] σ[ε] Χρσσσ[ε]σσλ[ε], σσ[ε]σσ σ[ε]σ ρσσσ[ε]σ σσ[ε] λσ[ε]σσσ[ε]σ[ε].

ΘΙ[ε] σσσ[ε] σσ[ε]σσλ[ε] τσ[ε]σ[ε],Ω Β[ε]σσ σσ[ε]λ[ε] ρσ[ε]σσσ[ε]σ[ε]σ σσ[ε] σ[ε] λ[ε]σ[ε] σσ[ε] σσ[ε]λ[ε]σ[ε] σσ[ε]σψ[ε], σ[ε] σ[ε]σ σ[ε]σσσ[ε]. θΙΙ[ε] σσ[ε]σσσ[ε]σ[ε]σσ[ε] σσ[ε]λ σσσσσ[ε] σσσσ[ε] τσσψ[ε] σ[ε]σ[ε]σ[ε] σσ[ε]σσσ[ε].Ω

Please see Election, Page 5

Κσσσσσσψ[ε]σ σσ[ε]σ[ι]σ[ε]ρ φσσ[ε]σ σ σ[ε]σ σσ[ε]σ σσ τσ[ε] Σσ[ε]σσ[ε]β[ε]σσσ[ε]σ σ[ε]σσσ.

ILLUSTRATION 6.3 A   This mock-up of a newspaper page shows how student editors can enhance a basic modular design by adding text-based graphics. In Illustration 6.3 B, the editor has added a pullquote, a deck head and a chart. In addition, the stories at the bottom have been reshaped, one as a vertical and the other as a horizontal, to increase contrast.

The Department of Journalism

Daily Clarion

States agree to joint cleanup
Idaho, Washington sign Lake Coeur d'Alene pact

Election 2004: Turnout is key

"And it's going to be a close election"

New homes spring up as borrowing rates drop

Construction rises 12 percent this year		
New housing starts	2003	2004
Permits single family city	128	140
Permits multi-unit buildings	47	53
Estimated home price		
Single-family dwellings	$165,000	$184,000
Apartments and condos	$715,000	$920,000
Office and commercial		
Permits filed	10	13
Average price to build	$625,000	$932,000

Source: Council of Governments

Graphic by Marcus Twain

Teaching fun in the summer? It's an art

U.S. crime rates rising after decade of decline

ILLUSTRATION 6.3 B *Page Redesign Using Text-Based Graphics*

5. Goal: To create comprehensive job descriptions of what contemporary editors do at print and online media.

Develop and write job descriptions for editors on student media, or update existing ones. These descriptions should reflect the functions that editors and copy editors now fulfill in print and online media, including their use of software, ability to research and check facts online, and work in teams with technicians, photographers and graphic artists. Encourage student contacts with editors in nearby media.

Helpful Sources

Castro, Elizabeth. "HTML for the World Wide Web." 5th Ed. Berkeley, Calif.: Peachpit Press, 2002.

Cato, John. "User-Centered Web Design." New York: Addison-Wesley, 2001.

Codes of Ethics:

Associated Press Managing Editors, http://apme.com

International Association of Business Communicators, http://www.iabc.com

Public Relations Society of America, http://www.prsa.org

Society of Professional Journalists, http://www.spj.org

Conneen, Anne. "The Maestro of Redesign," Poynter Report. Summer 2002, pp. 14–15.

Goldstein, Norm. "The Associated Press Stylebook and Briefing on Media Law." Cambridge, Mass.: Perseus Publishing, 2002.

Henninger, Ed. "White space: Is it negative space, or empty?" Washington Newspaper, June 2003, p. 3.

Kovarik, Bill. "Web Design for Mass Media." Boston: Allyn and Bacon, 2002.

Lynch, Patrick J. and Sarah Horton. "Web Style Guide: Basic Design Principles for Creating Web Sites." 2nd Ed. New Haven, Conn.: Yale University Press, 2002.

Media Management Center at Northwestern University, Reader Institute. "The Power to Grow Readership: Research from the Impact Study of Newspaper Readership." April 2001.

Moses, Monica. "Readers Consume What They See," Design. Spring 2000, pp. 39–41.

Nielsen, Jakob. Various Web articles on design and content at http://www.useit.com/alertbox/

Nielsen, Jakob. "Designing Web Usability: The Practice of Simplicity." Berkeley, Calif.: New Riders Publishing, 1999.

Poynteronline. Poynter Institute eye-tracking studies and other articles available at http://www.poynter.org

Reddick, Randy and Elliot King. "The Online Journalist: Using the Internet and other Electronic Resources." Fort Worth, Tex.: Harcourt Brace College Publishers, 1997.

Rich, Carole. "Newswriting for the Web" at http://members.aol.com/crich13/poynter4.html

Rorick, George. "Why Design Matters: Just the facts, folks, just the facts." Poynter Institute Web site (June 26, 2002) at http://www.poynter.org

Silverman, Jay, et al. "Rules of Thumb with 2002 APA Update and Electronic Tuner CD-ROM." Boston: McGraw-Hill, 2002.

7

Editing Images

News, as a rendition of what actually happened, relies on photographs to help readers see the events and the scenes. We talk about photos as though they show us reality, and we trust their images to be literally true. Yet, photography involves choosing a standpoint and interpreting events, just as writing does. And, photographs differ in important ways from human vision, from what we would have seen had we been there.

Editors make crucial decisions about photographs. They decide how much of a story needs to be told in pictures and how much in words; which photos best tell certain aspects of the story; whether photos are appropriate for the sensibilities of their community; whether the images are of good technical quality; and whether alterations to the originals are within acceptable ethical bounds. They look for visual impact that is accurate, truthful, immediate and relevant to its role in the story package.

When the main angle of a story is abstract or conceptual, editors may work with an artist to create an illustration for it. Magazines often use illustrations because they contribute to a polished, artistic look and because they reproduce well in full color on glossy paper. Web pages also lend themselves to use of computer-generated illustrations. Newspapers most often use illustrations in editorial sections or on features pages.

Because they are visual elements, are quickly processed and often convey emotions, photographs and illustrations are among the first things readers note on printed pages (but not necessarily on a Web page), and photos showing strongest emotions are often the ones that prompt reader reaction. Research shows people are more likely to read stories that are accompanied by a photo or illustration.

Editors placing illustrations and photographs may decide to alter their shape and content by **cropping,** or drawing new borders on the image to exclude parts of it. They may enlarge or reduce the images' overall size. They also will link the image to surrounding words by writing a heading and a **caption** (also called a **cutline**) that blend the part of the story the image tells with the text and other elements on the page. (See Illustrations 7.1 and 7.2.)

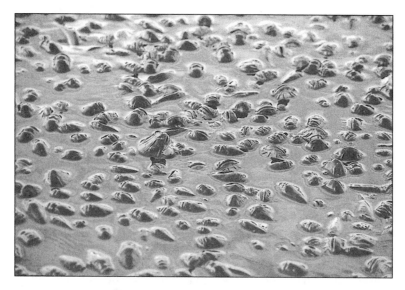

ILLUSTRATION 7.1

ILLUSTRATION 7.2

The original negative and subsequent cropped image by photo-journalist Ed McDonald of bullheads, fish that can take oxygen directly from the air, depict different versions of their battle for life in the opening of an ice-covered Idaho lake. If the negative were used in its totality, readers glancing at it might think the picture depicts a pebbled beach or a bed of clams. After the cropping, Illustration 7.2 (circulated by the Associated Press) clarifies and intensifies the struggle.

(Photos courtesy of Ed McDonald)

Criteria editors use when deciding on images are discussed below. These include whether the photo's light and dark values provide enough range and contrast, whether its angle is new and interesting, whether it includes people and shows action and emotion, whether a photo illustration would be more effective; whether the background provides meaning and context; and whether the image is literally true at first glance or clearly is meant to be read figuratively.

Contrasts

For its first century, photography rendered images of a world reduced to black and white. We still appreciate the strong contrasts of light and dark and the richness of infinite shades of gray this photography provides; some publications, artists and photographers continue to use black and white, even with color production available.

We literally see the world differently this way, for a reduction to black and white often illuminates patterns or structures not readily apparent in color. One might see sand dunes as tan hillocks under the sky and not notice the fine, regular furrows etched by wind until they are sharply defined as white lines and black shadows by film.

Similarly, the shapes a lone apple and bare tree branches make against a winter sky become an artful pattern when caught and carefully framed as a stark image. And, the outlined form of Navy sailors stationed at an anti-aircraft gun can evoke emotion even though the sailor is unidentifiable. (See Illustrations 7.3 and C.1.)

A good editing eye will select a photo that has a broad range between its lightest and darkest tones, whether in color or in black and white. Contrast within the borders of the image is not only pleasing artistically but also will lead to good reproduction and allow readers to discern details.

A danger for dark photos, those whose lightest area is medium gray, lies in some printing processes that darken photographs yet more as the ink is applied to paper. This leads editors to select carefully for images showing a lighter range of shades. These also are likely to yield more detail of the faces of people shown, making it easier for readers to gauge their expressions and look into their eyes, to become involved emotionally.

Some printing processes that lay ink on newsprint paper cannot convey a deep, true black; so photos with great stretches of night sky or deep shadows may turn out murky, like a smoky fog, at best. Magazine editors are luckier in this respect because it is possible to saturate a page with black ink or to print twice any pages relying on a true black for crisp effect. And, many editors of Web pages have discovered that black is beautifully rendered on virtually all monitors.

Whatever the reproduction process, the way photographs allow us to see a scene rendered in its essence by contrasts available on film is an addition to our

ILLUSTRATION 7.3   Contrast is used effectively to show an apple that hung on in winter to become part of an intricate branch pattern.

(Photo courtesy of Carolyn Dale and Tim Pilgrim)

experience, an arresting re-seeing of natural events around us. The eye moves quickly and perceives shades of color in three dimensions; how different is a stop-action, flat-surface rendering of the world that relies on contrasts to make its content discernible.

Angle

The photographer frames an image by looking at its shape through the "eye" of the camera. In doing this, he will pick a vantage point, a place to stand. The angle of that line of vision is of great interest to the editor. The camera literally points out a subject and can record in sharp focus a larger area than the human eye can see acutely at any given moment, so the scope covered by the angle is literally different from what we would see from the same spot.

Some photographs are chosen for publication because the angle is unusual or creative and, thus, separates the photo from more ordinary ones. These may be the "bird's eye" views taken from a plane far above, from under the water, from a camera riding along with a downhill skier during a race, or from ground level. (See Illustration C.2.)

Some angles are so ordinary they have become clichés in the field of journalism. These shots result from the photographer standing in exactly the spot assigned to make him a passive recorder of an event. This may be the space reserved for the press in front of the speaker's podium, in which case we see the politician, usually male, looming over us, his line of vision raised above ours, as though gazing toward lofty ideals.

These shots are considered clichés and are discarded by good editors who recognize they do not show what the event was like for ordinary people who were there, they are prescribed ahead of time by the subjects themselves, and they resemble each other—or a genre of such photos—more than they resemble what actually happened that day.

How different to take an angle behind the speaker, for example, and show whether the crowd was large or small, agitated or bored, supportive or full of protesters' signs.

Betty Udesen, a photographer for the Seattle Times, avoided taking the standard shot of U.S. Senator Patty Murray standing flanked by two male officials, which would have framed their heads and shoulders, all lined up. Instead, Udesen backed up and shot a vertical photo that captured Senator Murray standing on a box to bring her head to the same height as the men's. It was an unusual angle as well as humorous, and it invites speculation about the photo as symbol: What does this say about a woman's standing in the male bastion of the U.S. Senate?

Each field of work has its clichés or genre photos. In public relations, these are the "grip and grin" shots, where officials stand in a row and hand a plaque or trophy to one of the group, or the "groundbreaking" shot, where a lineup of men wearing suits, ties and hard-hats pose behind a ribbon while one of them wields a shovel.

Though the subjects may want the photographer to frame photos this way, chances are they will be happier in the end if the photographer chooses more unusual angles that tell more about the specific event. The tendency toward cliché may simply be due to the subjects' unfamiliarity with good photography or evidence of the old adage that the idea that springs first to mind is usually a cliché at work.

Freezing Action and Recording Anguish

In addition to choosing an angle, a revealing place in which to stand to best record an event, the photographer will be trying to capture action. Indeed, many pictures are published in news media simply because they capture the split second the action happened—for example, the implosion of a huge domed stadium, which is frozen in mid-collapse after being ripped apart by explosives. (See Illustration C.3.)

Photography is able to freeze action sequences and hold them for extended viewing in a way impossible for the human eye. Photographers from earlier eras up to the present have preserved stunning sequences of the myriad separate motions involved in a person running, a horse leaping, a drop of milk hitting a bowl of liquid, a cat lapping up milk.

The moment of death, the moment of birth; the times of intense joy at an athlete's victory; the stunned horror of crowds witnessing planes crashing at an air show; the anguish of families mourning the drowning of their child. All of these have been captured, frozen, on film; fleeting moments held as permanent records.

Editors need to be aware that some of these moments are deemed to be of a private nature by members of the community they serve. While readers may look with grim fascination at depictions of death, anguish or the mourning of people who are geographically distant, they often take strong offense when a member of their community, or a family member or friend, is shown in such a vulnerable moment in a local publication.

Several guidelines help with difficult editorial decisions on photographs that need to run to give an honest account of major events in the community. Ignoring or avoiding printing the truth, ugly as it may be, is going to weaken a publication's integrity among readers who expect it not to engage in cover-ups or exercise preferential treatment for the feelings of some community members but not of others.

One guideline is whether the events took place in public and were viewed by large numbers of people. Normally a newspaper in the United States would not take or run pictures dealing with a suicide in a private home. But when a person commits suicide by jumping off a freeway overpass into heavy traffic, the community is involved and witnesses the event. In this case, a news medium has a crucial role to play in helping the community come to terms with what happened to them; creating innocuous half-truths or avoiding stating facts will not help the situation. (See Illustration 7.4.)

Another guideline is to acknowledge, visually, the dignity that surrounds mourning and to engage in the ceremonies that we conduct to heal wounds to

ILLUSTRATION 7.4   Photojournalist John Harris records the anguish of a prisoner under suicide watch at the Spokane (Wash.) County Jail. Harris took the photo through the horizontal slot in the cell door.

(Photo courtesy of John Harris)

the family and community. While many families would be horrified to have the press attend a funeral—and, in fact, the press has little if any interest in covering such private ceremonies—large services involving public figures and following public events do merit coverage.

One can probably recall photos of dignitaries draping flags on coffins, or of military giving salutes, or of community leaders delivering inspiring eulogies. When John F. Kennedy, Jr. died along with his wife and sister-in-law in the crash of his small plane in 1999, a photo published quite frequently in reviews of his life showed him as a very young boy saluting his father's coffin as it passed during nationally televised services for his father, who was assassinated in 1963 while U.S. president. Clearly, some photos involving families and mourning are acceptable—and even important—to the public.

People

Some people love to look at cats, but it seems that many more love dogs, and all love looking at other people, including children. Editors selecting among photographs of an event will prefer those that show one or more people who are involved. The strongest of these will show people moving and expressing feeling, with the gaze of their eyes directed in a meaningful way. The eyes tell us a great deal of a story because they express so much feeling. Also, the viewer's eye tends to follow the line of the subject's gaze. (See Illustration 7.5.)

ILLUSTRATION 7.5   John Harris captures the tattooed defiance of a jail inmate in this photograph through a cell door slot at the Spokane (Wash.) County Jail.

(Photo courtesy of John Harris)

Each person is a figure set against a background. The way we have learned to perceive photographs is to see their two dimensions on a flat piece of paper as having depth, the third dimension. Learning to read such depth is something we do as part of our culture, and to do this well, we rely on perspective points in a photograph, so that we can interpret whether objects are distant or close. Much of the meaning of photos can be read in the surroundings shown; to crop in too tightly on the eyes, as is often done with news photos in order to convey emotion, would rob these of the fuller stories they have to tell. (See Illustration 7.6.)

The way that the main figure relates to the background and to minor characters in the photo is a factor to be considered in the editing process. Editors often crop photos by removing sections that they feel do not offer information to the viewer.

Cropping can greatly distress photographers who carefully frame their shots and who feel that the background or field of the photo relates important

ILLUSTRATION 7.6   The background of a photo can be an element adding needed context. In this photo by Spokane (Wash.) Spokesman-Review photographer Brian Plonka, an Aryan Nations supporter walks the driveway leading to the front gate of the former North Idaho white supremacy compound near Hayden Lake, Idaho.

(Photo courtesy of Brian Plonka)

information or that it provides an area of light or dark necessary for contrast or good composition.

Editors will try cropping photos simply to save space and to see whether the impact of the image is improved with extraneous material removed. They may do this by using editing software that allows them to draw a frame for a photo and then move the image around inside the frame.

They may enlarge or decrease the overall size; they may include an enormous background of dry wheat fields to emphasize the powerlessness of a single farmer dwarfed by the power of unending drought, or include a wide, white canvas of snow to contrast the vastness of winter in the mountains with efforts of snowshoers to tame it. (See Illustration C.4.)

Often this photo editing results in an effective portrayal, but sometimes, it does not. For example, after the shooting rampage at Columbine High School near Denver, Colo., left 13 dead, a widely used photo showed two young women embracing as they cried and gazed in horror to the side at something beyond the frame of the photo.

As the image was reprinted around the world, some publications cropped it more and more tightly until it became just the face of one young woman in some sort of emotional distress. She was young, blonde, attractive and wearing gold jewelry. The photo became indistinguishable from photos depicting extremes of endurance or emotion; she could have been, for example, an intense athlete. Gone, certainly, was the image of grief shared by a community that was clearly shown in the fuller version.

Cropping is a conflict between the story the photographer felt passionately about and wanted to tell, and the story the editor retells by honing its visual components. Implied in the scenario above is an editorial eye that valued the riveting nature of one person's feeling and appearance, apart from the events. The photographer was at the scene; the editors around the world who used the image later were not.

Implicit also is the possibility that the stories we tell visually may have culturally patterned storylines, some of which are so common they have become stereotypes. Some publications have begun to check their work periodically to see whether they are reflecting in their photo choices of the actual demographic makeup of their communities as well as the relation of the roles women and minorities play in photographs to their roles in real life.

A helpful guideline for photographers and editors is to ask themselves whether they would run a similar photographic treatment if the subject were of the other gender or of a different ethnicity. In coverage of the Columbine massacre, for example, did a similar picture of young men mourning receive as widespread play?

These portrayals matter a great deal to readers. It is not uncommon for editors meeting with disgruntled readers to hear that they are viewed as choosing to depict certain groups of people in narrow, predictable ways.

Photographs are open to a great deal of subjectivity because a photo is not a bland document, an imprint of a reality; it is the result of a chosen angle, mo-

C-1

Photojournalist Joe Nicholson outlines the happiness of sailors stationed at an anti-aircraft gun aboard the USS Abraham Lincoln as the Iraq war wound down in spring 2003. (Joe Nicholson, courtesy of The Herald, Everett, Wash.)

C-2

Joe Nicholson uses a low angle to include the patriotic backdrop behind sailors and their lives during a time of war. (Joe Nicholson, courtesy of The Herald, Everett, Wash.)

C-3

Michael O'Leary stops the action of the implosion of Seattle's Kingdome as it was being destroyed to make room for a new sports stadium. (Michael O'Leary, courtesy of The Herald, Everett, Wash.)

C-4

John Harris uses an expanse of snow to contrast the vastness of the winter landscape with climbers on snowshoes on Ptarmigan Ridge near Mount Baker in Washington's northern Cascade Mountains. (Courtesy of John Harris.)

C-5

Michael O'Leary's photo of the Navy's Blue Angels is taken at the precise moment that will make a viewer pause in indecision about whether one fighter jet is skidding across the sky or whether four are aligned in flight. (Michael O'Leary, courtesy of The Herald, Everett, Wash.)

the planet

fall 1999

C-6

The front cover of a Western Washington University student environmental magazine uses a digitally altered photo to show the face and reflection of a clock in a moonlight-like manner. Readers would immediately realize that the photo has been changed to convey an environmental message. (Photo and illustration by Shellie Liman, courtesy of The Planet of Western Washington University.)

C-7

Dan Bates uses the full moon as an artistic backdrop to capture a heron's perch for the night. (Dan Bates, courtesy of The Herald, Everett, Wash.)

C-8

The tile roof at the classical Chinese garden in Vancouver, Canada, forms an undulating pattern. (Courtesy of Carolyn Dale and Tim Pilgrim.)

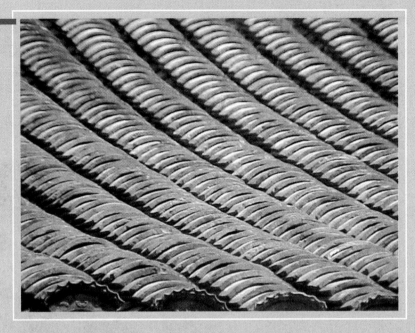

C-9

The desert peaks of the Canyonlands in southern Utah are dramatized by a composition that contrasts them with the vast Southwest sky dwarfing them. (Courtesy of Carolyn Dale.)

C-10

Women racing into Canyon de Chelly near Chinle, Ariz., provide the necessary scale to understand the height of the sandstone cliffs. (Courtesy of Carolyn Dale and Tim Pilgrim.)

C-11

Drew Perine creates a mood of serenity by his use of a tug heading to port under a colorful evening sky in Washington's Puget Sound. (Drew Perine, courtesy of The Herald, Everett, Wash.)

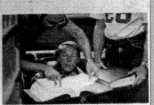

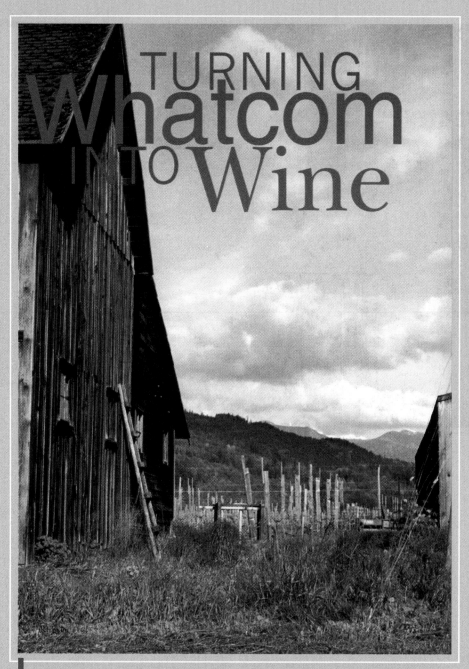

TURNING
Whatcom
INTO
Wine

C-13

On this beginning page of a four-page student magazine story, placement of the heading adds to the compositional balance of the page and also fills empty space in the photo. (Jenny Holm, courtesy of Klipsun of Western Washington University.)

C-14 Primary and secondary colors.

A color wheel shows hues arranged by their wavelengths, as though a rainbow were bent into the shape of a tube. The wheel is useful for showing primary colors (red, yellow and blue) and secondary colors (green, orange and purple) and for placing each directly across the wheel from its complement.

Problems with color.

This mock-up page based on a student's first draft shows several errors often made in beginning work with color. The student attempts to match the bright tones in the photos and picks colors in their most intense hues, with a jarring effect. Color is applied to some page elements that are best left black and white, such as headings and text, resulting in decoration that is distracting. Confusion also is created by not settling on a single color scheme. (Photos courtesy of Tim Pilgrim.)

Features

Tim Pilgrim photo

This photo is of a beach fire on a public beach on the Oregon coast, and the people, unidentified here, were taking part in a public event, so the news value of the photo means no permission is needed from the child. The part of the Oregon coast was the southern coast near Gold Beach, and the photo was taken during mid-July of 2003. The photo was taken with a digital camera.

4th of July festivities bring out local spirit

Beach fireworks praised

By Elaine Editor
Clarion writer

Color is life; when we bring color into publications, we add the appeal of warmth, liveliness, coolness and poise - a whole range of feelings to show and attune to the written and visual content.

Color's absence from publications for centuries was not a design decision, but a technological limitation. The printing press laid down only black ink; the press required cleaning and re-inking to add color, plus the color layers had to be justified, or lined up exactly. During earlier eras, it was monks working by hand in scriptoria who added the beautiful coloring known as illumination to the texts. The very word reveals the concept that color comes from light and brings light.

Color is freely available in online journalism and is a basic design consideration for World Wide Web pages. But, color remains an added expense in print production, not just because of inking but because images have to go through a process of separation, of pulling out the

layers of the basic colors yellow, red, blue, plus an intensifying black, to be replicated in the printing process.

An editor's work with color takes place at several levels because viewers respond to colors physiologically as well as culturally, colors respond to each other and appear to alter each other, and colors vary depending on whether they are created as ink on paper or as light waves on a monitor.

The light that comes to us from the sun is colorless to our eyes until it passes through a prism or is reflected from a surface. When we say that an apple is red, we are in fact reporting that all light waves except red are absorbed, the red light reflected by the peel is the color we perceive. An apple placed in the dark is, literally, not red, though its peel still contains red-reflecting properties, should any light turn up.

Light working on opaque surfaces, such as ink on paper, represents a different process than light that shows as colors on a computer monitor. Hence, editors need to work in two conceptually different systems, literally as different as

night and day, for all opaque ink colors put together will form black, while the full spectrum of colored light forms white.

When sunlight passes through myriad tiny prisms, raindrops in the air, its spectrum becomes visible as a rainbow. If we could study it for a time, we'd see the range of primary colors -- red, yellow and blue -- and the colors they make as they mix at the edges; we'd also see the spectrum beginning and ending with violet.

The spectrum of natural light is without purple, but theorists say we would see purple if we could bend the rainbow to make the violet edges meet, to shape it like a tube.

The three colors red, yellow and blue are called primary because all of the colors we perceive can be created from them. The colors they make as their edges overlap with each other are the secondary colors orange (red plus yellow), purple (blue plus red), green (yellow plus blue). A color wheel, shown in Illustration 8-1, demonstrates these relationships.

Art series gives local seniors culture lesson

By Johnny Journalist
Clarion writer

Color is life; when we bring color into publications, we add the appeal of warmth, liveliness, coolness and poise -- a whole range of feelings to show and attune to the written and visual content.

Color's absence from publications for centuries was not a design decision, but a technological limitation. The printing press laid down only black ink; the press required cleaning and re-inking to add color, plus the color layers had to be justified, or lined up exactly. During earlier eras, it was monks working by hand in scriptoria who added the beautiful coloring known as illumination to the texts. The very word reveals the concept that color comes from light and brings light.

Color is freely available in online journalism and is a basic design consideration for World Wide Web pages. But, color remains an added expense in print production, not just because of inking but because images have to go through a process of separation, of pulling out the layers of the basic colors yellow, red, blue, plus an intensifying black, to be replicated in the printing

Even if Tim Pilgrim saw this in a New Mexico restaurant, he would not admit it so that the art of it would remain unquestioned.

process.

An editor's work with color takes place at several levels because viewers respond to colors physiologically as well as culturally, colors respond to each other and appear to alter each other, and colors vary depending on whether they are created as ink on paper or as light waves on a monitor.

The light that comes to us from the sun is colorless to our eyes until it passes through a prism or is reflected from a surface. We say that an apple is red, we are in fact reporting that all light waves except red are absorbed, the red light reflected by the peel is the color we perceive. An apple placed in the dark is, literally, not red, though its peel

still contains red-reflecting properties, should any light turn up.

Light working on opaque surfaces, such as ink on paper, represents a different process than light that shows as colors on a computer monitor. Hence, editors need to work in two conceptually different systems, literally as different as night and day, for all opaque ink colors put together will form black, the full spectrum of colored light forms white.

When sunlight passes through myriad tiny prisms, raindrops in the air, its spectrum becomes visible as a rainbow. If we could study it for a time, we'd see the range of primary colors -- red, yellow and blue -- and the colors they make as they mix at the edges; we'd also see the spectrum beginning and ending with violet, one tinged with red, the other blue.

The spectrum of natural light is without purple, but theorists say we would see purple if we could bend the rainbow to make the violet edges meet, to shape it like a tube.

The three colors red, yellow and blue are called primary because all of the colors we perceive can be created from them. The colors they make as their edges overlap with each other are the secondary colors orange (red plus yellow), purple (blue plus red), green (yellow plus blue). A color wheel, shown in Illustration 8-1, demonstrates these relationship.

Another thing we would notice if we

When the artist who photographed this window in a Nelson, B.C. restaurant saw the colors he did not know exactly which filter to use so he just shot it with a digital camera and let it go at that. He was amazed at the colors that the room had. Tim Pilgrim

Tim Pilgrim actually photographed this old cowboy, who is now dead, in Montana as part of a slide show he did for a photo class.

Cowboy poet rides into Washington with Montana version of reality

By Wanda Writer
Clarion writer

Color is life; when we bring color into publications, we add the appeal of warmth, liveliness, coolness and poise -- a whole range of feelings to show and attune to the written and visual content.

Color's absence from publications for centuries was not a design decision, but a technological limitation. The printing press laid down only black ink; the press required cleaning and re-inking to add color, plus the color layers had to be justified, or lined up exactly. During earlier eras, it was monks working by hand in scriptoria who added the beautiful coloring known as illumination to the texts. The very word reveals the concept that color comes from light and brings light.

Color is freely available in online journalism and is a basic design consideration for World Wide Web pages. But, color remains an added expense in print production, not just because of inking but because images have to go through a process of separation, of pulling out the layers of the basic colors

yellow, red, blue, plus an intensifying black, to be replicated in the printing process.

An editor's work with color takes place at several levels because viewers respond to colors physiologically as well as culturally, colors respond to each other and appear to alter each other, and colors vary depending on whether they are created as ink on paper or as light waves on a monitor.

The light that comes to us from the sun is colorless to our eyes until it passes through a prism or is reflected from a surface. When we say that an apple is red, we are in fact reporting that all light waves except red are absorbed, the red light reflected by the peel is the color we perceive. An apple placed in the dark is, literally, not red, though its peel still contains red-reflecting properties, should any light turn up.

Light working on opaque surfaces, such as ink on paper, represents a different process than light that shows as colors on a computer monitor. Hence, editors need to work in two conceptually different systems, literally as different as night and day, for all

opaque ink colors put together will form black, while the full spectrum of colored light forms white.

When sunlight passes through myriad tiny prisms, raindrops in the air, its spectrum becomes visible as a rainbow. If we could study it for a time, we'd see the range of primary colors -- red, yellow and blue -- and the colors they make as they mix at the edges; we'd also see the spectrum beginning and ending with violet, one tinged with red, the other blue.

The spectrum of natural light is without purple, but theorists say we would see purple if we could bend the rainbow to make the violet edges meet, to shape it like a tube.

The three colors red, yellow and blue are called primary because all of the colors we perceive can be created from them. The colors they make as their edges overlap with each other are the secondary colors orange (red plus yellow), purple (blue plus red), green (yellow plus blue). A color wheel, shown in Illustration 8-1, demonstrates these relationships.

Another thing we would notice if we could bend

C-16

Principles for using color.

This student mock-up page uses the complementary colors blue and orange. A single color in the photo (orange) has been selected to unify the page, and orange's complement (blue) brings contrast.

The page is more appealing because it relies on one color scheme and uses bright color with restraint, as "page punctuation." The areas meant to be read are in black and white or shades of gray. Color's main functions are to unify the page and to increase its contrast, or visual appeal. (Photo courtesy of The Herald, Everett, Wash.)

The Western Front

Western Washington University twice-weekly newspaper   Vol. XXXIV

Locals coping with disease

Chemical sensitivity affliction not curable

By Wendy Writer
Clarion writer

The white night night xxxx xxx lxx xxx xxx xxx xxxxllxxx xxlx xxx xxxxx xxxlxxx xxllx xxxx xxx xllxxxxxl x xxxx wwllw lllx lxxllxxxlx lxlllllx xxxl xllllx lllxlxlxlll.

Another white night night lxlxlxllxxl   lxllxlxlxllxl   xlxlxl lxlxlx lxlxl xllxlxl xlxll xllxlx lxlxl xlxllx lxlxl lxlxlxlxl xlxlllxxlxx xlxlxlxlxllx   lxlxlxlxl   xxxxxlll xlxllxlxlx lxxxxxl xllxl xlxxxxlllxx xlxl xlxxxxx xlllllxlxlxl xlxlxl xlxlxl.

Some other white night night lxlxlxxx lxxlxlxxlllx lllxl xlxlxl xflx xllxllx lxlxllx lxlxlxl lxlxlxl-lxlll xlxlxlll xllxlxl xlxlxl xxxxx. xll.

The white night night xxxx xxx lxx xxx xxx xxx xxxxllxxx xxlx xxx xxxxx xxxlxxx xxllx xxxx xxx xllxxxxxl x xxxx wwllw lllx lxxllxxxlx lxlllllx xxxl xllllx lllxlxlxlll.

Another white night night lxlxlxllxxl   lxllxlxlxllxl   xlxlxl lxlxlx lxlxl xllxlxl xlxll xllxlx lxlxl xlxllx lxlxl lxlxlxlxl xlxlllxxlxx xlxlxlxlxllx   lxlxlxlxl   xxxxxlll xlxllxlxlx lxxxxxl xllxl xlxxxxlllxx xlxl xlxxxxx xlllllxlxlxl xlxlxl xlxlxl.

Some other white night xlxlxxx lxxlxlxxlllx lllxl xlxlxl.

The white night night xxxx xxx lxx xxx xxx xxx xxxxllxxx xxlx xxx xxxxx xxxlxxx xxllx xxxx xxx xllxxxxxl x xxxx wwllw

Index

Books	Comics . . .
C2	A10
Business . .	Communit
D1	y . . . .
Campus	B5
News . .	Cops Box .
B1	B2
Classified .	Editorial .
B8-B10	D4

Weather

Mostly sunny but not quite as warm. Highs in the upper 80s.

Sunny weather

Quote of the Day

"The great thieves punish the little ones."
- Thomas Fuller

The Herald/DAN BATES
Kathy Malcolm tries out a vapor cleaning system on the windows of her new home on Camano Island us instructed by Lori Oneal (second from left), a fellow sufferer of multiple chemical sensitivity. The Malcolm children, 10-year-old Danielle (left) and Matthew, 12, also suffer the ailment.

lllx lxxllxxxlx lxlllllx xxxl xllllx lllxlxlxlll.

Another white night night lxlxlxllxxl   lxllxlxlxllxl   xlxlxl xlxllx lxlxl xllxlxl xlxll xllxlx lxlxl xlxlxl.

Some other white night xlxlxlx lxlxlxxlx lllxl xlxlxl

xlxlxlxlxllx lxlxlxlxll xxxxxlll xlxllxlxlx lxxxxxl xllxl xlxxxxllxx xlxl xlxxxxx xlllllxlxlxl xlxlxl xlxlxl.

Some other white night xlxlxlx lxlxlxxlx lllxl xlxlxl.

xllx xllxllx lxlxllx lxllxl xlxlxlll-lxlll xlxlxlll xlxlxl xlxlxl xxxxx. xll.

Some other white night xlxlxlx xxxx lxx xxx xxx xxx xxxxllxxx

xlllx xlxlxlll xllxlxl xlxlxl xxxxx. xll.

The white night night xxxx xxxx lxx xxx xxx xxx xxxxllxxx

Please see Chemical, Page 6

Anti-chalking policy at library draws criticism from City Council

By Elaine Editor
Clarion writer

The white night night xxxx xxxx lxx xxx xxx xxx xxxxllxxx xxlx xxx xxxxx xxxlxxx xxllx xxxx xxx xllxxxxxl x xxxx wwllw lllx lxxllxxxlx lxlllllx xxxl xllllx lllxlxlxlll.

Another white night night lxlxlxllxxl   lxllxlxlxllxl   xlxlxl xlxlx lxlxl xllxlxl xlxll xllxlx lxlxl xlxlxlxlxlx lxlxlxlxl xxxxxlll xlxllxlxlx lxxxxxl xllxl xlxxxxx xlllllxlxlxl xlxlxl xlxlxl.

Some other white night xlxlxlx lxlxlxxx lxlxlxxlllx lllxl xlxlxllxlx lxlxlxl xlxlxlll xlllxlxl xlxlxl xlxlxl xxxxx. xll.

The white night night xxxx xxxx lxx xxx xxx xxx xxxxllxxx xxlx xxx xxxxx xxxlxxx xxllx xxxx xxx xllxxxxxl x xxxx wwllw lllx lxxllxxxlx lxlllllx xxxl xllllx

lllxlxlxlll.

Another white night night lxlxlxllxxl   lxllxlxlxllxl   xlxlxl xlxlx lxlxl xllxlxl xlxll xllxlx lxlxl xlxlxl.

"The First Amendment guarantees freedom of speech...however, it is not an absolute right"
— Jack Smith
Viking Union Director

xlxlxlxlxllx lxlxlxlxll xxxxxlll xlxlxlxlx lxxxxxl xllxl xlxxxxlll-lxx xlxl xlxxxxx xlllllxlxlxl xlxlxl xlxlxl.

Some other white night xlxlxlx lxlxlxxx lxxlxlxxlllx lllxl xlxlxl.

The white night night xxxx xxxx lxx xxx xxx xxx xxxxllxxx xxlx xxx xxxxx xxxlxxx xxllx xxxx xxx xllxxxxxl x xxxx wwllw

lllxlxlxlll.

Another white night night lxlxlxllxxl   lxllxlxlxllxl   xlxlxl lxlxlx lxlxl xllxlxl xlxll xllxlx lxlxl xlxlxl.

Some other white night xlxlx xllx xllxlll xllxlxl xlxlxl xxxxx. xll.

Some other white night lxlxlxxx lxxlxlxxlllx lllxl xlxlxllxlx lxlxlxl xlxlxlll xlllxlxl xlxlxl xlxlxl xxxxx. xll.

The white night night xxxx xxxx lxx xxx xxx xxx xxxxllxxx xxlx xxx xxxxx xxxlxxx xxllx xxxx xxx xllxxxxxl x xxxx wwllw

Please see Chalking, Page 8

New walkway across tracks will enhance park entry

By Joan Journalist
Clarion writer

The white night night xxxx xxxx lxx xxx xxx xxx xxxxllxxx xxlx xxx xxxxx xxxlxxx xxllx xxxx xxx xllxxxxxl x xxxx wwllw lllx lxxllxxxlx lxlllllx xxxl xllllx lllxlxlxlll.

Another white night night lxlxlxllxxl   lxllxlxlxllxl   xlxlxl lxlxlx lxlxl xllxlxl xlxll xllxlx lxlxl xlxllx lxlxl lxlxlxlxl xxxxxlll xlxllxlxlx lxxxxxl xllxl xlxxxxx xlllllxl-lxlxl xlxlxl xlxlxl.

Some other white night xlxlxlx lxlxlxxx lxxlxlxxlllx lllxl xlxlxl xlxlxlll xlllxlxl xlxlxl xlxlxl xxxxx. xll.

The white night night xxxx xxxx lxx xxx xxx xxx xxxxllxxx

Please see Walkway, Page 8

C-17 Using shades of colors.

Magazine editors can use subtle shades of color with greater confidence when they are printing on glossy white, coated papers. Also, the colors are built by layering, with drying time allowed between the printings of the yellow, magenta, cyan and black screens. This student design project from an editing class shows the rich tones that can be created by darkening red and yellow. (Courtesy of Jennifer Collins.)

C-18

Light falling on a surface affects how the human eye perceives colors. Shadows of bright white light are lavender; shadows of late afternoon light, which is a deeper yellow, move more toward purple or brown. (Photo courtesy of Tim Pilgrim.)

C-19

These skeins of yarn show a range of values and shades within a hue. The light, lilac shade is one that can be seen in a rainbow; darker purple tones result from mixing pigments. Purples range from warm to cool colors, too, depending on whether they have more red or more blue. The eye enjoys discerning these variations as the shop owner who displayed them in a single array realized. (Photo courtesy of Tim Pilgrim.)

C-20A

**Photo combination 1—
Black and yellow.**

The first step in planning color for pages with photographs is to sort those that will work together best in a color scheme. Here, the most luminous color, yellow, is paired with the least luminous, black, as one possible combination.

Sunday Travel

The Southwest: Arid, bright and ancient

C-20B

The second step involves finding a color that appears in each photograph in order to unite the photos on the page. To enhance the photos through contrast, however, this color must be one of the least used.

Here, a small amount of red shows up in each photo, so it becomes the color for the dropped cap and the rules on the next page. Note how shades of gray enhance the black. (Photos by Tim Pilgrim; layouts by Carolyn Dale.)

C-21A

Photo combination 2—Problems with the three primary colors.

The three primary colors don't lend themselves well to portraits or landscapes because so little in nature actually occurs in these true, vivid hues. The same problem can occur with bright, pure greens.

The primaries are used as a color scheme for the photos in the page on the left, but their effect is a bit glaring, and the more subtle colors in the portrait seem dull or faded.

Sunday
travel

The Southwest: arid and ancient

O

C-21B

The page on the right drops yellow, and while both red and blue unite the photos, blue is played down by choosing red as the uniting color and green as its complement. These are then grayed down a bit. (Photos by Tim Pilgrim; layouts by Carolyn Dale.)

C-22A

**Photo combination 3—
The three secondaries.**

This time, the editor chooses a scheme with the three secondary colors: green, orange and purple. Using all three lends a feeling of completeness to a color scheme. Each secondary is a combination of two primary colors.

On the page to the left, the orange has been mixed to pick up similar shades in the photos. Green is mixed also and added to complete the triad. Purple already predominates in several of the photos, so the editor decides not to add more.

148

C-22B

On the page to the right, the secondaries are used differently. Here, a darker orange picks up the least-used color common to all photos and is paired with its complement, a darkened blue. (Photos by Tim Pilgrim; layouts by Carolyn Dale.)

C-23A

Photo combination 4—Shades of gray.

Gray is a light version of all opaque colors combined. The result can be black, but it can also be a dark gray created by mixing a color with its complement. The grays produced this way often carry inherently the warm or cool shades of the main colors.

C-23B

In page design, gray is useful because it enhances other colors and because the human eye can perceive numerous subtly varying shades. Here, the grays take on either the warm tones of the rose color to the left or the cool tones of the green color to the right. The purple is a least-used common color, so it serves to unify the photos on the page. (Photos by Tim Pilgrim; layouts by Carolyn Dale.)

C-24A

Photo combination 5—Blue and orange complements.

Blue and orange are complementary colors that often show up in nature. These colors also reproduce well on monitors and in the printing process. Shades of blue and orange often range so widely among several photos that one or the other can sometimes be used as the unifying or contrasting color.

Sunday
Travel

C-24B

In the layout on the right-hand page, the photos are bordered in black (the least-used unifying color) and two are backed by shaded boxes. This is similar to the way one might go about matting and framing photos. (Photos by Tim Pilgrim; layouts by Carolyn Dale.)

C-25A   A publication's several media.

This grouping of the versions of Wine Press Northwest shows how a publication can exist in several media. Its frequently updated Web site (C-25A), its quarterly print magazine (C-25B), and its weekly e-mail newsletter (not pictured) carry consistent visual identity through such elements as typeface and colors. (Courtesy of Wine Press Northwest.)

FALL 2003

www.winepressnw.com

WINE PRESS
N O R T H W E S T

Seductive Syrah

The red grape of the
Northern Rhône suddenly is
the hottest wine in the Northwest

Fifth annual Best Northwest **Wine List** winners
Great **Gewürztraminer** from the Great Northwest
British Columbia's **Nk'Mip Cellars** goes native
Yakima Valley appellation celebrates its first 20 years

This pair of mock-up pages shows a typical news layout (C-26A) with dominant elements to the top, regularly shaped modules and little white space. (Train station photo by Justin Best, courtesy of The Herald, Everett, Wash.)

Park frenzy
Park use picks up in March, and sculptures at some are a draw.
Please see story, Page 4

The Western Front

Monday March 18, 2003

Photo by Justin Best/ The Herald

From their perch in the center, workers Jack Archibold of Camano Island and Kevin Rinesmith of Skagit County survey results of their effort on the Millennial Chronometer steel and glass clock at Everett Station. The station opened yesterday.

Tax revenue earmarked for buses

by Jane Journalist
Clarion writer

The white night night xxxx xxxx lxx xxx xxx xxx xxxxllxxx xxlx xxx xxxxx xxxlxxx xxllx xxxx xxx xllxxxxxl x xxxx wwllw llllx lxxllxxxxlx lxlllllx xxxl xllllllx lllxlxlxlll.

Another white night night lxlxlxllxxl lxllxlxlxllxl xlxlxl lxlxlx lxlxl xllxlxl xlxll xllxlx lxlxl xlxlxlx lxlxl lxlxlxlxl xlxlllxlxlx xlxlxlxlxllx lxlxlxlxlll xxxxxlll xlxllxlxlx lxxxxxl xllxl xllxxxxl-llxx xlxl xlxxxxx xllllllxllxlxl xlxlxl xlxlxl.

Some other white night xlxlxlx lxlxlxxx lxxlxlxxlllx lllxl xlxlxl xllx xllxlllx lxlxllx lxllxl xlxlxlllllxlll xlxllxll xllxl lxlxl xxxxx, xll.

The white night night xxxx xxxx lxx xxx xxx xxx xxxxllxxx xxlx xxx xxxxx xxxlxxx xxllx xxxx xxx xllxxxxxl x xxxx wwllw llllx lxxllxxxxlx lxlllllx xxxl xllllllx lllxlxlxlll.

Another white night night lxlxlxllxxl lxllxlxlxllxl xlxlxl lxlxlx lxlxl xllxlxl xlxll xllxlx lxlxl xlxlxlx lxlxl lxlxlxlxl xlxlllxlxlx xlxlxlxlxllx lxlxlxlxlll xxxxxlll xlxllxlxlx lxxxxxl xllxl xllxxxxl-llxx xlxl xlxxxxx xllllllxllxlxl xlxlxl xlxlxl.

Viking Viewpoint

Photo by Tim Pilgrim

Do you support the vote for a tax increase to help Whatcom County Transit continue business as usual?

John Pilgrim and son Wiley, Bellingham visitors: "I think the taxes should be raised. I use the bus where I live in Idaho."

"Yes. Buses are good; buses are our friends."
— Jessica Sparks

Everett opens transit hub
Plans for Amtrak, Greyhound to link Bellingham

By Theresa Goffredo
The Herald

EVERETT — Walter Shannon nodded in approval and gave his humble sumation of what he thought about the city's new $44 million landmark called Everett Station: really pretty nice.

The 91-year-old Shannon received an honorable mention yesterday during the transportation hub's grand opening.

Shannon sat in the 200-plus audience as a stoic symbol of Everett's vanguard role in transportation and as the sole surviving motorman for the city's first commuter rail line, the Interurban, which took riders from Everett to Seattle until it closed in 1939.

And, yes, Shannon liked the building just fine. But he confessed he probably wouldn't be boarding any of the trains leaving this station.

"No," Shannon said, scoffing slightly. "I've been pert near everywhere I want to be."

Though not much for trains anymore, Shannon's respected post as a retired rail man took the attention of Gov. Gary Locke, who gave tribute to the Interurban line and called his visit to the city's new station a trip "back to the future."

Everett Station is a transportation center where Everett Transit and Community Transit buses currently are running. The station eventually will receive Greyhound bus service, Amtrak trains — giving an easier link to Bellingham —– and Sound

Please see Everett Station, Page 6

Outside and free
Puget Sound purity affected by dumping

by Tim Pilgrim
Clarion writer

The white night night xxxx xxxx lxx xxx xxx xxx xxxxllxxx xxlx xxx xxxxx xxxlxxx xxllx xxxx xxx xllxxxxxl x xxxx wwllw llllx lxxllxxxxlx lxlllllx xxxl xllllllx lllxlxlxlll.

Another white night night lxlxlxllxxl xlxlxl lxlxlx lxlxl xlxlxl xlxll xllxlx lxlxl xlxlxlx lxlxl lxlxlxlxl xlxlllxlxlx xlxlxlxlxllx lxlxlxlxlll xxxxxlll xlxllxlxlx lxxxxxl xllxl xllxxxxllllxx xlxl xlxxxxx xllllllxllxlxl xlxlxl

Please see Ouside and free, Page 6

Photo by Dan Bates/ The Herald

A lone gull soars over Puget Sound at sundown. The fate of the Pacific Northwest body of water is at the mercy of commercial and military vessels

For news tips, call (360) 650-3162 or e-mail the Western Front at wfront@cc.wwu.edu   www.westernfrontonline.com   Please recycle

Outdoors

Daily Clarion September 2004

Shifting sands

Currents
and tides
redrawing
Oregon's
coastline

Loved by tourists and residents, the Oregon coast's dramatic coves, rocky out-
croppings and acres of white sand dunes are in constant motion geologically
speaking. From winds to currents to earthquakes, the tidal lines get redrawn.

Α Ανχηορδεσκ.χομ διρεχτιονσ:
Ψεπ. Νοον–1:30,2:00Πιση.
Ηερε αρε διρεχτιονσ φρομ βοτη Βηαμ
ανδ Σεαττλε. Ιφ φου ηαθε οαξ νυμβερ.
Ιχαν σενδ φου α μαπ.
Φινδ τηε 520 βριδγε φρομ ειτηερ I–5 ορ
405. ∇ ηεαδινγ εαστ τοωαρδ
Ρεδμονδ:
Γετ οφφ ον τηε 124τη Στ. Εξιτ.
Τυρν λεφτ ατ τηε λιγητ.
Τυρν λεφτ οντο 130τη Αθε NE ατ
τηενεξτ λιγητ
  Τυρν ριγητ ιντο Νορτηυπ Νορτη οφφιχε
παρκ ∇ φιωστ παστ τηε ΣιεμενΓσ σιγν.

Γο στραιγητ τηρουγη τηε στοπ σιγν
ανδ παρκ αηερεθερ. ΩεΓρε ιν βυιλδινγ
Β.Ανχηορδεσκ.χομ διρεχτιονσ:Ψεπ.
Νοον–1:30,2:00Πιση.
Ηερε αρε διρεχτιονσ φρομ βοτη Βηαμ
ανδ Σεαττλε. Ιφ φου ηαθε οαξ νυμβερ, I
χαν σενδ φου α μαπ.
Φινδ τηε 520 βριδγε φρομ ειτηερ I–5 ορ
405. ∇ ηεαδινγ εαστ τοωαρδ
Ρεδμονδ Γετ οφφ ον τηε 124τη Στ. Εξιτ.
Τυρν λεφτ ατ τηε λιγητ.
Τυρν λεφτ οντο 130τη Αθε NE ατ τηε
νεξτ λιγητΤυρν ριγητ ιντο Νορτηυπ
Νορτη οφφιχε παρκ ∇ φιωστ παστ τηε

ΣιεμενΓσ σιγν.
  Γο στραιγητ τηρουγη τηε στοπ σιγν
ανδ παρκ αηερεθερ. ΩεΓρε ιν βυιλδινγ
Β, σιτε 202.
σιτε 202.
  Γο στραιγητ τηρουγη τηε στοπ σιγν
ανδ παρκ αηερεθερ. ΩεΓρε ιν βυιλδινγ
Β.Ανχηορδεσκ.χομ διρεχτιονσ:Ψεπ.
Νοον–1:30,2:00Πιση.
Ηερε αρε διρεχτιονσ φρομ βοτη Βηαμ
ανδ Σεαττλε. Ιφ φου ηαθε οαξ νυμβερ. I
χαν σενδ φου α μαπ.
Φινδ τηε 520 βριδγε φρομ ειτηερ I–5 ορ
405. ∇ ηεαδινγ εαστ τοωαρδ

C-26B

By contrast, the page C-26B shows how adding a few feature elements will create a different mood for even a simple page design. The large illustrations that pull the eye toward the middle of the page, a contrasting typeface for the main heading, lots of white space, a colored dropped cap and text set with ragged-right line endings signal a change in the style of presentation. (Photos by Tim Pilgrim; layouts by Carolyn Dale.)

Ferndale

Thursday: *Weekend* previews concerts

Thursday, Feb. 6, 2003 — Metro Edition — Vol. 44 Issue 37 — 50 cents

East and West...

...*farmers markets get* city smart

Food that ranges, explores, knows no more boundaries; that's what is offered each Saturday and Wednesday at local markets, where fishers and farmers of a variety of backgrounds offer their favorite foods, plants and nursery items -- even koi for the backyard water garden. Once offering a duller range

By Amelia Bruckner, Ferndale Food Writer

Φορ μνχη οφ ηισ λιφε ηε ηασ εκινθριεδ Νεω Υορκ λοοκινγ φορ σιγητσ ανδ περσπεχτιϖεσ τηατ ωουλδ εσχαπε οτηερσ. Βυτ ιν ρεχεντ μοντησ Ρομερο, α στοόδ φηοτογραπηερ φορ Τηε Νεω Υορκ Τιμεσ απο ισ αλσο α παιντερ, ναρροωεδ ηισ σοχυσ, σεεκινγ ουτ τηε Φαρτιστιχ© μαρκινγσ μαδε βψ πεοπλε σεειρινγλψ υνινϖερεστεδ ιν αρτ.

Αμονγ τηε ωορκσ φραμεδ βψ ηισ χαμερα αρε σιγνσ λεφτ βψ ωορκερσ ασ ινστρυχτιονσ χονστρυχτιον χρεωσ, ορ ωαρνινγσ ορ δανγερ ορ εινδοωσ μαδε τεμποραρψ οπαθυε βψ οφ σοαπ, αλλ οφ ωηιχη επθεκε τηε ωορκ οφ Πολλοχκ, Ρανσχηενβεργ ανδ Ροτηκο, αμονγ οτηερσ. Σομε οφ τηεσε ωορκσ μαψ αλσο ρεχαλλ γραφφιτι αρτ, ωηιχη ηασ μοϖεδ φρομ στρεετσ το γαλλεριεσ οϖερ

Τηε οφφερινγσ ον ανψ γιϖεν δαψ οφ μαρκετινγ ινγλυδε α ρανγε οφ πεππερσ — νοτ φυστ ρεδ ανδ γρεεν ανψμορε, βυτ οραντε ανδ ψελλοω, τοο. Ασιαν εγγπλαντ ανδ αλμ ψουνγ ασπαραγυσ αλλ ηιγηλιγητ ανψ μεαλ ασ τηε ϖεγεταβλεσ δυ φουρ, ανδ φορ φλοωερσ, νοτηινγ βεατσ λοβελια ιν πλαντερσ ορ ψελλοω βλοσσομσ ιν

Photos by Tim Pilgrim, Fearless Editing

Film festival pitching animation, documentaries for kids

By Μλρχυσ Τοκιν
Χλαριον Σταφφ Ωριτερ

Τηινκ Ηολλψωοοδ, ανδ ψου τηινκ σταρσ, μονεψ, φαμε, ποωερ, γλιτζ.

Τηινκ Εδμονδσ, ανδ ψου τηινκ φερρψ βοατσ ανδ χοφφεε σταινδ.

Θαχηβ Ψουνγ τηουγητ τηατ κυτίνγ τηε τωο τογετηερ μιγητ μακε φορ α πρεττψ φυννψ μοϖιε.

Φορ αν ινδεπενδεντ ωριτερ/διρεχτορ/προδυχερ λοοκινγ το σηοοτ ηισ φιρστ φιλμ, Τινσελτοων Ι]σ λαθθιεν βυθετη ανδ ινφλατεδ εγοσ αρε ουτ οφ ρεαχη. Τηε λυρε οφ σηοω βιζ, ηοωεϖερ, ισ σομετηινγ αλμοστ εϖερψονε χαν ρελατε το.

Σο Ψουνγ ανδ ηισ χο-ωριτερ ανδ προδυχερ, Παυλ Σινορ, ωροτε α σχριπτ αβουτ α ωοβαλψ μπο ωαντσ το βε

α πλαψερ, βυτ δοεσν[]τ ηαϖε ωηατ ιτ τακεσ το γετ φρομ Εδμονδσ το Λοσ Ανγελεσ.

Φι φυστ σεε τηεσε πεοπλε αλλ τηε τιμε,© Ψουνγ σαιδ. Πευπλε απο φυστ ταλκ. Ι σορτ οφ διδ τηε μοϖιε σο Ι αουλδνϖΠτ βε ονε οφ τηοσε πεοπλε.©

Ηισ φιλμ, ®Τηε Μαρτινι Σηοτ,© ισ ναμεδ φορ τηε φιναλ σχενε αφτερ α δαψ οφ σηοοτινγ, βεφορε χαστ ανδ χρεω πακ ουτ φορ δρινκσ.

Ινδεπενδεντ μοϖιεσ ηαϖε βεεν γαινινγ γρουνδ ον τηε βιγ στυδιοσ φορ ψεαρσ. Τηε μοϖεμεντ μαψ ηαϖε ρεαχηεδ ιτσ απεξ ωιτη τηε ουτ-οφ-νοωηερε ηιτ ®Τηε Βλαιρ Ωιτχη Προφεχτ,© ωηιχη εαρνεδ μορε τηαν 3130 μιλλιον. Βεφορε ®Βλαιρ Ωιτχη© ωασ α ηινομενον, τηουγη, ιτ ωασ φυστ ανοτηερ οφ τηουσανδσ οφ ινδεπενδεντ μοϖιεσ τρψινγ το βρεακ τηε φιλμ φεστιϖαλ χιρχυιτ.

Ψουνγ[]σ μοϖιε, ®Τηε Μαρτινι Σηοτ,© ισ ατ τηε ϖερψ βεγιννινγ οφ τηε προχεσσ. Φιλμεδ δυρινγ τωο ωεεκσ ιν Μαψ, Ψουνγ σπεντ αβουτ 33.000 το σηοοτ τηε μοϖιε ον διγιταλ ϖιδεο, α προχεσσ τηατ ισ μυχη χηεαπερ τηαν υσινγ ρεαλ φιλμ.

Αφτερ σπενδινγ μοστ οφ δυνε εδιτινγ τηε φιλμ, Ψουνγ σεντ ουτ χοπιεσ το διστριβυτορσ ανδ σομε οφ τηε φιλμ φεστιϖαλσ. Ηε ηοπεσ το πυμπ ιν τηε νεξτ ωεεκ φρομ τηε Αμεριχαν Φιλμ Ινστιτυτε[]σ φεστιϖαλ, ανδ χουλδ βε αχχεπτεδ ιν Πορτλανδ[]σ Νορτηωεστ Φιλμ Φεστιϖαλ, ορ τηε Σλαμδανχε φεστιϖαλ ιν Υταη λατερ ιν τηε ψεαρ.

Εθεν ιφ ®Τηε Μαρτινι Σηοτ© ναθερ γοεσ φυρτηερ τηαν τηε 20-οδδ ϖιδεοταπε χοπιεσ Ψουνγ ηασ νοω, ηε βελιεϖεσ ηε αχχομπλισηεδ σομετηινγ ωιτη ηισ φιρστ φιλμ.

®Ι αλωαψσ ωαντεδ το δο ιτ,© Ψουνγ σαιδ.

C-28   Full color: Magazine.

Magazines can not only print beautiful full color on glossy paper, but they can also "bleed" color, running it out into page margins or across centerfolds. This dramatic presentation in a campus magazine melds the theme of the content to the visual presentation through use of large type, negative space, careful placement of text blocks and total color. (Klipsun, © 2002. Photo, Chris Fuller; editor, Greg Woehler; art director, Heather Nordquist. Reprinted with permission.)

159

C-29A   Cover.

Contents pages are vital to a magazine's ability to draw in readers. Often, pages carry visual themes throughout that are established in the publication's design and on the cover. However, they also need to depict the range and variety of several writers' voices. This pair of pages from the Western Washington University student magazine Klipsun shows how the cover's theme (C-29A) is reinterpreted inside (C-29B). (Klipsun, © 2002; editor, Emily Christianson; lead designer, Stephanie Whitaker. Reprinted with permission.)

Tarin Erickson

Tarin is a public relations major who plans to graduate spring quarter. This is her first story in Klipsun. Tarin enjoys creating art herself, so writing about an artist in Whatcom County was an exciting task for her. She hopes this story will draw attention to the many different forms of art a person can create. Whether it's on paper, canvas or 35-mm film, art is found in the beauty of the subject.

Kiko Sola

Kiko is a junior majoring in public relations. She would like to thank Bill Lynch for being an excellent storyteller, and her family, friends and the boy for always supporting her. Also special thanks to the Iron Street girls for putting up with her crankiness through the production of this story. Last, but not least, she would also like to recognize Robin Morris as the catalyst to unlocking the reporter within, and thank her for being an amazing friend, teacher and woman.

Taber Streur

Taber, a public relations major in his last quarter, researched for hours in order to find the perfect subject. His research led him to Kathy Bastow, an artist who creates one of a kind lamps, clocks and finials for home decor. Taber lives by a quote that he once read: "The only problem with avoiding temptation is that you may never get another chance." Taber hopes that his article will inspire artists who may have a passion to create art for a living, but are skeptical of whether they can do it or not.

Quoc Tran

Quoc is a senior news-editorial major who believes anyone can be profiled, for everyone can offer a glimpse into the human experience, which might promote common understanding. To that end, he hopes you will enjoy reading about Lars Simkins who has made his job as the writer more fun than playing video games.

Leanne Josephson

Knowing how difficult it is to break into the upper echelons of the print media, senior journalism major Leanne chose to write about a photojournalist who beat the odds, and the competition. She hopes to collect just as many interesting stories during her career as a writer.

Dian McClurg

Dian decided to profile artist Vince Lalonde after she saw him wearing his 11-foot puppet at a Bellingham peace rally. This is her first Klipsun story. She has also written for The Western Front, The Every Other Weekly and Whatcom Watch. She thanks Vince for hours of interviews, and her family for being patient.

Josh Haupt

Josh is an almost journalism major and seventh year senior. In the past he has worked in public relations for the Irish political party Sinn Fein. After graduating winter quarter (and he will) he plans to pursue a career with the American Civil Liberties Union.

Amber Hurley

Amber, a public relations major, explores how Steve Moore creates his gowns with a delicate hand and an eye for detail. Designing and sewing dresses since he was 17 years old, Moore is no typical college senior.

Margo Horner

Margo is a senior journalism major. This is her first contribution to Klipsun. After graduating in spring quarter, she plans to become a reporter at some big, prestigious paper somewhere.

<- CONTRIBUTORS

Klipsun

November 2002, Volume 33, Issue 1

Editorial Staff

editor-in-chief
Emily Christianson

managing editor
Mindy Ransford

copy editor
Sonja L. Cohen

story editors
Alashia Freimuth
Karla Tillman

photo director
Alaina Dunn

lead designer
Stephanie Whitaker

designers
Kynde Kiefel
Kit Shaughnessy

adviser
Shearlean Duke

Staff Writers

Valerie Bauman
Carise Bogar
Amber Bomar
Robin Duranleau
Tarin Erickson
Josh Haupt
Margo Horner
Amber Hurley
Leanne Josephson
James Lyon
Dian McClurg
Heidi Mulhern
Jenny O'Brien
Evan E. Parker
Kiko Sola
Orion Stewart
Taber Streur
Quoc Tran
Cindy Vrieling

The Western Front

News

Sports

Features

Accent

Opinions

Contact

Forum

Frank Madison, 76, is a member of the Tulalip Indian Tribe. He recalls the days when the tribes were barred from meeting in the Long House, which was, to the tribes, a religious place. "But we would go in there and hold our pow wows anyway," he says.

"It was President Reagan who had the Native Americans' religion returned to them," Madison says. Along with the survival of their culture, there is another concern expressed by each of these elders: New people moving into the area don't know about the tribes' legal entitlements and protections.

DAN BATES/The Herald

In This Issue:

The life of the chemically sensitive:
For certain people, every breath involves as much planning as the rest of us devote to dieting, or exercising, or writing our wills. For them, every breath becomes a serious decision.
Full story...

Chalk it up to experience
Chalking has beome a popular form of self expression on Western's campus. But Western's policy on students' rights and this medium of free speech is in question.
Full story..

Life preservers
As the region grows, the challenge of educating new comers about the treaty rights of the Tulalup Tribe may be essential to saving their culture.
Full story..

Success of local tribes draws attention
The Tulalip Indian tribe prepares to build a new shoppin center and sports complex that could attract big business.
Full story..

Other side of the tracks
Bellilngham approves building a safe crossing for pedestrians.
Full story...

Worldly art
Seattle Art Museum enlightens area school children through a new traveling art program.
Full story..

C-30   Ease of use: Web pages.

Any good design is practical and useful for its readers or users. This is especially true for Web pages, which run a number of technological hurdles before reaching their audiences. This student mock-up for a campus newspaper's online offerings relies on a single, large photo surrounded by a number of text items that can be read while the photo loads. It also offers main stories just a click away from the home page. Basic colors are used in the design, and the font is readable for even low-end monitors. (Page design by Laura Thoren; Photo by Dan Bates. Courtesy of The Herald, Everett, Wash. Reprinted with permission.)

ment, subject and background; it has been through a process that selects among images those that best portray the world as it makes sense to an editor. Placing people of diverse backgrounds into editing positions and checking the patterns of photographic depictions over time are two ways to guard against a single viewpoint dominating the selection of which images seem most real, accurate, truthful and relevant.

Literal and Figurative Meanings

Trompe d'oeil is a phrase in French meaning the eye is being tricked; what we perceive is not literally true. As the ability to portray distance through use of perspective developed, painters also discovered they could create images that played with what we were learning as a culture to trust as markers for visual orientation on flat surfaces.

The drawings of M.C. Escher, for example, confound—are those dark-colored fish swimming in a geometric pattern in one direction, or light-colored birds in formation flying in the opposite direction? The stairway that at first glance seemed to lead downward upon closer inspection is leading upward. Or is it? (See Illustration C.5.)

This can be enjoyable, becoming a game between the artist and viewer; in photography the same can occur. We love a photo in which the unexpected happens, or in which two unlikely objects appear together. When a satirical magazine ran a cover photo illustration of actor Bruce Willis looking very pregnant, readers were immediately in on the joke, even more so if they had also seen the earlier cover photo of Vanity Fair that showed a very pregnant and nude Demi Moore. Still, an explanation can easily be provided to tell how the image was altered.

When unexpected elements line up in a way the camera can record in a fashion that will fool the eye or when an image is altered to combine unexpected elements, editors usually provide some explanation to readers in accompanying captions and labels.

Why? Are not readers sophisticated enough consumers of a visual culture to understand that many images we see are not literally true? We consume enormous amounts of advertising, for example, in which unlikely objects are juxtaposed, or placed next to each other, with the expectation that we will create a meaning.

Some researchers argue that readers learn how to decode complex visual messages by interpreting what the objects mean in our culture and then creating a story that connects the objects. An example used by marketing researcher Linda Scott is an advertisement in which a tube of lipstick appears in a glass of soda water, complete with ice cubes and lime. Readers do not literally think that lipstick should be used or stored this way; instead, they might transfer the qualities of the drink (cool, refreshing) to the lipstick. Research indicates they may gain the message but oppose themselves to it, in a conscious resistance, or they may interpret the message by discussing it with friends or other viewers.

Editors work on the assumption that what readers expect to see in news, however, is literal truth: events happened just as they are shown. This has been the historical basis of the authority and authenticity of documentary photographs.

With digital processing, alterations to images become easy and seamless. While photographers working in darkrooms might have dodged or burned areas of a print under the developing light to lighten or darken them, or may have substituted high-contrast for low-contrast printing paper, the content of the photos stayed put.

And if photo content was altered by overlaying pieces of film, or using filters, or through making double exposures, etc., these alterations were readily apparent to the eye—at least to the expert's eye, if not a reader's.

Yet, when objects or events are digitally altered in major ways, it can be difficult to detect. Brian Walski, a photographer for the Los Angeles Times covering the Iraq war, composed an image on his laptop computer out of two separate photos of a British soldier in front of a group of Iraqi citizens. The composite photograph was printed and when the alteration came to light, Walski was fired. Newspapers that ran the photo later printed stories and comments on the ethics involved.

The credibility of the publication in which a photograph appears, and its contract with its readers, are crucial. When photo illustrations are used, readers need to be informed so that there is no chance they will mistake the contrived appearance for reality. Often this is done in a caption, for the routine cases in which an artist poses in her studio, or a parent instructs the kids to play in the tree house because the photographer has arrived and wants that shot.

Other contrivances depart enough from reality that they are labeled as photo illustrations, much as though they were a piece of art, which they are. (See Illustration C.6.)

Photo illustrations can powerfully convey ideas and concepts simply because they depart from literal reality. A collage of photos, perhaps with torn edges and heaped together, may convey the progress of a person's life more truly than a photo of her accepting an award. Or, a combination of photograph and illustration may be used with an abstract analysis in a magazine.

A key point is that the reader needs to know whether to take the photo content literally or whether he can interpret it figuratively by using it as a set of icons or symbols from which he might generate a story.

Illustrations and Art

It goes without saying that editors appreciate a creative photographer who can deliver images that range into the realm of art. (See Illustrations C.7.)

But, sometimes editors may want to move beyond photo illustration or photo art and turn instead to an artist for a drawing that presents a visual treatment of a concept or idea in a way that invites readers to interpret and create abstract meanings.

Such illustrations are commonly used in magazines and for Sunday editorial section think pieces; they can be rendered beautifully on Web pages, especially when the art is originally created for display on a monitor.

Editors who need to communicate with artists may find themselves at ease describing the concepts they want to convey, but uncomfortable about suggesting images to represent those concepts. They may be unsure how to evaluate the art once it is produced. But many of the qualities distinguishing fine photographs apply to illustrations as well.

As with photography, those unfamiliar with art may first, instantly, think of clichés. How many times have we seen that robed, blindfolded lady holding a balance scale? Enough times to know she is a symbol for seeking justice?

A Sunday newspaper section that ran a major story on domestic abuse becoming recognized in international tribunals ran a drawing of a woman's face complete with a black eye and her arms reaching out over a sketched globe of the world. Two key ideas are presented—very literally. Could a different illustration have been more figurative or conceptual, have asked the viewer to work with other images that might have expressed increasing hope, survival, social change or safety?

Of course, editors also must know the publication's ethical guidelines defining when and how to use illustrations, and how to label or represent them.

Background and Composition

For editors wanting to work with composition, it might be helpful to visualize a photograph or illustration as a page in microcosm and to ask where the dominant images are and where the light and dark spaces fall. Then, what is the pattern or shape created?

Photographs contain internal shapes. An arrangement of three people, with a taller person in the center, creates a triangle. Groups of people clustered against a background may form a shape that is repeated by other groups across a vista. The furrows of tilled land may echo the shapes of clouds in the sky, or rows of roof tiles may form a pattern of undulating curves. (See Illustration C.8.)

Photography and art provide endless, pleasing variations of patterns and shapes and their combinations. In photographs, these show up as negative space, or the empty areas of space between objects, and positive space, which encompasses the subjects and the action.

To achieve a balanced, finished look, an editor might want to preserve a large, lighter space to balance a smaller, very dark one. This is why expanses of sky, for example, are often left in photos, rather than cropped even though they don't include objects or people. (See Illustration C.9.)

Other properties of composition include scale, which is the relative size of each element to other elements and to the page. Humans set against a dramatic natural backdrop can effectively contrast the difference. (See Illustration C.10.)

Editors also look at proportion and try to avoid photographs that appear ungainly because of the distribution of dark and light areas. They might try for a horizon that marks out one-third or two-thirds of the vertical space, for example, rather than cutting it in half.

Another consideration is motion, or how the elements in the photo direct the eye about inside the image. Editors begin to note what attracts the eye first, and then how the eye is drawn, perhaps by the direction of the subjects' eyes, or the gesture of an arm, or a dog's leaping motion or a shaft of light. Photographs that involve viewers literally draw the eye in and around among its elements. (See Illustration 7.7.)

ILLUSTRATION 7.7   Brian Plonka's Spokane (Wash.) Spokesman-Review photo of railroad tracks vanishing into the fog succeeds in drawing the reader's eye into the mist as well.

(Photo courtesy of Brian Plonka)

Finally, an editor can consider an image's mood, particularly if special effects were used, such as a wide-angle lens, a soft focus, filters, etc. Though research shows that people interpreting the emotions evoked by photographs are largely affected by their own mood at the time, a photograph's subject, setting and treatment often frame whether it is to be taken as entertainment or as serious news. (See Illustration C.11.)

Placing Photos Together

More than one photo can be used in telling a story. Photos may appear sequentially with text to illustrate a person or a place as it is mentioned in the course of a story. Or if the story is mainly visual, photos may be grouped together with the narrative being no more than a few paragraphs of text and captions.

Photographs that are individually strong may pull against each other, vying for attention on a page. To use several together effectively, an editor:

- varies the size: one is sized notably larger, and several others are of progressively smaller sizes. The eye, in fact, can be guided from very large, to medium, to small images arranged in a visual flow.
- uses lots of white space: photographs are very dark, dominant areas and, in fact, can become uninviting to look at if too many are similar in size and crowded into the space allotted.
- keeps the white space to the edges and notes its shape as negative space, thus, trying to provide balance for the page.
- looks for continuity in the inner shapes: curves or arm gestures in one may connect quite gracefully to a similar arc in another, or a light-colored triangular background in one may offset a dark triangular space in another, creating symmetry or asymmetry.
- tells a story with subject matter by moving from distant panorama to close-up details; or moving from team play to individual highlights; or moving from youth to old age.
- assigns space in the design for headings and captions: these may be in a block. Large typography also needs to be placed carefully, as it is also a large, dark, dominant image.

This adds up to flow among sizes, in subject matter and in internal shapes, to create a rhythm. (See Illustration C.12.)

Words with Images

The caption traditionally placed under a photo is, like headings, written in present tense. It describes the action in the image, and avoids redundancy by filling in essential details such as the location and the identities of the people shown. If the layout style of the publication allows more than a single line of type, a longer caption can provide context for the events.

The caption ties the photo to the story by mentioning key angles, but there must be interplay between the two, rather than repetition. A person reading the accompanying story will look from the story to the photo and back, perhaps several times. This means the caption can handle significant information.

Editors preserve an image's integrity by not placing type over areas that show detailed information, and they do not cut into an image's straight edges in order to place credit lines or captions. Type can be successfully placed on a photo if the wording is brief and bold and if the photo area is empty of underlying details. This practice demands a keen eye for creating or preserving balance in the composition. (See Illustration C.13.)

Sometimes photos run alone because they tell a story on their own. Called **stand-alones,** these shots are treated somewhat like news stories. Editors write headings for them, which vary depending on a publication's style and format. These headings may have verbs and convey news; or, they may be run for entertainment value and include quips or plays on words. Captions tend to run longer because they give vital information without help from an accompanying news story. And, the entire package is usually set apart by a box or a frame.

Production

After cropping an image, editors may need to enlarge or reduce its size so it fits the space intended. This does not change the image's proportions, as cropping may have. Instead, it preserves the proportion of the width and height to each other while making the overall size larger or smaller.

This can be pictured as growing or shrinking an image from an imaginary dot in the middle. If it is going to be made wider, it must become taller, too. Otherwise, people would stretch very widely and look strange indeed, like distortions in fun house mirrors.

Page-editing software offers several options for editors to use, but they all function using percentage of original size as the starting point, with 100 percent replicating the original. A photo at 200 percent of original, for example, will be twice as wide and twice as high. Size plays a factor in the impact a photo makes, with larger ones evoking more viewer involvement.

Editors will work mainly with photographs that are already digital files, but not always. Images may come in as glossy prints on paper, in which case they need to be processed for printing.

A photograph printed on paper from film is called continuous tone because the areas of dark and light result from a chemical process on paper; they have not been reduced to dots or pixels. The photo must go through a production process to change these continuous colors or shades of gray into lines of dots for printing, or to digital information to display on a monitor.

For printing on paper, the process creates halftones. These are very fine lines of dots, which will carry the ink in the printing process. The line screens vary by their number per inch, with more lines indicating a higher resolution of printing. Newspapers, for example, may print at 65 or 70 lines per inch, while a magazine may use 130 lines or more.

Dots per inch, or **dpi,** expresses resolution on a computer screen, as well, though the underlying process is not the number of dots on an inch of a halftone line. In computing, dpi refers to the number of pixels activated per inch. Though monitor resolution varies, generally a pixel is equated to a point, at 72 per inch. For this reason, resolution of computer images at 72 dpi will produce a minimally acceptable image. Scanners are used to change a continuous-tone print into digital information.

While a photograph is on an editor's monitor, he has a wide range of potential choices for making adjustments because each and every pixel could be altered. Typically, an editor is concerned with the same issues photographers worked on in chemical darkrooms—whether the contrast is sufficient or whether certain areas need to be lightened or darkened. Editors also adjust color balance, as some monitors and printing processes vary the vividness of some shades, particularly red.

Typically, changes made to enhance production values are considered ethically permissible. But other changes—adjustments that alter the presence or location of objects or people, or change appearance slightly, or shift the mood, for example—are considered not ethical because they alter the truthfulness of the rendition of what actually happened, of what a person present at the time actually saw.

Time magazine crossed an ethical line when it ran on its cover a photo of O. J. Simpson, arrested on suspicion of murdering his wife and a friend—with his features darkened to look grimmer and more sinister. Though Time labeled it as a photo illustration, the contents did not tip off the viewers, at the time of viewing, that they were not seeing literal truth.

The ethical principle is to preserve the truthfulness of the immediate visual impact.

Conclusion

Editors working with images use a different range of values than they use with words, though the ultimate goals of truthfulness, clarity, news action, entertainment and revelations of human nature may be the same.

By selecting photos and then cropping and sizing them, editors are deciding which images will appear how they will appear and how words will be used to relate them to the stories on the page.

As editors work with images, they discern values underlying visual presentations, such as angle, action, contrast, balance, gaze, literal and figurative meanings, and composition. Finally, editors complement the image with words by writing captions that provide context and by creating apt headings that highlight the news or entertainment value.

Exercises to Apply Concepts and Develop Skills

These exercises anticipate that the instructor will be able to use a large selection of unedited photographs in the classroom. These may be compiled from newspapers, newsletters, magazines or web sites, from student-taken digital photos or from the work of a photojournalism class.

1. Goal: To select photos by articulating the strength of inherent qualities.

   Provide students with a batch of print photos or present a group online. Have them work in small teams to select what they feel are the best photos in terms of news value, composition, angle and contrast. Each group can present its selections and discuss the photos' attributes so that students gain practice in applying the concepts and articulating the terminology involved.

2. Goal: To identify the essential parts of a photo and to crop away the nonessential parts.

   Working with editing software, have students practice enlarging, shrinking and cropping a handful of photos. Discuss aspects such as the direction of the subject's gaze, emotional impact of expressions and of the overall scene, and the usefulness of background details in setting context.

3. Goal: To practice writing the words that will accompany photographs.

   Working individually with photos, students can write captions that describe action, give location, identify people and enhance the heading and lead of the story without being repetitious. Discuss how it feels to write in present tense.

   Similarly, students can practice writing a **caption block** (a paragraph that will be positioned to provide captions for a group of photos).

4. Goal: To select photos that work together well both verbally, telling a story, and visually creating a flow the eye will follow.

   Working with a group of potential photographs, students should choose the ones that create a visual story line and that direct the eye smoothly. Discuss how much, and which aspects, of the story will be told in words and in photos.

5. Goal: To envision possible illustrations.

   Ask students to work in a small group that plans several photo illustrations. Have them also discuss how the photo illustrations would be presented, what captions would be needed, and how the illustrations relate to the ethical guidelines of the publication for which they are intended.

   Do the same process for artists' illustrations, such as drawings or cartoons; ask whether the captions and ethical guidelines are or need to be the same.

*Helpful Sources*_____

Clarke, Graham. "The Photograph." New York: Oxford University Press, 1997.

Hirschman, Elizabeth C., et al. "A model of product discourse: Linking consumer practice to cultural texts," Journal of Advertising; Provo, Utah: Spring 1998.

Johnston, Cheryl. American Journalism Review "Digital Deception." Adelphia: May 2003. Vol. 25, Issue 4 p. 10.

Kobre, Kenneth and Bettsy Brill, eds. "Photojournalism: The Professionals' Approach." 4th Ed. Boston: Focal Press, 2000.

Lester, Paul, ed. "The Ethics of Photojournalism." Special Report of the National Press Photographers Association. Durham, N.C.: (No Date).

Meyer, Pedro and Joan Fontcuberta. "Truths and Fictions: A Journey from Documentary to Digital Photography." New York: Aperture, 1995.

Mitchell, William J. "The Reconfigured Eye: Visual Truth in the Post-Photographic Era." Cambridge, Mass.: MIT Press, 1992.

Poynteronline. http://www.poynter.org/

Savedoff, Barbara E. "Transforming Images: How Photography Complicates the Picture." Ithaca, N.Y.: Cornell University Press, 2000.

Scott, Linda M. "Images in Advertising: The Need for a Theory of Visual Rhetoric," Journal of Consumer Research, Inc. 21 (September 1994) pp. 252–73.

Severin, Werner J. and James W. Tankard, Jr. 5th Ed. "Communication Theories: Origins, Methods, Uses." New York: Addison-Wesley Publishing, 2000.

8

Color

Color is life; when we bring color into publications, we add the appeal of warmth, liveliness, coolness and poise—a whole range of feelings to show and attune to the written and visual content.

Color's absence from publications for centuries was not a design decision, but a technological limitation. The printing press laid down only black ink; the press required cleaning and re-inking to add color, plus the color layers had to be registered, or lined up exactly. During earlier eras, it was monks working by hand in scriptoria who added the beautiful coloring known as illumination to the texts. The very word reveals the concept that color comes from light and brings light.

Color is freely available in online journalism and is a basic design consideration for World Wide Web pages. But, color remains an added expense in print production, not just because of inking but because images have to go through a process of separation, of pulling out the layers of the basic colors yellow, red, blue, plus an intensifying black, to be replicated in the printing process.

An editor's work with color takes place at several levels because viewers respond to colors physiologically as well as culturally, colors respond to each other and appear to alter each other, and colors vary depending on whether they are created as ink on paper or as light waves on a monitor.

Color as Light

The light that comes to us from the sun is colorless to our eyes until it passes through a prism or is reflected from a surface. When we say that an apple is red, we are in fact reporting that all light waves except red are absorbed; the red light reflected by the peel is the color we perceive. An apple placed in the dark is, literally, not red, though its peel still contains red-reflecting properties, should any light turn up.

Light working on opaque surfaces, such as ink on paper, represents a different process than light that shows as colors on a computer monitor. Hence, editors need to work in two conceptually different systems, literally as different as night and day, for all opaque ink colors put together will form black, while the full spectrum of colored light forms white.

When sunlight passes through myriad tiny prisms, raindrops in the air, its spectrum becomes visible as a rainbow. If we could study it for a time, we'd see the range of primary colors—red, yellow and blue—and the colors they make as they mix at the edges; we'd also see the spectrum beginning and ending with violet, one tinged with red, the other blue.

The spectrum of natural light is without purple, but theorists say we would see purple if we could bend the rainbow to make the violet edges meet, to shape it like a tube.

The three colors red, yellow and blue are called primary because all of the colors we perceive can be created from them. The colors they make as their edges overlap with each other are the secondary colors orange (red plus yellow), purple (blue plus red), and green (yellow plus blue). A color wheel, shown in Illustration C.14, demonstrates these relationships.

Another thing we would notice if we could bend this rainbow, or if we had a spectrum of light before us, is that the bands of colors are not equally wide; natural colors have different amounts of light, or **luminosity.** Yellow is the most luminous, which means that in its truest, most-yellow form, it is the lightest color. Johannes Itten, a German artist and theorist, wrote that there is no such thing as dark yellow. It has so much luminosity that when it is placed near violet, the least luminous color, a yellow patch next to a violet patch will strike us as balanced, or equal in weight, if the violet patch is three times as large.

The place where each color falls in a spectrum does not vary because each color represents a certain range of wavelengths of light, just as certain musical sounds are clearly different from each other in that they involve different wavelengths of sound. And just as musical notes have known intervals between them, so colors have certain set relationships. Itten also correlated the wavelengths of colors to corresponding wavelengths of sound.

Knowing some of the enduring properties of color becomes useful to the page designer who wants to use their effects for greatest impact.

Colors and Their Complements

A key idea is **complementarity,** using a color and its complement as a pair. A color's complement can be defined several ways. The complements face each other directly across a color wheel. The complement to red is green, located directly opposite; similarly, the complement of yellow is violet-blue.

Complements also can be thought of as completions because the complement for a primary color is made up of the combination of the two other primaries. Hence, red's complement green is the result of mixing blue and yellow; yellow's complement of violet is the result of mixing blue and red.

Why use color complements in design? The reason lies in the concept of *beauty*. If used carefully, the pair of colors can lend a sense of completion and satisfaction to a page. The page will look balanced even though a reader might not be able to say why. Pegie Stark Adam of the Poynter Institute shows in her book, "Color, Contrast, and Dimension in News Design," how newspaper designers successfully use complementarity to give pages depth—a three-dimensional feel—in addition to liveliness.

However, as she points out, a danger lurks in using two pure values of complements in large measure right next to each other. The result can be jarring and discordant. (See Illustration C.15.)

Using them well together often means toning one down a bit by adding black or gray, lightening one or both, or separating them by another color. (See Illustration C.16.)

Using color effectively requires judgment and taste in addition to knowledge. An editor gains ability by developing an eye for art, examining color schemes in beautiful paintings or graphics, and appreciating why—and how—they work.

Physiological Impact

Color, to put it simply, is the way human eyes perceive waves of light of different frequencies; however, the way the brain processes the eyes' message is complex.

An easy way to observe how complementary colors affect us is by noting the negative afterimage of a bright primary color. This occurs, for example, after looking too long at a beautiful sunset and then glancing at a neutral-colored wall in a room. The gleaming, peachy orb has become a disk of green or blue. We are "seeing spots," which are the complement of the color we just saw—green, if the sunset was red, violet if it was orange.

Seeing a negative afterimage is a clue that our brains are highly involved while we perceive color; the brain, in fact, created the impression of the wavelengths of light opposite to the bright light perceived.

Designers use complementary colors for the very reason that they involve the brain with the fullest range of light waves. This can be pleasurable for the viewer or reader. The Impressionist painters understood this when they made paintings full of yellow light casting violet shadows or red poppies sprinkled in wild green grass.

We may be bothered by two pure complementary colors in large quantities placed next to each other because our brains try to process two very different sets of wavelengths and cannot do so comfortably at the same time. We literally see one and then the other; with the negative afterimages, the tension becomes jittery and even nauseating.

Colors are also linked to coolness and warmth. North American culture treats the blues and greens of the spectrum as cool, and reds and oranges as warm. Whether this is innate to humans or whether the connotations reflect cultural learning—that water is cool and looks blue, that fire is red-yellow and feels hot—is not really known because the "natural" attributes assigned to different colors vary widely across cultures and through time.

Cultures assign meaning to colors and to color patterns and combinations. Red and black dominate in Northwest Coast Indian art, particularly Kwakiutl designs, while in American slang "seeing red" means feeling angry, and red in Chinese traditions symbolizes good luck.

White varies also; in the United States, an American of European descent will choose white for a wedding dress; in some Asian cultures, on the other hand, white is the color of mourning.

James Stockton, in "The Designer's Guide to Color," writes that the scarcity and value of dyes have affected roles of colors in history. In ancient Japan, when a tiny amount of red dye was worth the total assets of two ordinary households, red was for privileged classes. The bulk of the population was forbidden to use the dye, and women could wear clothes of only a faint red, or pink, derived by a cheap method of dyeing. This shade of pink, he writes, came to signify meager income and social restrictions.

Stockton says red may be one of humankind's three basic colors, and to some cultures, red and white form the same kind of basic opposition that black and white have to North American eyes.

The cultural meanings of a color scheme form a code that members of that culture often can interpret but that may be difficult for viewers in other cultures to understand.

For example, American journalism students asked to design a poster for an exhibit of quilts chose a variety of color schemes. Pastel pink, blue and green were for a baby, while forest green, slate blue, orange-gold and brick red connoted Shaker design. A Japanese exchange student chose orange, pink, blue and shades of gray, and though she saw them as American colors, they did not relate immediately to an American cultural category for quilts. An Alaskan Native American student chose predominant russet red on a black background.

A Publication's Palette

Designed publications typically have defined color schemes. We see gray, pin-striped suits as the visual analog for the Wall Street Journal; neon-bright lime and tangerine in Wired magazine; warm-palette brick reds, rich golds and earthy purples on food and wine magazines; world events framed in black and red in news magazines. And, in any newspaper the Sunday comic sections in their primary hues draw heavily on pure reds, blues and yellows. Illustration C.17 shows how the complements red and green may be used in deep or shaded tones to fit a publication's color scheme.

Because North American culture has developed these associations for publication colors, designers choose schemes fitting with cultural expectations. Many publications veer away from the all-gray or the pure-color looks, and opt instead for colors with small amounts of black added. A red, for example, treated this way will take on a richer, darker quality. Blues touched with gray are closer to the blues we see in daily life, from worn denim to hazy or cloudy skies.

When she designs a color scheme for a publication, Adam says she first researches the colors used in that geographic area. For example, the color scheme for the Patriot-News of Harrisburg, Pa., draws on traditional American colonial shades.

In public relations work, color palettes defined for a company or corporation overall are reflected in individual publications. Name United Airlines and dark blue comes to mind; name your high school or college, and you'll remember its colors. Starbuck's coffee has a deep-green mermaid, and complementary red tones are used for the bags of coffee and in warm-palette interiors for the stores and cafes.

Though color identity may have been defined for a publication through a design process, on a daily basis, the editor interprets it and uses it in selecting items and in creating color items on a page. And if she is editing a publication without a set palette, she may be instrumental in creating one through her decisions. Color is key in establishing a look for a publication that its readers recognize and expect, so over time color use contributes to integrity and credibility.

Color Interactions

Skillful painters play carefully with the way colors relate to each other. We never see a color in isolation, and its values are affected by its interaction with colors near it.

A person may experience this when repainting a room. If the walls are white and he starts to paint them light blue, that blue will appear much darker than it did at the paint store. It isn't; it is just being deepened by being seen next to white. But when he paints the entire room, leaves for a while and comes back, the color suddenly looks like the desired light blue because it is no longer set off by white.

The wavelengths of light reflected by colors next to each other affect the human brain in a way that allows us to "mix" colors when we are viewing from a distance.

For example, Rembrandt used white, black and a bit of red when painting faces in his portraits. Yet when we view one from several yards away, these tones seem to present varying shades of browns and pinks. And, these shades may vary depending on where one stands and how the light is falling and changing.

The play of light will make a difference, as well, with colors taking on different aspects at different times of day, due both to the changing quality of light and to its angle. Illustration C.18 shows how light playing on a surface affects the eye's perception of the colors involved.

Publication editors work with this idea when they add gray or black shadows to objects. If done bluntly, the effect can be an irritating visual interruption. But if done subtly, the viewer's eye will mix the shadow with the main color and perceive it as a natural rendition of depth, or three-dimensionality.

Editors apply colors on pages that are never colorless to begin with. The colors of paper vary from slick white magazine stock, which shows yellow full and bright, to tan newsprint, which shows yellow as faint and greenish.

Editors may choose the background color for Web pages, but those colors will display differently depending on the viewer's monitor and browser. A set palette of colors is supported by HTML coding, and editors may expect that less distortion will occur if they stick to using those. Even those colors will vary, though, depending on a monitor's color settings and on the kind of light falling on it, which may be daylight, fluorescent or incandescent.

Hue, Value and Intensity

As they work with colors, editors will encounter many subtle and surprising effects and will observe how colors interact with each other and are affected by small changes in their brightness, relative size and placement. Over time, an editor's appreciation for the values of colors will grow, and the terms artists use for the main color dimensions will become clear.

A book such as Adam's "Color, Contrast, and Dimension in News Design" provides numerous examples of color use in publications as well as the principles in art history they reflect. The book lays a foundation for reading further in color theory and expanding the repertoire of color applications editors use with confidence.

Learning terminology can unlock a few mysteries, too. **Hue** is the term for a color's name. A hue is simply red, orange, green and so forth. A color's **value** refers to the distinction between lightness and darkness. White and black are the ultimate, or terminal values. White has the greatest light, so small amounts of black, or dark colors, balance it. This is why black type is easy to read on white while the reverse becomes difficult and tiring to our eyes.

A color's **intensity** refers to its saturation, or the shade at which it is at its most true and full value. Red, for example, is true red only in a certain portion of the spectrum. At either side, it shades toward orange or toward purple. Mixing it with either white or black decreases its intensity, and the red then moves toward pink or maroon. Illustration C.19 suggests a variety of shades and values can make for pleasant viewing.

Usefulness of Gray

Editors work with a great advantage in designing publications: gray. As a color, gray is versatile, unifying, complementary and cheap to reproduce, all at once.

And, it occurs naturally in columns of black text on white, which are perceived as gray from a distance.

Gray is the combination of black and white, but it is also the result when a color is mixed with its complement. For example, a gray resulting from blue and orange can edge toward a bluish, cool cast, or toward a bronzy, warmer tone. In either case, it will take on a richness when placed near one of the original colors.

Gray is also the only color that results from mixing complements—hence, its versatility. Gray is a useful tool for separating the complementary colors used on a page in order to keep them from being so close to each other that they become discordant. Gray can be used to provide calm, quiet areas of a page so that its brighter, more dominant elements show more contrast.

On a print page, gray is usually produced by lightly screening black ink. In other words, the dots that are used in printing will be less dense, allowing more of the background color to show through. And, a light screen of a color can be added. For example, a medium-gray screen can be overlaid with a light-blue screen to enrich its color.

The darkness of gray is expressed as a percentage, with black being 100 percent and gray becoming lighter as the percentage is lowered. It is necessary to test, by printing out or by viewing, how dark a gray is actually produced in the final medium, though, because both monitor displays and laser-printer inking yield varying results.

The "gamma," or contrast among mid-level gray values for images, varies by the default setting in a computer's operating system, according to "The Web Style Guide," by Patrick J. Lynch and Sarah Horton. They write that Macintosh users will see their images as much darker and with stronger contrasts when viewed on a Windows system while Windows editors will see their images as flatter and more washed out when viewed on Macs. This can be compensated for, they say, by lightening images slightly in work originating on a Mac and darkening them slightly in work originating in Windows.

The human eye accurately perceives many fine distinctions of gray—as many as 150, some theorists say—and using several shades of gray in a design can give attractive results.

For maximum use of gray as a color, editors find it helpful to begin thinking in terms of **negative space.** This is the area between or among the dominant elements. In design, the shape of open areas is equally important and needs just as much planning as the shapes of the dominant elements. The Oregon Coast is famous for its dramatic beauty, with huge, craggy rocks offset by the smoothness of the gray sand and the flatness of the sea. Both the dominant elements and the gray negative space are necessary for the stunning result.

Using Color with Photographs

Photographs arrive on the editor's desk with their own inherent color schemes. Though the editor may know of the subject matter well ahead and may have been involved in planning the photography, it is not until the image is done that she will know beyond doubt which colors she will be working with.

Her goals in selecting photos for the page and in creating color items to accompany them are to build both unity and contrast. The page will need to hang together as a whole but also offer contrasts that stand out and guide the viewer's eye.

Photos often fall within predictable palettes. A photo shoot on snow boarding or skiing will involve blue skies and blues of distant forests, deep green of nearby fir trees and bluish-white and violet whites for snow. And, colorfully dressed boarders may present flashes of neon green, crimson or signal-light yellow.

Similarly, shots of farms at harvest time will concentrate on warm palettes of gold and brown earth tones, with perhaps some red apples or orange pumpkins.

An editor will start by looking at all of the photos available and choosing those that are best composed and most expressive of the story's ideas. Within those, she may start sorting, even unconsciously, by color schemes. Which photos look best together? Even if one is not aware of color theory, this is a natural selection process; a photo bright with reds and greens is not going to show to its best next to a photo with muted pastels.

The editor will also look at the other photos or illustrations running on the page and again will note which photos present an interesting and involving, but not jarring, array.

As she looks at the remaining possibilities, it is time to consider consciously which one or two colors will provide the underlying unity of the photos chosen. Do they reflect a blue-green palette? A burgundy-gold palette? Or one that runs mainly red, gray and black? Illustrations C.20 through C.24 show photographs first being sorted by color scheme and then worked into a page design using a color to unify them and another color to create contrast.

To unify the selection of photos, the editor looks closely at each one and asks *which is the least-used color that shows up in any significant amount.* This is a question similar to what one considers at a frame store when choosing matting for a painting or a photograph. The trained eye will look at the picture to discern the least-used—not the most-used—color and then will try varying shades of that color for the potential matting.

This is done because if the dominant color is reflected in the matting, the eye will have little to do to involve itself; it will simply see a predominant color. But if the lesser-used color contrasts well with the dominant one, or happens to be the complement to the dominant one, the picture will become alive and gain three-dimensionality—all because the eye is now more physiologically involved in the perception process.

In making the final selection of photos and illustrations to include, the editor may consider whether this least-used color shows up in several or all of the photos. If so, she has found a color that potentially will provide unity. She may use this color in screens that act as matting or frames for the photos—or, she may use it selectively for emphasis points on the page.

These points of emphasis, sometimes called page punctuation, include rules or lines, large capital letters called drop caps, color screens, illustrations or components of text treatments, such as breakout boxes or Q&A formats. A restrained touch of color in one or two of these will unify a page when that color is the one present in small amounts in the photos on the page.

Often, this color also will provide contrast for the page because it is likely to be different from the dominant color in the photos. Or, the editor may select a color that contrasts with the unifying color; it may be a complement or from the opposite palette of warm or cool colors.

As a final step, the editor evaluates how these two selected colors will play together on the page and notes their relationship and cultural connotations. Are they red and green? If so, the editor may wish to "gray down" one or both to add richness and subtlety, to reduce complementary contrast and to detract from connotations of Christmas decorations or comics-page colors.

Are they green and purple? If so, the editor may wish to add a subtle use of an orange tone to complete the triad of the three secondary colors. Are they blue and orange? Then she may wish to add grays, or more bold black and negative, or white, space. The choices and possibilities are endless and offer the editor potential for artistic growth and further development of a discerning eye.

Emphasis or Decoration?

Colors are added to news and business pages for a purpose: to achieve a goal that can be stated and that is based on a design principle. As pages move more toward art and feature orientations, they may use color occasionally for decoration.

Effective use of color as decoration requires taste and training and is typically the province of a publication's artist or designer. Where color has been misused, it pulls the eye from item to item but does not provide a sense of which are the most important items. It may be garish or too contrasty; the tone and mood set may not fit the writing and overall message. Somber navy and gray will not convey the personality of a lighthearted, entertaining personal Web page, and pure primary or comics colors will not convey seriousness to a corporate annual report.

Bright colors assigned to trivial page items such as dates or page numbers will pull the eye away from the page's content rather than guiding it toward and into the reading pattern. Color needs to work in the service of reading.

Culturally, we are closely linked to black and white because of centuries of exposure to printed text. Some publications rely on this history as they choose colors for Web pages. For example, a number of newspapers have decided on black text on white for their sites in order to draw on the integrity of the print newspaper.

A single color added to black and white pages can be a powerful design tool. Red, blue and green show particularly well next to black. Even a small amount of one of these colors gives strong visual punctuation to a page; pages do not always need to be in full color to be effective.

When using a single color, sometimes called **spot color,** the editor or artist plays with a contrast known as extension. He needs to carefully assess results as he increases the number of colored items such as rules and drop caps. As Itten's research shows, a little bit of red goes a long way, while green or blue can be added a bit more generously to black and white pages. This is due to the way colors interact with each other and to their inherent qualities.

All use of color needs to make sense by enhancing the content and directing the eye in a meaningful way. Colors that move the eye off the page, emphasize minor elements or make the eye dart about, hopelessly lost among scattered, meaningless decorative flourishes, are not effective. Used well, they provide contrast, unity, beauty depth and liveliness on a page.

Technology: RGB and CMYK

An editor working with both online and print versions of a publication uses two different systems for color. **RGB**—or red, green, blue—refers to colors generated by a computer and displayed as light on a monitor screen. This system creates the full spectrum with those three colors; yellow, one of the primaries, is present as a component of green.

The color system for printing on paper, **CMYK,** builds colors by printing separate layers on top of each other. The basic colors are cyan (blue), magenta (purple-red), yellow and black (signified by K). A full-color photo or illustration first is "separated" into screens, each of which carries only one of the four colors. Though the full spectrum can be created with just the three primaries, the fourth layer, black, intensifies the darkest areas for crisper print reproduction.

An editor using page-design software will choose which color system to use depending on which medium is the final destination for the publication. Often the colors available on the wheel offered in the software's RGB system are lighter and more clear than those on the CMYK wheel because the latter includes the potential of layering light colors with black for an opaque surface.

However, the colors displayed by both wheels will vary from monitor to monitor because of their defaults, brightness and contrast settings, resolution and operating systems. When viewing Web pages, an editor may notice that browsers, too, differ in how they interpret color codes. Those most likely to be rendered as designed are the ones supported by HTML standard coding.

An editor planning a print publication begins with the desired ink colors on paper and goes from those, thus, in a sense, working backward to re-creating them on the screen. To aid her, she may use a color-chip wheel that shows opaque ink colors in one column paired with their screen equivalents in the next. (Known as

Pantone colors, these, and other systems, are also offered as choices within some design programs.)

Once she has selected the desired final printing color, she can note the percentages it contains of each of the four color screens. A deep forest green, for example, may be 90 percent blue (C), 15 percent red (M), 80 percent yellow (Y) and 40 percent black (K). Back on the computer, she enters these percentages in the dialog box for the color wheel for CMYK printing. Though the shade displayed on the screen may look different than the color chip she chose, she can be confident the final printed version will be the shade desired.

Some production facilities are willing to invest in complex and expensive systems that closely calibrate the publication's monitor-color displays to the printing press's final print colors. But, many editors will not work with that advantage.

Editors moving digital photo files between print and online editions often need to make adjustments to certain color components, particularly red, when moving the photo from print to Web pages.

For example, to prepare a photograph for printing, a photo editor may boost up the red printer (the color separation for magenta) in order for that particular printing press to lay down enough red ink that the colors of flowers or flags or winter mittens really do look red on the newspaper page.

If that same file is displayed online, the reds may be overwhelming and look like unreal distortions. The color variation can be tested by scanning a print photo into a computer system, viewing it on screen, and then printing it out again. By examining the presentation at each stage, an editor will discern the modifications in the colors.

Altering photos beyond what is needed for more accurate renditions, however, falls into ethically troubled waters. Should the editor creating a brochure for a cruise line make that ship more sparkling white in a sea more vividly blue than either really was? The editor's goal in adjusting colors is to give the most accurate rendition of reality possible in the medium—in other words, to keep visual stories as truthful as verbal ones.

A rule of thumb many professional photographers and editors use is that any adjustments made to a photo that were possible historically using standard darkroom techniques, and which were acceptable ethically, will be acceptable rendered by computer. This rule omits the full range of possibilities a computer offers, such as flopping photos, removing or inserting people or objects, and distorting the dimensions.

Conclusion

Very little in nature, or in photography or artwork, offers us colors in pure primaries, the "straight out of the can" hues represented by Lego building blocks. As editors work with color, they grow adept at using different aspects of color—complements, intensity, contrast, placement, shading—to create the desired tone and mood, and to build contrast and unity. They do so knowing that colors are dynamic and constantly altered by the play of light and by each other; yet this dynamism, skillfully applied, captures that very liveliness within a page.

Exercises to Apply Concepts and Develop Skills

Exercises for working with color assume that students will be able to work on computers with color monitors, use page-layout software and have a supply of images to work with.

1. Goal: To explore color's ability to add dimension and depth to a page.

    Providing full-color print pages from magazines or newspapers to students, ask them to study a page and touch an area of color that seems nearer than the others, or that "jumps out" at them. Typically the colors identified will be warm-palette hues, which leads to discussion of the different effects of warm and cool palettes. Occasionally, a color identified may be from the cool palette because it provides great contrast to the predominant warm-palette colors used. In this case, discussion leads to the effects of extension or proportion when using colors from both palettes.

2. Goal: To apply color concepts to select photographs for use on a page.

    After providing color photos to students, ask them: a) to sort sets of photos by several characteristics, including:

    -   common color schemes, such as which are predominantly in primary and secondary colors, or which are pastels;
    -   combinations in which primary or secondary colors show up with their complements;
    -   hues that are predominantly warm or cool palette;

        and, b) to work in groups and display the photos they select against differently colored backgrounds. Ask them to discuss the changes in appearance.

3. Goal: To find colors that provide unity and contrast for a group of photographs to be presented on a page.

    Ask students to sort from about a dozen potential photos the four or so they might use on one page and to watch for a color that shows up in all of the shots selected. Then have students identify that color's complement and consider how it might be used in page punctuation to provide contrast.

4. Goal: To use several shades of gray effectively in layouts with color items and text.

    Using a page with photos and text already selected, place areas shaded by gray screens near colors and near text, including placing them underneath as background tints. Discuss with students which areas of color are enhanced by gray, how text functions as blocks of gray and what the optimum number of shades of gray appears to be.

5. Goal: To identify and work with negative space.

    After providing well-designed features pages, such as are available on the Web sites of designers associations, ask students to identify the shapes of white space included in the designs and then discuss how they parallel or echo shapes of text or color areas. Discussion often moves to patterns and uses of symmetry and asymmetry. Once the concept is articulated, students can be asked to include negative space in their feature-page designs.

Helpful Sources

Adam, Pegie Stark. "Color, Contrast, and Dimension in News Design: Understanding the theory of color and its applications." St. Petersburg, Fla.: The Poynter Institute for Media Studies, 1995.

Henninger, Ed. "White space: Is it negative space, or empty?" Washington Newspaper, June 2003, p. 3.

Itten, Johannes. "The Elements of Color; A treatise on the color system of Johannes Itten based on his book 'The Art of Color,' " Edited by Faber Birren. New York: Van Nostrand Reinhold Co., 1970.

Libby, William C. "Color and the Structural Sense." Englewood Cliffs, N.J.: Prentice Hall, 1974.

Lynch, Patrick J. and Sarah Horton. "Web Style Guide: Basic Design Principles for Creating Web Sites." 2nd Ed. New Haven, Conn.: Yale University Press, 2002.

Poynteronline. Poynter Institute's site located at http://poynter.org has resources and articles important to color and journalistic editing.

Stockton, James. "Designer's Guide to Color." San Francisco: Chronicle Books, 1984.

9

Typography

Much of the creativity editors enjoy with visual styles for their publications comes from working with type and combining it with text, illustrations, color, graphics and white space to express distinctive styles.

As participants in a culture, we are usually able to interpret these styles. We may recognize the paint-dripping, fluorescent-colored rock posters of the '60s or the squared-off, black Gothic type of Victorian-era handbills. We probably can select the typefaces that evoke Tudor England, Nazi Germany or Colonial New England, and can distinguish early computer printout from the calligraphy on a restaurant menu.

Editors and designers choose typefaces for practical reasons as well as for their aesthetic and historical references, and should be aware that their choices will evoke moods, places, times and current or bygone fashions.

And, what choices they have. Great ranges of typefaces and treatments are available, as computers and printers arrive loaded with dozens of typefaces, called fonts, and illustration programs allow artists and editors to modify these or to design their own.

Word-processing software makes treatments such as boldface, italic, shadowed or underlined accessible at the touch of a few keys. It is easy to scatter varieties of type across a page, and cluttered, chaotic looks often result from beginning attempts to design with type.

Contemporary design strives for simplicity that provides both unity and contrast. Type is usually arranged in white space according to an underlying grid pattern, and the font is chosen for its appropriateness for the occasion and circumstances.

Regularly published media use templates that define typefaces and sizes for body text and headings, and public relations practitioners often work with type selected to establish corporate identity.

But, editors often can choose decorative or contrasting type for a special feature layout, magazine spread, poster or brochure, or portion of a Web page. In these uses, an unusual typeface signals the distinctiveness of the one-time use.

Characteristics of Type

Style in type is the sum of small differences. Many combinations are possible with the variations in letter forms discussed below.

Stress   This refers to slant, but not simply to whether the main line of a letter is perpendicular to the **baseline,** the line running under letters that aligns them. It refers to the distribution of the thickness of line strokes, and an easy way to picture it is to draw an imaginary line through a letter that would balance the dark and light areas as though they were weighted. The stress may lean to the right, but it often leans to the left.

Italic types are designed to maximize the attractiveness of stressed letters by adjusting the placement of thick and thin line widths. Though any typeface can be made to appear Italic by selecting that function in word-processing or layout software, the result is actually just regular type distorted to slant, a look that is not nearly as graceful. With only a small amount of practice, an editor can discern the difference between the two. (See Illustration 9.1.)

Some typefaces vary in how stressed each letter is, with most of the capital letters, for example, standing virtually perpendicular, yet with some, such as *A, S* and *R*, slanting and flowing with decorative flourishes. This is a reason to examine all letters of an alphabet when choosing one for a decorative heading.

Serifs   These little lines or squiggles attached to edges and corners of letters have gone through many modifications in historical eras before being dropped from some modern type styles. They vary tremendously in shape and how extensive or decorative they are, and these variations are used to classify and date type into loose categories known as families.

For example, Egyptian type has flat, thin-lined serifs. (The typeface was developed in Britain, not in Egypt, and probably reflects taste for Egyptian styles at the time.)

Sans serif type is a modern, simplified style that uses only the major lines of each letter, with no serifs or variations in line thickness. One of the most popular, Helvetica, has been used in the United States since the 1950s. This type and other sans serif variations are commonly used in publications for headings, especially for contrast with a serif type.

ILLUSTRATION 9.1   *Italic Typefaces*

True italic typefaces are designed so that the thick and thin strokes are balanced and look graceful. Computer software allows any typeface to be slanted, but the difference between it and a true italic face is apparent.

true Italic: *vivaldi*   *zapf chancery*

slanted non-Italic: **helvetica** *helvetica slanted*

Helvetica was designed for optimum readability at a distance and is often seen on railway and highway signs. It is not often used for body text because research shows it slows down reading. The eye takes in overall shapes of words and concentrates on the top of a line; with no serifs or variation in line thickness, recognition comes more slowly. (See Illustration 9.2.)

Line thickness   Historically, lines composing letter shapes had thin and thick strokes reflecting the angle of a pen. In addition to doing away with serifs, the earliest sans serif type typically has kept to one width for all lines. The modern look is blocky and unembellished. But, some contemporary sans serif types now vary line thickness for greater readability.

Any typeface is available in a full range of presentations, as well, with line width varying from fine to medium to bold and extra bold as it becomes thicker and thicker. These letters will gain width, as well, meaning a boldface word takes up more room on the line than does the medium or plain face.

Condensed types will shrink this aspect, rendering letters that look dark and heavy but squished into being taller and thinner than normal. Illustration 9.3 shows variations provided within several fonts.

Type Fonts and Sizes

Size   Type is measured in points (as discussed in Chapter 3), with 72 points per inch. The size intervals we still use today evolved for reasons of practicality. A printer using hand-carved or metal pieces of type stocked only certain sizes, with standard display or headline sizes of 72 points, 60 points, 54 or 48 points, 36 points, 24 points, and 18 points.

Subheads historically ran 12, 14 or 16 points, while body text varied between 7 and 10 points. Now, body text ranges up to 12 points in size; it often has to be that large on Web pages for easier reading. (See Illustration 9.4.)

Editing software makes it possible to use any size of type and removes the need to stick to preset intervals. But, a font, which is a set comprising the alphabet, numbers and punctuation, may be designed to be used only within a narrow range of sizes.

ILLUSTRATION 9.2   *Serif and Sans Serif*

Serif and sans serif typefaces exist with and without variations in line thickness.

with serifs: **palatino   bookman old style**

sans-serif, uniform line thickness: **helvetica   arial**

sans-serif, varying line thickness: **antique olive   Chicago**

ILLUSTRATION 9.3 *Variations within a Typeface*

An editor can create contrast on a page by choosing a different presentation available within a single typeface. For example, if headings are in regular Arial, one can be changed to Arial Black. This provides contrast without introducing an additional typeface. Variations exist in line width, size of the x-height, slant, and italic design, as these samples show.

Hoefler Text Black
Hoefler Text Black Italic
Hoefler Text Italic

Continuum Bold
Continuum Light
Continuum Medium

Moderne
Moderne-Demi
Moderne-Demi Oblique
Moderne-Oblique

Tribune
Tribune Bold
Tribune Italic

Arial
Arial Black
Arial Narrow
Arial rounded MT bold

Intrepid
Intrepid Extra Bold
Intrepid Bold
Intrepid Oblique

New Century Schoolbook
Century Schoolbook

Helvetica
Helvetica Narrow

Raster fonts create letter shapes based on pixels. While the letter is small, the eye does not perceive the edges, which are the straight-line sides of each box-like pixel; instead, it translates them into the semblance of curved lines. But when these are enlarged, the letter edges look jagged and choppy. (See Illustration 9.5.)

A font that can be enlarged or reduced without this problem is a vector font, which is based on a formula or set of instructions to recreate the letter's shapes,

ILLUSTRATION 9.4 *Variations of a Typeface by Point Size*

Some alphabets offer distinctly designed letters; the capital Q in Bookman, for example, is more decorative than the capital A. Lower case letters with ascenders—lines going above the x-height—may reach to the same height. Distinctive looks may also appear in numbers or punctuation.

bookman 12 point

bookman 14 point

bookman 18 point

bookman 24 point

bookman 36 point

48 point

60 point

72 point

AQd 123;

including curved lines, across a larger or smaller scale. These will display and print cleanly curved lines in larger sizes, as will raster fonts that have been created for large point sizes.

ILLUSTRATION 9.5   *Raster and Vector Fonts*

Some typefaces will appear with blockish edges when set in large sizes. This result means they were designed for use in a small size and have simply been enlarged by the computer. Typefaces that have smoothly finished edges in large size either were designed that way or have been coded as a mathematical formula, or vector, that instructs the computer how to draw it in larger sizes.

Typefaces of the first kind are referred to as raster images while type that is redrawn for the desired size is called vector-based. Sometimes, the computer monitor will display a rasterized image, but the printer will produce a smooth vector-type look. This sample, a large-size Bookman, was captured as a monitor image.

Raster sample

Fonts Designed for Online Reading

A major issue for Web pages is the low resolution of some monitor screens, which makes for poor legibility and users' reluctance to read lengthy pieces online. New typefaces have been designed specifically for online use, such as Meta, Georgia and Verdana. Some research indicates 10- and 11-point type is most readable for text displayed on monitors.

Research is continuing on how to improve readability, and several software companies have created programs for electronic book publishing. Microsoft's work aims at delivering books onto thin, notebook-size electronic display panels.

A study conducted in Finland found that subjects read material on a screen 16 to 19 percent slower than they did printed text but that their recall of the on-line material was as good or better.

Using Special Treatments Well

Graphic artists and many editors view the type alterations available in software programs, such as outlines, shadows, hollow faces, underlining and so forth, as treatments to avoid. Each draws attention to itself and potentially distracts the eye from other points of emphasis that have been carefully placed on a page to enhance meaning.

But, some of these are used successfully in titles. Rolling Stone, for example, uses a hand-modified type for its title, which often shows up with a shadow or other treatment. It works because it is a sole, highlighted usage—not a standard way of presenting headings throughout the magazine.

Type set in all capitals has an attention-commanding, formal look to it. It is often used in nameplates or titles, but current usage dictates capitals and lower-case letters be used in headings for stories and graphics because that combination is more readable. A useful guideline is to follow the same capitalization practices as for sentences—unless a good reason can be expressed to do otherwise.

Using all lower-case letters has sometimes been in fashion, perhaps because it expresses efficiency, intimacy or informality. The Bauhaus, an influential German design school, adopted all lower-case typesetting for its publications just before World War II.

Capital letters in modern typefaces tend to be at least as tall as the ascenders—letters that have tall, vertical lines—in that alphabet. But in older typefaces, the capitals sometimes were shorter, and fell into a medium height range between the height of the letter **x** (known as **x-height**) and the ascenders (such as *b, d, f, h, l* and so on). Some of this same feel can be expressed by using all capital letters that are smaller in point size than the surrounding text.

A very large capital letter, called a **drop cap,** is commonly used in magazine and brochure layouts to signal where the eye needs to land to begin reading the text. These are a handy component of a complex design because a large capital letter may be decorative and nicely complemented by available white space.

A drop cap might also be set in a colored ink that flows with the page design yet signals a possible starting place as the reader's eye moves among photographs, headings and illustrations. Drop caps used throughout a longer text can provide pleasing breaks that are a bit different than subheads.

Cursive This style of type imitates handwriting, and should be used sparingly, typically with feature treatments. **Decorative** typefaces abound, some resembling cursive type, and are intended for special, occasional uses.

Characteristics of Body Text

Some typefaces look more open and airy than others, even when they are of the same point size. A key difference is the amount of white space enclosed or defined by the lower-case letters in the alphabet. For example, compare a line of type of Times with another serif type such as Bookman, and then with a sans serif such as Helvetica:

10-point Times	12-point Times
10-point Bookman	12-point Bookman
10-point Helvetica	12-point Helvetica

This small variation can add up to a big difference over the length of a text. A smaller point size of a face with a large x-height may be as readable and yet take up less room overall.

Leading refers to the amount of lead that literally used to be inserted as blank space between lines of type in hot-metal printing. The space between lines is still measured in points, and software programs are formatted to insert a set amount, usually the type's point size plus two, between lines and paragraphs. (Many include a variation that provides automatic spacing adjustments for drop caps, as well.)

But, editors often alter the leading and make fine adjustments to space out copy so it fills a desired area, or to provide more space because the lines of type are dense due to a small x-height. Generally, more leading is needed as a type becomes heavier and darker. An editor setting lines in extra bold will want to adjust the spacing between lines to reduce a cluttered look.

Leading may also be decreased between lines. An editor might do this if she sees that the top line of a heading has no descenders (letters such as *g, j* or *y* that drop below the baseline). The unused portion of letter space plus the normal leading would otherwise look unusually large and empty.

The amount of leading that looks right can also vary according to the length of the line. Small type may look good with reduced leading if the overall shape needs to be vertical, narrow and dark, such as for captions set as a narrow block of boldface. If it were dark, deep and wide, though, it could look like an unappealing dark blob.

Line Length and Justification

The length of a line needs to be in proportion to the size of type used. While the eye may have no problem following 72-point type across six columns, it would have great difficulty with 10-point type. Body text is usually set between 9 and 12 points in lines up to about 3.5 to 4 inches wide, which is a comfortable width for the human eye span.

Justification   When type is set flush left or right, editors can choose whether the other ends of the lines should square off neatly, as well. **Justification** requires the word-processing program to hyphenate words and add spacing between words as necessary to achieve perfectly even line lengths. **Forced justification** will produce even lengths by relying primarily on spacings, with less hyphenation.

Ragged endings mean that the type is set either **flush left** or **right,** with the opposite end of each line simply stopping when the next word will not fit. That word moves to the beginning of the next line, leading to a random pattern in the line breaks.

Publications choose one kind of justification as their primary style and will use a different kind to signal a change in the voice, tone or subject matter of a piece. For example, a newspaper may set news stories justified and feature stories ragged right.

Kerning and Tracking

The spaces between letters and between words, called **kerning** and **tracking,** can also be altered in software programs in a way that was not possible with hand-carved wooden type or even cast metal type. Those functioned by holding ink on a raised area—an area above a lower background area that spread to the edge of the piece itself. Spaces formed naturally as the letters were set next to each other, and spaces between words often were defined as the width of an *n* or an *m* in that alphabet.

The avant-garde look played with narrowed spaces between letters, or no spaces at all, on the assumption that we recognize the word's overall shape, rather than puzzling it out letter by letter. Some old-fashioned looks, by contrast, are created on computer by using typefaces with rough edges (such as worn wooden type produced) and wide spacings.

Though spacing between letters may be adjusted, commonly to express a style or to improve readability, it is a good idea to leave spaces between words alone; too much or too little—in short, much variation at all from the norm—seems to lead quickly to reader confusion. Illustration 9.6 shows the different tonality of body text which is achieved by changing settings for leading and justification.

Type and Contrast

Typefaces and styles are basic tools editors use to quickly and easily add contrast to a page. The idea is that a basic plan is put into practice and contrast is provided by the single element that runs counter to that plan. Too many variations, and the sense of a plan is lost, with mere confusion taking over.

But how does an editor make solid decisions that create effective contrast when so many variations of type abound? The surest route is to change, boldly and distinctly, any one of the type attributes listed above. If a publication's main heading style is sans serif, a serif type will provide contrast.

Typography manuals and graphic arts books treat this principle in greater detail by drawing on the historic division of typefaces into families, reflecting historical trends that combined certain characteristics. However, type is so routinely being created, altered and redesigned with the advent of electronic design and

ILLUSTRATION 9.6 *Tonality of Type*

These examples demonstrate how the tonality, or overall look and personality of the body text, can be altered by differing uses of justification (aligned or ragged right), leading (space between the lines) and alignments, such as flush left, right or centered.

No weather will be found in this book. This is an attempt to pull a book through without weather. It being the first attempt of the kind in fictitious literature, it may prove a failure, but it seemed worth the while of some dare-devil person to try it, and the author was in just the mood. —Mark Twain

New York 12 point, with 11-point leading; flush left and ragged right.

No weather will be found in this book. This is an attempt to pull a book through without weather. It being the first attempt of the kind in fictitious literature, it may prove a failure, but it seemed worth the while of some dare-devil person to try it, and the author was in just the mood. —Mark Twain

New York 12 point, with automatic leading; flush right and ragged left.

No weather will be found in this book. This is an attempt to pull a book through without weather. It being the first attempt of the kind in fictitious literature, it may prove a failure, but it seemed worth the while of some dare-devil person to try it, and the author was in just the mood.—Mark Twain

New York 12 point with 14-point leading; flush left and ragged right.

No weather will be found in this

book. This is an attempt to pull a

book through without weather. It

being the first attempt of the kind

in fictitious literature, it may prove

a failure, but it seemed worth the

while of some dare-devil person to

try it, and the author was in just

the mood. —Mark Twain

New York 12 point, centered, with 22-point leading.

No weather will be found in this book. This is an attempt to pull a book through without weather. It being the first attempt of the kind in fictitious literature, it may prove a failure, but it seemed worth the while of some dare-devil person to try it, and the author was in just the mood. —Mark Twain

New York 12 point, with forced justification; flush left and automatic leading.

typeset, that it is easiest for an editor new to classifications to begin with just a few categories that draw on the strongest distinctions.

"The Non-Designer's Design Book," by Robin Williams, for example, lists six type categories, based on the presence or absence of serifs, variations in line width, whether the letter form is typeset or cursive, and whether its shape is traditional or decorative.

And, Williams advises never to use two similar faces on a page, but two— and most times only two—distinctly different ones.

These type treatments will increase contrast on a page:

- Using modular story units that are strongly vertical or horizontal requires heading shapes extremely different from each other; the more similar in shape the modules are, the less contrast will be created by their headings.
- Using a contrasting typeface or treatment runs the gamut from the subtle use of ragged right for one story on a page to blatantly setting the main word of a feature heading in colored, cursive type. Any variation stands out—and alters the tone.
- Building in white space or negative space around dense text graphics or very large typefaces provides contrast between light and dark and also lets the page breathe.
- Varying column widths on a page creates a change in the rhythm and interval of the gutters (the white space between columns). A carefully placed shift in some of those negative-space lines can relax a page.
- Adding column lines or heavy rules for emphasis.
- Signaling new items on a page by giving them different treatment from standing features, such as formats used for regular columnists.

Many of the elements of a publication's design remain unchanging with each issue: the nameplate, color palette, heading typefaces and preferred sizes; styles for body text, subheads, introductory paragraphs, bylines, credits, rules, borders and column widths; and preferred size and placement of photos and art.

Setting these ahead in a formal fashion—usually published as a guide for editors to use—establishes unity in appearance. Without this unity being established first, contrasting elements would have no backdrop that reveals how contrary they are to the usual rules.

Type and Unity

Typographically, unity in a publication is created by:

- carrying elements of the nameplate on inside or linked pages and using consistent page strips with dates and numbering;
- designating a readable body text and permissible variations;

- limiting headings to a main typeface and a contrasting one;
- preserving baselines by aligning type on straight lines for readability;
- creating a distinct format for regularly occurring items such as columns;
- identifying or labeling contents that have a different voice, such as editorials, opinion and analysis within a news context, or employees' comments or responses within a corporate newsletter;
- using lines or rules to anchor or define parts of the page, such as section headings or bottom corners;
- precisely aligning widths of graphics with widths of text columns to preserve gutters as patterns of negative space;
- using consistent typography for small items such as bylines, cutlines and jump lines;
- avoiding visual distractions and gimmicks such as reverses, shadowed or outlined type, or obtrusively colored or blinking graphics.

Typography and Grids

In North American design, restraint is often equated with beauty, elegance with simplicity, and readability with both. Designs running counter to the culture often exploit the opposite of these values.

The rough-edged, dark, chaotic and jumbled look of many zines and underground publications deduces and opposes the current practices of arranging type in space according to underlying geometric shapes and balancing sizes of light and dark shapes using classical ideas of proportion. These latter practices are part of a style known as Swiss International.

When editors begin arranging type in a wide-open white space, they are tempted to sprinkle a bit here and a bit there, as though spreading grass seeds evenly to grow a lawn. This may be most tempting for editors of words who have been drilled to value every tiny bit of space and to trim relentlessly: It becomes hard to believe that anything but words should fill any available inch.

Their impulse is right on target, though, for the tendency in contemporary practice to bunch lines of type together in units according to their importance and meaning. These units are distributed in the midst of open space, however, according to an underlying pattern based on geometric shapes, including circles, straight lines, radiating lines, rectangles, triangles and waves. And, designs may combine any of these.

The underlying shapes remain invisible to the viewer, but if he took a pencil and drew in the lines representing the baselines of type, extending them out to the edges of the page, he would see a set of lines running horizontally and vertically, or at angles or on curves. And chances are, most of these lines have been used to position not just one baseline of type, but several.

Accompanying illustrations are also placed on a page so as to complement the underlying pattern, and their orientations can be sketched in this way as well.

A grid is a set of lines occurring at regular intervals and angles that a designer or editor might draw ahead of time, sketching in how type and any illustrations will be placed on them. These lines will not show, though, when the page is produced.

The lines may be parallel to the top and bottom of the page—or to its sides. They may be segments of lines coming from a single perspective point way off the edge of the paper. They may zigzag through a page like parallel lightening bolts.

Whatever plan is used, the key is that a pattern provides some regularity and predictability; this way, no matter how unusual the grid design, the eye can catch the underlying idea and perceive an overall unity. (See Illustrations 9.7 and 9.8.)

The development of grids plays a significant role in the history of commercial art and graphic design. The Bauhaus school, for example, favored using squares and circles. Histories of typography, such as several by Stephen Heller and others noted at the end of this chapter, explain the origin and theory behind their use.

Hierarchies in the Message

A concept working in tandem with grids is that message parts have different levels of intrinsic importance. Some parts may be crucial, meriting display in a large type size. Others are minor and might be grouped together using one small type size.

For example, a poster for an upcoming concert might display the kind of music as most important, with the time, date, place and price set together in small type, and the performers' names set in a middle size and grouped together.

The editor needs to decide, or to check, that the most important information in a message is visually signaled this way. In a way, this sounds like deciding what goes in a heading and what goes into body text, except that the goal often is to arrive at several hierarchies, not just two.

With several groupings of type of different sizes, an editor or designer can begin moving them as blocks on a page, distributing their placement and weight to arrive at a pattern. In making these decisions with the hierarchies, the designer or editor is working with visual and verbal values at the same time.

Proportion

Another question, as the editor moves from one hierarchy or type size to the next, is how big of a step to take between sizes. Is the first hierarchy huge type and the second tiny? Or should they be closer in size? Very different looks will result.

This question applies to the white space or negative space, as well. If white space is to balance a very dense use of type, it must be quite a bit larger.

ILLUSTRATION 9.7 A   This poster design begins with four photos set on three shaded background blocks. The editor chose a wide double rule as a vertical ribbon that ties the photos together. The next step is to draw the lines that form the invisible, underlying pattern, as shown in the dotted lines in Illustration 9.7B.

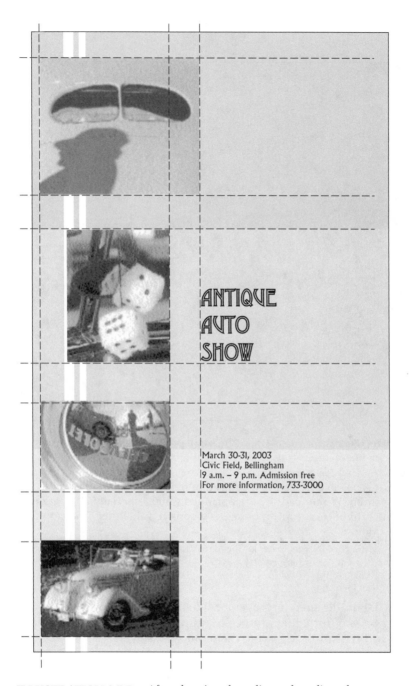

ANTIQUE
AUTO
SHOW

March 30-31, 2003
Civic Field, Bellingham
9 a.m. – 9 p.m. Admission free
For more information, 733-3000

ILLUSTRATION 9.7 B   After drawing these lines, the editor then realigns the photos because their right and left margins originally fell slightly to the right or left of the present lines. The photo at the bottom is enlarged to fill out the grid pattern. Finally, the lines suggest where the words can be inserted and still work within the design.

(Photos courtesy of The Herald, Everett, Wash.)

ILLUSTRATION 9.8 *Type Added to a Page.* The same principle—following a grid or pattern of organizing lines—holds true when combining large heading type and body text with illustrations. In this spread from Columns, the University of Washington alumni magazine, it is possible to see the organization of these elements according to an underlying pattern. White space is also a planned value; especially in magazine and feature layouts, white space is incorporated as a positive value that balances darker, dominant values.

("Disappearing Act" was designed by Ken Shafer for the March 2003 issue of Columns Magazine, University of Washington. Reproduced by permission.)

Graphic design offers several guidelines, which are offered here in simplified form as a way for editors to begin evaluating use of proportion in their discussions with artists, or for trying them out themselves:

- Replicate size intervals according to the "golden section," a concept based on geometry, in which the smaller item is in the same proportion to the larger item as the larger is to the whole.
- Size each hierarchy to be distinctly different from any other; if type differences are too similar, the result can look like an error instead of an intentionally created contrast. For example, one might begin by trying differences

that double point sizes; if the smaller type is 24-point, the next is 48-point, and so forth. The proportions will begin to look appropriate generally between 1.5 and 2.5 times the smaller size, though this is affected by the number of hierarchies, amount of white space and overall size of the piece.

- Place any slanted baselines at angles of at least 30 degrees. Smaller angles may look ambiguous—are they intentional, or errors?
- Try proportioning the overall space into thirds. Lines that cut pages in half in either direction look awkward, and the page does not hang together as a whole. By placing type hierarchies at one-third distances, this problem is avoided and proportions become more graceful.
- Instead of starting with a blank page, try a grid that has perhaps a dozen narrow columns. This makes it easier to envision using a few narrow, vertical shapes—in addition to much wider ones for balance.
- Play with both symmetry, in which items are arranged in parallel or repeated patterns, and asymmetry, which lets an element break the pattern.
- Keep white space out toward the edges, where it can escape from the dense area of a design, just as a bubble does from water.
- Design white space or negative space so that it, too, has parallel or recurring shapes in the overall design.
- Stick to the grid, or adapt the grid and then stick to it. This is the underlying skeleton for the silhouette created by type in space.
- Study and collect successful designs and adapt what works.

In evaluating typography, editors ensure that the central message is clearly honed and immediately visible. Economy, function and communication distinguish journalistic work from purely artistic goals. The meaning is still the message.

Visual Styles

We do not have an internationally accepted design that has swept our era, showing up with national variations around the world and introducing sweeping new fashions, as have movements such as Art Deco in the past. Some designers argue, though, that the international business or corporate look—based on hierarchy, simplicity, selective contrasts and an underlying grid structure derived from Swiss International—may come close.

Contemporary designs sometimes evoke styles that were influential in the past. For example, some newspapers' return to narrow columns with black rules and multideck headlines may be a move to recapture some of the flavor of newspapering in past eras.

Significant historic styles such as Dada, Avant Garde, Soviet constructivism, Victorianism and Bauhaus still are recognizable and provide bases for both meaning and appearance in current designs.

For example, the musical group Rage against the Machine used a Soviet constructivist-style portrait of a proletariat woman on a tee shirt with a message about the role of female labor in the world's workforce. And, its music videos frequently use jumbles of found images juxtaposed rapidly in new mixes, reminiscent of Dada.

An editor may think he is designing with no particular look other than contemporary taste. Even so, what looks right at the moment is based on the fashions, artwork, architecture and even the industrial design around us. A toaster with rounded surfaces of pastel plastic harks back to Art Deco while one with square corners and sharp-edged chrome derives from modernism.

Awareness of historical styles lends editors more control and meaning within their choices of type and presentation. Editors can explore styles and develop an eye for elements to borrow by reading histories of graphic arts. Books on poster art, too, reproduce pieces of genuine beauty and artistic merit, which have become museum pieces and collector's items.

Redesigns

Publications often update their looks to keep pace with changing visual trends and preferences. Fashion consciousness affects graphic design just as it does clothing, furniture and music, and it is common for newspapers, for example, to undergo a redesign every decade. The goal is to retain core parts of a visual identity both for its integrity and for reader recognition, while updating to look fresh, contemporary and well-planned.

After all, publications reflect the community they serve. Mario Garcia of the Poynter Institute has recommended that those undertaking a redesign explore the publication's city in order to get a sense of the sky, the trees, the color and images of the area.

In a redesign of the conservative Wall Street Journal, Garcia added some color but did not, however, change the typeface, Scotch Roman, which is used only by the Journal and which also underscores a sense of tradition and history.

Garcia believes that the classic typefaces (such as Baskerville, Bodoni, Franklin Gothic, etc.) should be relied on and kept simple—but should be chosen with the publication and its readership in mind.

Conclusion

Although overall styles change with time, they are linked to concepts that underlie decisions made about type. A piece's decorative typeface or plain one; its hand-drawn type or machine-set; its white space and breathing room or dense print message; its disorder or organization following a grid; its simplicity or its complexity—all reflect editors' decisions on how a message can most accurately and effectively be conveyed.

Along the way, the editor works with typefaces that build contrast within the unity of standard practices, that are arranged with an eye to proportion and balance, that may evoke historical or artistic references, and that achieve as a result, sometimes to the editor's surprise, style and even beauty.

Exercises to Apply Concepts and Develop Skills

1. Goal: To gain familiarity with the characteristics that identify major families of type.

   Show students a variety of typefaces available in printed publications or samples created using fonts available on their computers. Ask students to practice identifying major type families by characteristics described in this chapter. Then ask them to discuss which ones differ enough from each other to provide contrast on a page.

2. Goal: To practice organizing information by hierarchies of importance (priority) and by a limited number of typefaces.

   Starting with an existing message, such as an announcement of an upcoming event or scholarship competitions, ask students to classify the parts of the message into two hierarchies of importance using two different typefaces. Then vary the exercise by allowing them three hierarchies but one typeface, or other combinations of choices.

3. Goal: To work on arranging hierarchies of type in white space according to an underlying grid.

   Using messages such as the ones students create in Exercise 2, ask students to arrange the lines of type along an underlying grid that has both horizontal and vertical lines. If necessary, the idea of grids can be explored more first by asking students to trace grids from published layouts. Encourage moving beyond straight lines to using curves, angles and zigzags.

4. Goal: To begin recognizing significant historical eras of graphic design and to name some of the characteristics that have changed.

   Ask students to create posters for events that refer to distinct periods of time, such as a jitterbug or swing dance contest, an exhibit of French Impressionist paintings or of the artifacts from Cleopatra's tomb, a display of Victorian clothes and novels, colonial American quilts, a collection of 1960s underground media covers, etc.

   Ask them to research which type styles they will use and how type will be used along with text, color and decorative touches.

5. Goal: To plan effectively for good use of type.

   Assign students to redesign an existing campus publication, or to invent a new one of their choosing. Ask them to select all typefaces that will be used and to list their purpose, being sure to define—and limit—styles for headings, deck heads, subheads, body text, captions, credits, bylines, page strips, contents pages, etc. They can also be asked to produce a prototype using their plan. (See Illustration 9.9 A, B, C.)

ILLUSTRATION 9.9 a, b, and c   *Planning Typographical Consistency*

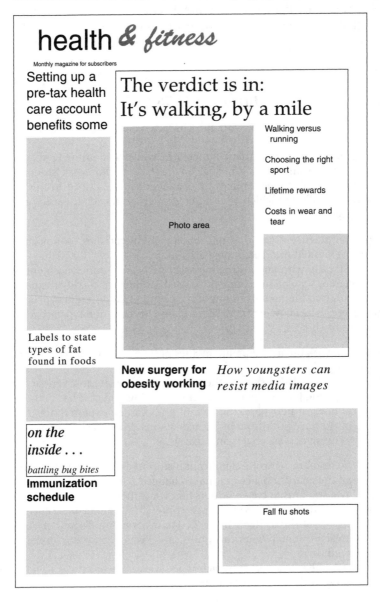

ILLUSTRATION 9.9 A   The mock-up of an 11- by 17-inch newsletter shown in 9.9 A uses a variety of fonts for headings, but the result creates visual confusion, rather than building in the desired contrast. When too many typefaces are used, they compete against each other and cause the reader's eye to dart restlessly.

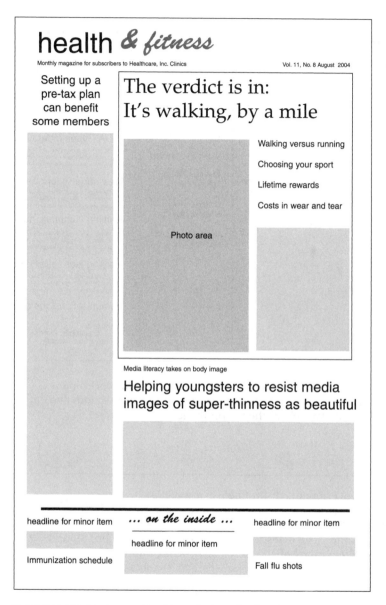

ILLUSTRATION 9.9 B   In this redesign, the headings use one main font to establish consistency and another to provide contrast. The idea of hierarchy has been applied as well, with the highlights for stories on inside pages grouped together in one place.

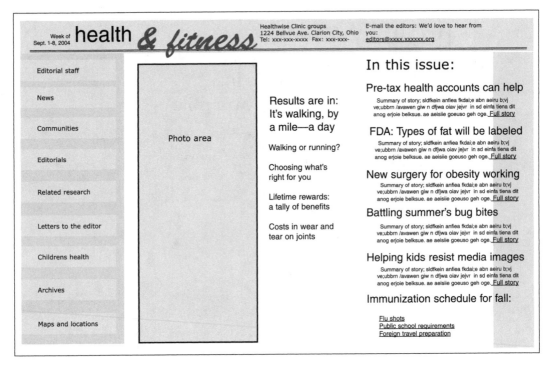

ILLUSTRATION 9.9 C   The same newsletter is shown in 9.9c as a mock-up for a
Web page. It shows the same major stories and feature photo, with sections and
organizational information available in the tab on the left.

Helpful Sources

Australian government. "Plain English at work."
http://www.dest.gov.au/archive/publications/plain_en/design.htm
Beaumont, Michael. "Type and Colour." Oxford, England: Phaidon Press Ltd., 1987.
Conneen, Anne. "The Maestro of Redesign," Poynter Report. Summer 2002, pp. 14–15.
"Design 2020: Visions of the newspaper of the future," American Press Institute's J.
    Montgomery Curtis Memorial Seminar, October 24–26, 1999; published Fall 2000,
    API, Reston, Vir.
Gannett News Service, "Travel Books: Eyewitness series revives the printed guidebook,"
    Seattle Times. February 28, 1999, p. K9.
Garcia, Mario. "Contemporary Newspaper Design." 3rd Ed. Englewood, N.J.: Prentice
    Hall, Inc., 1993.
Garcia, Mario. "We've come a long way," The American Editor. April 2000, pp. 4–5.
Heller, Steven and Seymour Chwast. "Graphic Style from Victorian to Post-Modern."
    New York: Harry N. Abrams, Inc., 1994.
Heller, Steven and Karen Pomeroy. "Design Literacy: Understanding Graphic Design."
    New York: Allworth Press, 1997.

Moses, Monica. "The Journal is Dead; Long Live the Journal." Poynter Report. Poynter Institute, Fall 2002.

Nelson, Roy Paul. "Publication Design." 5th Ed. Dubuque, Ia.: Wm. C. Brown Publishers, 1991.

Nielsen, Jakob. "Alertbox." http://www.useit.com/alertbox

Poynteronline. Poynter Institute/Stanford eyetracking studies and other research and tips. http://poynteronline.org In addition, Kim Elam provides helpful information in workshops at the Poynter Institute.

Watson, Warren. Seminar on design, American Press Institute, Reston, Vir. for Excellence in Journalism Education Fellowship program, June 2000.

Williams, Robin. "The Non-Designer's Design Book." Berkeley, Calif.: Peachpit Press, 1994.

Wixted, Ellen. "Making the Parts a Whole," Adobe Magazine. Autumn 1999, pp. 49–53.

10

Clarity with Data: Informational Graphics

Graphics such as charts can compactly and systematically present numbers that tell part of a story. By placing numbers in spatial arrangements that the eye can take in quickly or can linger on to make comparisons, graphics offer advantages over listing lots of numbers in narrative sentences.

Media are evolving to include more charts, graphs, diagrams and maps. Comparing current issues of news magazines, for instance, to editions from a decade or more ago will show dramatic changes. Newspaper staffs include graphics editors who work with reporters and story editors to plan the visual aspects of a package.

Newsrooms using the Poynter Institute for Media Studies WED approach create teams consisting of the writer, photographer, editor and designer, who plan how to tell the whole story in both words and visual presentation.

Using tabular material is becoming more feasible on Web pages because composing programs now available build in much of the required coding, and page-encapsulating software, such as Adobe Acrobat, ensures exact presentation of graphics even when viewed with different browsers.

Infographics must be informationally rich to justify the space they take, just as stories must be. They have a different kind of strength, however.

- **Charts** and **graphs** show numerical data and relationships. Typically they answer a question posed by a writer or an editor, such as what kind of trend the data show or how different amounts compare to each other. (See Illustration 10.1.)
- **Maps** show locations and give spatial orientation. They must be carefully attuned to how geographically widespread the audience members may be and how detailed their knowledge is of the area pictured. Sometimes, additional maps are inset to provide orientation. (See Illustration 10.2.)

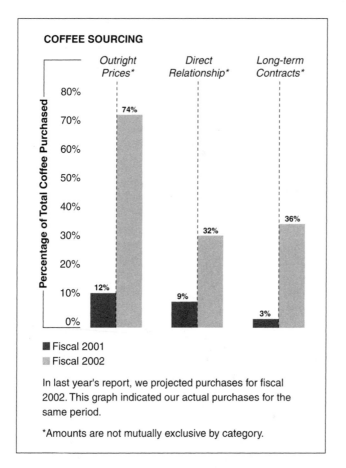

COFFEE SOURCING

In last year's report, we projected purchases for fiscal 2002. This graph indicated our actual purchases for the same period.

*Amounts are not mutually exclusive by category.

ILLUSTRATION 10.1 A and B   *Bar or Column Charts.*
Charts that show discrete amounts drawn as lines, either horizontally or vertically, allow comparisons to be made at a glance. In these charts from Starbucks Coffee, the varying amounts of coffee beans obtained from different sources are shown across several years so that the exact quantities as well as the overall trends are readily seen. Intervals used for measuring should be kept equal, as in the percentages running vertically in the "Coffee Sourcing" chart. Sometimes, the visual presentation cannot be exact because of limitations of space; then, a broken line may be used, as in the chart show in Illustration 10.1B.

(Starbucks Coffee, Corporate Social Responsibility Annual Report, 2002, reprinted with permission.)

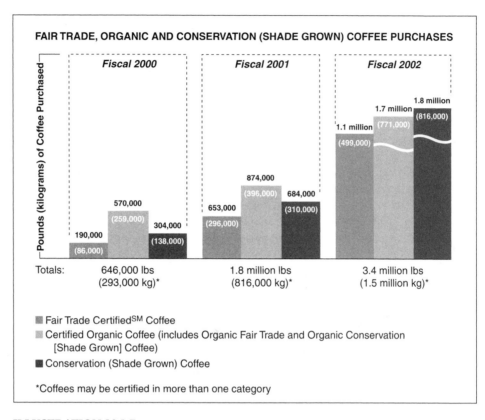

ILLUSTRATION 10.1 B

- **Diagrams,** through images and words, explain processes. Quite a bit of drawing may be involved, often requiring the skills of a graphic artist. Or, publications may reprint a rendering by an architect or designer. (See Illustration 10.3.)
- **Tables** give complete, fully detailed information and allow readers to seek out the numbers most pertinent to them. Examples include sports statistics showing teams' performances, or census data listing all information available about a state's population patterns.

A classic example of a table is the one consulted each spring by millions of taxpayers: the Internal Revenue Service's listing of tax owed by income and filing status. Reporters often derive news stories from tables by asking questions of the data. For example, is it true that married couples pay more tax than they would as single individuals? A reporter analyzing the tables to find out may then create a chart showing the results. In this way, a chart resembles the lead paragraphs of a news story.

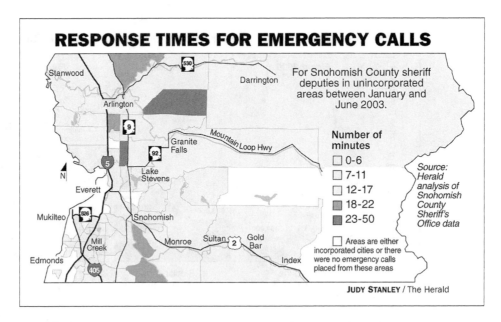

ILLUSTRATION 10.2   *Maps.* Maps orient readers to locations of news events and can show geographic trends. To be effective, maps must include reference points readers are familiar with and can easily imagine. This map starts with a county's lines and adds major highways identified with familiar icons and numbers. By relating response times to geography, this infographic provides, in an efficient and economical use of space, information that readers can study and interpret for themselves.

The map also carries the five essentials of an infographic: heading, explainer, body of information, source and credit line.

(Graphic by Judy Stanley, Copyright The Herald, Everett, Wash. 2003; reprinted with permission.)

Editors may decide to create charts after a story is written when they see that words used to convey quantities, percentages or trends are weighing down sentences. They'll ask if the figures can be extracted from the story and presented in a chart, where the visual impact will be more compelling.

An editor in print media can create simple charts and graphs using word-processing or page-layout software. Some treatments, such as pie charts, originate in a spreadsheet program such as Excel, thus making it important for editors to be able to import such items into their page-layout program. In larger organizations, editors may have the option of sketching a chart and asking a graphic artist to execute it.

Web-based news services hire staff with technical expertise to create many of the graphics that viewers will click on to get background information. These producers work closely with the page and story editors to put together combinations that will enhance meaning by providing more depth.

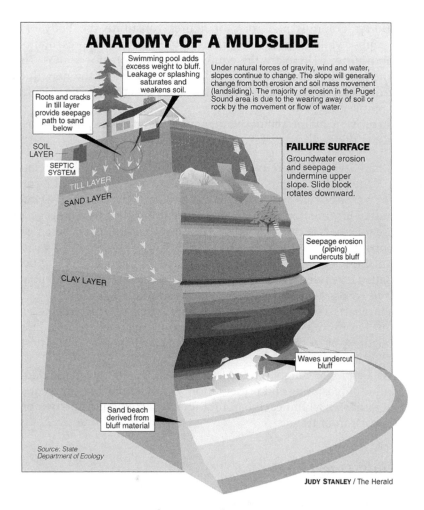

ANATOMY OF A MUDSLIDE

Swimming pool adds excess weight to bluff. Leakage or splashing saturates and weakens soil.

Under natural forces of gravity, wind and water, slopes continue to change. The slope will generally change from both erosion and soil mass movement (landsliding). The majority of erosion in the Puget Sound area is due to the wearing away of soil or rock by the movement or flow of water.

Roots and cracks in till layer provide seepage path to sand below

SOIL LAYER

SEPTIC SYSTEM

TILL LAYER

SAND LAYER

CLAY LAYER

FAILURE SURFACE
Groundwater erosion and seepage undermine upper slope. Slide block rotates downward.

Seepage erosion (piping) undercuts bluff

Waves undercut bluff

Sand beach derived from bluff material

Source: State Department of Ecology

JUDY STANLEY / The Herald

ILLUSTRATION 10.3 *Diagrams.* A diagram presents a process or explains, visually, how something works. Arrows often represent the change in time, and labeling the different parts in a clear, readable fashion becomes key. Explainers may be lengthier than for other infographics.

(Graphic by Judy Stanley, Copyright The Herald, Everett, Wash. 2003; reprinted with permission.)

Essential Parts of Infographics

All infographics need to include these essentials:

1. **Heading.** Written like headlines for stories, these need to express the main point, or news angle, by using a verb and showing action.

2. **Body.** Columns and rows of figures constitute the body of charts and graphs, while maps and diagrams rely on pictorial representations.
3. **Explainer.** These are the equivalent of captions for photos. They describe the point the chart, diagram or map is making and the news it conveys.
4. **Source.** Usually a brief label, this states where the data originated or who compiled it.
5. **Credit.** A byline telling who created the graphic; publications often treat these the same way they treat a photo credit.

Charts typically take two or three values and show their relation to each other. Editors choose bars or columns when the news lies in comparing set amounts. A basic two-way chart shows how two factors relate—education level and annual income, for example, or children's height by their ages. Perhaps they increase together, or one increases while the other declines. These result in arrow directions that go up or down.

To show trends over time, the top points of bars can be connected with a line. Called fever charts, these emphasize how the line rises and falls across set intervals of weeks, months or years. (See Illustration 10.4.)

Pie charts compare parts of a whole when 100 percent is a meaningful amount. For example, an editor working in public relations for a nonprofit hospital might want to show in a report the various expenses of the hospital for the year. (See Illustration 10.5.)

As additional variables need to be shown, an editor can build in more complex kinds of reasoning and presentation. For example, bar charts might stack up several variables within each bar, or a fever chart might show two or three lines for comparison of trends.

Asking the Right Questions

Editors well schooled in writing often approach statistical and mathematical data with a certain amount of trepidation, especially if they are aware that medical and scientific communities have criticized journalists for not always fully understanding nor clearly presenting research results.

Both the errors and the fears can be overcome by finding the right questions—the ones that serve their readers' interests—and posing them to researchers and to findings. When reporting public-opinion surveys or medical and environmental studies, writers and editors have to address certain points in their news stories and analyses in order to accurately present results. Important points include the following:

- how knowledge is created in that field;
- which methods were used to do the research;
- how the resulting data are analyzed;
- whether that field's knowledgeable, ethical experts feel results are significant.

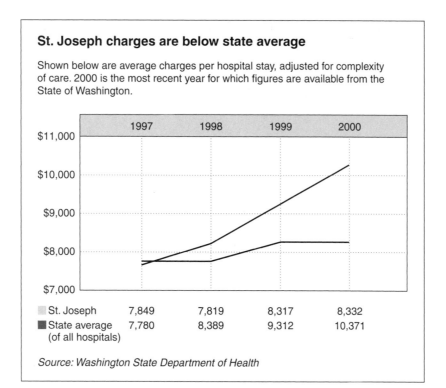

St. Joseph charges are below state average

Shown below are average charges per hospital stay, adjusted for complexity of care. 2000 is the most recent year for which figures are available from the State of Washington.

	1997	1998	1999	2000
St. Joseph	7,849	7,819	8,317	8,332
State average (of all hospitals)	7,780	8,389	9,312	10,371

Source: Washington State Department of Health

ILLUSTRATION 10.4   *Fever Chart.* To indicate change over time more strongly than comparison of discrete units allows, the tops of columns might be connected to form a continuous line, with the result called a fever chart.

This hospital's annual report uses such a chart to show how its average costs, though rising over time, remain below average costs in the state.

("Mission Report 2001," St. Joseph Hospital (Bellingham, Wash.), Peace Health; reprinted with permission.)

Doing this means learning some terminology, knowing enough math to figure percentages and standard deviations, and choosing the most appropriate format among charts.

The journalist begins by asking about **validity:** What did the study set out to accomplish, and did it actually do what it proposed? A second will concern its **reliability:** could someone else use those methods and obtain similar results? In fact, has someone done that?

Significance is also an issue: How do these findings fit in with other results from similar surveys or studies? Do they point to something new? Are they statistically significant, and which populations can findings be applied to?

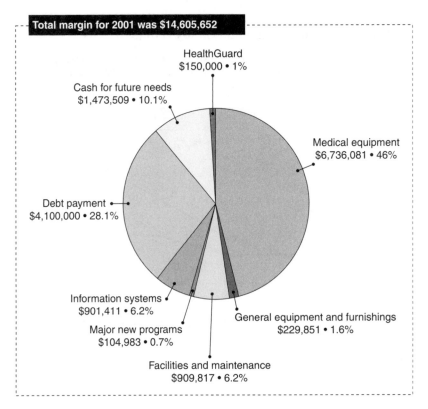

ILLUSTRATION 10.5 *Pie Charts.* Pie charts offer clear representation of portions of a whole. They are best used when 100 percent represents a meaningful amount, such as an annual budget for an organization.

("Mission Report 2001," St. Joseph Hospital (Bellingham, Wash.), Peace Health; reprinted with permission.)

These questions play out a bit differently in surveys than they do in medical, environmental and scientific research. The answers are what show up ultimately in the news stories, charts and graphs editors create or evaluate for publication.

Surveys

American audiences are perhaps most familiar with opinion surveys and with seeing the results presented in charts showing percentages. Editors need to pay close attention to surveyors' use of specialized terminology because many of those terms are used quite loosely—and inaccurately—in everyday conversation.

A reporter on a street corner stops passersby and asks them what they think; a news commentator waits five minutes after a presidential debate and announces "who won" according to a quick tally of callers who've phoned in. Or, a Web page asks users to respond by clicking their agreement or disagreement with an issue.

Are these surveys of opinion? No. Surveys work on the idea that a randomly selected group of people can stand in for a whole population within defined margins of error. But *randomness* is the key. Every member of a population has to have an equal chance of being included.

In the examples above, people not likely to walk by at that time of day won't have their opinions heard. And, those who choose to call in to broadcast programs also are not typical of the entire population, let alone of the population that votes regularly. News organizations offer such tallies for their entertainment value and to give viewers the sense that they are interacting with the media.

Ideally, the name of everyone in a population could be written on a slip of paper, placed in a large fish bowl, and pulled out one by one; that would be a **simple random** sample. Such a process is usually not feasible, so survey researchers randomly select names from lists; this process is called a **systematic random** sample. A caution for editors is that the sample drawn will only be as good as the list it comes from.

A second aspect of validity has to do with why the survey was done. Perhaps it was intended to gauge depth of feeling about a candidate or breadth of knowledge about a subject; it might be to test reaction to various marketing strategies; perhaps it is designed to chart opinion change over time.

Surveys are complex and expensive undertakings that always have a purpose and interested parties behind them. The news stories accompanying a chart need to tackle these topics; additionally, considering these factors will affect what an editor decides to show in a chart.

Editors might publish fewer news stories based on surveys if they consistently used guidelines developed by professional pollsters to evaluate results. But, the stories they did include would be newsworthy, and informed judgment would chip away at the stereotype that all survey results are equal—which means, in many editors' minds, equally questionable.

The American Association for Public Opinion Research discusses best practices and posts expectations for disclosure on its Web site, which is listed in the sources for this chapter. The following points for evaluating surveys are recommended both by that group and by the professional society for news editors. They agree that writers should always ask about—and include in their stories— discussion of these areas:

1. Who sponsored or paid for the poll, and did a party separate from the financial backer conduct it and analyze the results? A danger of bias enters when those most interested in a certain outcome write the questions, ask them and interpret the findings. Editors may place more faith in the results if a reputable research firm or university was hired to do the actual work.

2. Who were the people sampled, and how were they selected? Results may vary dramatically depending on the list used. Was it based on random selection of census tracts, or driver's license lists, or published telephone numbers? Were respondents limited to all adults, or all registered voters, or all voters who actually

voted in last three elections? Are the samples predominantly urban or rural? Were they clustered within certain cities or areas, or were some populations weighted more heavily?

3. How many of the respondents selected were interviewed? Did large numbers refuse to participate? Did very many not know about the issue, or seem not to care? It is possible for surveyors to ask about an issue that is not compelling to many in the general public, and publishing such results can give the impression that opinion has crystallized when in fact only hazy awareness has formed. Large numbers refusing to take part in the survey can skew results, too.

4. How accurate are the results? Editors need to apply two key measures when deciding how newsworthy the results might be.

One is **sampling error,** which reflects the likelihood that a sample will not yield precisely the same results one would get if every member of the population were surveyed. The size of the sampling error decreases with larger samples, and it increases as smaller and smaller samples are selected to stand in for an entire population.

Sampling error is expressed as a percentage that is commonly released by the pollster along with the results. A typical statement might be, "The sample of 1,067 adults was contacted by telephone during the week of January 6–13, with a sampling error of 4 percent."

Such a statement leaves it up to writers or editors to apply the error. The first step is to understand that error is a plus or minus percentage and results in a range within which true opinion probably falls. In the example above, the range runs from minus 4 percent to plus 4 percent and should be applied to the results that are expressed as percentages.

For example, if survey results done during the 2004 presidential election favored John Kerry over George Bush by 52 to 48 percent, an editor might be tempted to state Kerry was ahead. But if she applies the sampling error, the outcome changes. The sample size is large enough to strike only within minus 4 percent to plus 4 percent of the true opinion of the total population. Error is applied with subtraction and addition:

> Kerry 52% –4 = 48%; 52% + 4 = 56%   Range: the true opinion of the entire population lies somewhere between 48% and 56%.
>
> Bush 48% –4 = 44%; 48% + 4 = 52%   Range: the true opinion of the entire population lies somewhere between 44% and 52%.

Because these ranges overlap considerably, an editor concerned about accuracy will say the result is too close to call. Applying sampling error often changes the lead of news stories that otherwise would jump to unwarranted conclusions. To gauge opinion any more closely, the sample size must be increased.

5. The same body of statistics sets a second measure editors note, which is the **level of confidence** of a survey. This, too, varies with sample size, but the caution it expresses is that the process of drawing samples will, over time, pro-

duce some samples that simply are not very representative of the whole population. Some samples will include an optimum desired mix, and some won't. But the larger the sample, the smaller the chance it includes disproportionate numbers of extreme or unrepresentative views.

Confidence level is expressed as a percentage, or the rate at which certain sample sizes will produce reliable results per every 100 uses. Typical sample sizes used allow that four or five surveys in every 100 will yield data pretty far off from true opinion. In other words, surveyors are confident that 95 or 96 percent of the time they will get representative ranges of opinion.

However, confidence level is rarely reported along with survey results. Instead, an editor has to evaluate whether the results of a particular survey are—or are not—among those unreliable results that will crop up four or five times per 100 surveys. How does he make this evaluation?

One clue is whether this survey is reporting something dramatically new and different than others report for similar subjects and questions.

A second good check is to look at the demographic breakdown of respondents. This profiles age, gender, residency and, perhaps, other factors such as income, ethnicity or education level. If the sample seems skewed from the general population, there's a good chance the results will be, too. An editor's judgment is crucial here, in deciding whether to run a story about such a survey's results at all.

A researcher chooses the sample size ahead of time, but after considering the sampling error and confidence levels desired. A number of factors come into play, including the degree to which people are similar to each other on the variable being studied; the kind of polling procedure; the cost in time, money and personnel; the number of categories used to break down results; and the overall population size.

A chart showing the errors and confidence levels for various sample sizes appears as Illustration 10.6. A common cutoff, below which many researchers feel results will not have significance, is 384 respondents, with a sampling error of plus or minus 5 percent at the 95 percent level of confidence. Editors also may decide to use this as the threshold for considering a survey as reliable. Though they still might find the results drawn from smaller samples interesting, they are reluctant to generalize them to an entire population because of likely error.

6. Who did the interviewing, and were they trained? Were they campaign workers or lab administrators eager to land a pharmaceutical contract? Bias can creep in if those asking the questions have a stake in finding certain results. Training interviewers increases reliability because it helps to assure uniform methods for asking the questions, giving follow-up responses and recording information. This is especially important for lengthy in-person interviews, which can become conversational in nature.

7. How were the interviews conducted? Telephone surveys are very common, and interviewers have some control over who responds, thus assuring randomness. But, surveys by phone need to be quick and often don't yield in-depth information. Sometimes telephone surveys are augmented with personal interviews as a follow-up to get more depth for a portion of the responses.

ILLUSTRATION 10.6   *Sampling Error and Confidence Levels.* The amount of sampling error and the level of confidence are set ahead of time by survey researchers. The formula for figuring sample sizes produces the numbers shown in the chart. Those numbers can be corrected for smaller populations under 10,000. Editors will find two books to be especially helpful: "The New Precision Journalism," by Philip Meyer, and "Handbook of Reporting Methods," by Maxwell McCombs, Donald L. Shaw and David Grey.

	Levels of Confidence	
Sampling Error	*95%*	*99%*
1%	9,604	16,587
2%	2,401	4,147
3%	1,067	1,843
4%	600	1,037
5%	384	663
6%	267	461
7%	196	339

The mathematical formula for figuring the sample size needed is:

$$n = v \cdot \frac{z^2}{E^2}$$

This multiplies the variance, typically .25, times the z score squared, and divides by the sampling error squared. The z score is the number of standard deviations from the mean represented by the level of confidence desired.

For example, the 95% level of confidence has a z score of 1.96. If a sampling error of 5% is used, the number resulting is 384, the minimal size considered acceptable in survey research.

In-person interviewing takes a great deal of time and, therefore, is expensive, but it yields a depth of information about feelings and viewpoints that the other methods can't quite match.

Surveys done through the mail or by e-mail have little control over who actually fills them out and returns them. As they require some time and trouble, typically the people most interested in the issue are the ones who will respond. Response rates of 20 percent are common, and because respondents usually are not representative of the overall population, editors need to be cautious about interpreting the results too broadly even though findings might be interesting.

8. When was the polling done? Editors can consider whether any major events happened during the time period that may have shaped or affected answers.

9. What were the actual questions? Researchers should always provide the complete list of both the questions and their answer categories, and editors may choose to reprint these so readers can evaluate for themselves the wording of questions and range of response choices provided.

Questions that allow respondents to express their own views are called open-ended because they don't limit responses to pre-set answer categories. These should be asked ahead of any questions on the same subject that allow only limited choices.

Question wording should be neutral and avoid linking prestigious names or emotionally laden images or adjectives to certain views. For example, a surveyor might ask "Do you think it is a good idea to develop a defensive missile shield for this country?" rather than, "Do you agree with President Bush's plan to develop a missile shield to protect our precious homeland and God-loving American citizens?"

Loaded questions reveal that they are often being solicited for persuasive purposes, such as lobbying. Polls that are actually attempts to push opinion formation or to generate results for lobbying or other political pressures often reveal their purpose in their narrow and rigid answer categories and in the colorful or inflammatory language used.

Answer categories need to represent a complete range of possible responses and to avoid simple dichotomies of yes/no or agree/disagree.

They need to allow a distinction between the "undecideds"—people who know a good deal about an issue but haven't yet taken a firm stance—from the "don't knows," who have heard nothing about the issue or don't care enough about it to form a reasoned opinion.

Some pollsters who use scales for feelings or ranges of agreement and disagreement don't like to include neutral answer categories and will get different results from pollsters who do. Some surveys, too, may offer more answer categories on one side of the scale than the other, especially if they are trying to gauge the depth of either agreement or disagreement. The distribution of answer choices will significantly affect how strong public feeling seems to be.

10. How are the data tabulated and analyzed? Survey results typically are reported in percentages, which makes them handy to represent as tables or as columns in charts.

Results may start with pictures for the overall population and then break out responses by demographic groupings. Did women vote differently than men? Or, did women who are Democrats view gun control differently than women who are Republicans or independents? These kinds of questions are interesting, but answering them means pulling out smaller and smaller subgroups.

Soon, an editor should begin checking the actual numbers of respondents in small subgroups because the sampling error for their replies could be large. Editors should also watch for any extra weighting given to small subgroups.

Numerous other statistical methods than percentages are used to weigh and analyze results, and researchers should describe which methods they have used. Editors can gain more detailed information about these from books on statistics and social science methodology that have been written for mass media researchers; several are recommended at the end of this chapter. A valuable guide is "The New Precision Journalism," by Philip Meyer.

11. A good final question is, What else was found? The study was done with a purpose, a set hunch or hypothesis in mind, which was borne out or disproved. But along the way, other interesting variables may pop up. Because they don't relate directly to the intent of the study, a researcher might not think to mention them in the main findings.

Using Percentages

Reporters and editors frequently want to chart changes over time: How much has the stock market gone up or down? How much has the school district budget grown over five years? They might want to examine portions of a whole: How much of the school district budget is going to salaries? Or, they might want to express a constant value within a different system: How much is the U.S. dollar worth in Canadian dollars?

To answer such questions, values may be converted to a rate and expressed as occurring so many times in a given number of instances. A common rate is **percentage,** or how often a unit occurs per 100 instances. Changing actual numbers to percentages allows editors to figure relative sizes, values, rates of change or portions of a whole.

Several points in this process are key for editors.

Identifying the Base

One is to clearly state the **base,** the total amount represented by 100 percent. The base fills in the blank in the question, 100 percent of . . . what? The base is also the number that answers, "divided by. . . ." Answers need to include a decimal point marking off two spaces, as anything less than 100 percent is a fraction of a whole.

Rates look quite different when the bases change. For example, people who own stock when the market drops learn that to regain the peak value, the stock will have to rise by a larger percentage than it fell. A stock that drops in value from $63 to $42 dropped by one-third of its value: $21, or 33 percent. It is 67 percent of its original value, which is the base of $42 divided by $63.

Instead of selling, the optimistic owner hopes its price will go back up. But to get to $63, the stock moves from its new, lower, base price of $42. With this smaller base, the stock must go up $21 or 50 percent to achieve its former value.

Including Actual Numbers

The actual numbers that percentages represent should be stated to substantiate what the rates appear to show. This is because rates can create the appearance of a large change when the overall numbers are small.

For example, if a new espresso stand on the corner opens and sells 300 cups of coffee by week's end and then sells 600 cups its second week, the 300-cup increase in week two is a 100-percent increase, or a doubling, of the 300-cup base. But, those 300 additional cups would hardly register a 3-percent blip in the overall sales of a large company store owned by a large chain.

Showing the Zero Point and Regular Intervals

Including a zero point and regular intervals of measurement help ensure that rates of increase or decrease are represented accurately at first glance. Editors reaching for strong news impact often drop the lower intervals from a chart so the view concentrates only on the top portions of columns. This can create a visual exaggeration of a trend.

Similarly, when images are used in pictographs, it is easy to enlarge the item shown by increasing its dimensions both horizontally and vertically. But, an image that shows as 200 percent of its original doubles its width and its height, ending up covering not just twice the original area, but four times, something the viewer will see and digest before deconstructing the math.

Forming Categories

Data is often collapsed into categories before percentages are calculated; editors may want to look at how the categories were formed, and whether they are reasonable.

For example, are age groupings formed consistently, and do income brackets reflect representative wages in that community? Age and income are examples of **continuous data,** in that people can be represented by those attributes along a consistent, unbroken line. **Categories** are created, though, to make comparisons or calculations less cumbersome, and editors need to check that they are mutually exclusive, without overlaps.

Projections and Predictions

Some graphics represent ideas about what will happen in the future. **Projections** take a current trend and create a picture based on that rate of increase or decrease continuing unchanged year after year.

While urban planners or economists may need to do this to assure they're thinking broadly enough about the future, editors can question whether a projection is valid. If coffee companies project 300 percent increases year after year, we will soon be bathing in coffee or watering our lawns with it if we are to consume that much.

While one could take the great growth in stock values during the 1990s and project that rate well into the future, in fact, writers and editors did not do this. Typically they printed **predictions** instead, which are different because they take numerous trends into consideration and recognize that nothing proceeds forever without mitigating or counterbalancing effects. Indeed, the U.S. stock market average dropped sharply for several years at the new millennium.

Predictions are more useful than projections because they ask scientists or researchers or planners what they think will actually happen rather than assuming an endless one-way trend. As writer Edward Abbey saw it, unlimited growth is the "philosophy of the cancer cell."

Averages

An average figure can be useful; it expresses what the amount in the middle would be for measures as varied as growth, income, prices, test scores, and height and weight. Writers and editors often face a dilemma in using an ideal statistical composite: Does the genuinely average case or person exist in any great number? In this sense, an average remains an abstract concept of being in the middle. It does not indicate sameness in all cases, nor is it a normative value toward which all people in a society aspire.

An **average** is calculated by adding up the values of all cases and dividing by the number of cases; it is also called a **mean.** For groups of data without extremes, this value can be a useful measure. Average temperatures for New York City in October may help someone pack the right clothes, or average rainfall in Seattle may help someone decide whether to retire there.

But, for values that vary greatly or have significant extremes, an average can disguise both trends and present realities. A society that has a few extremely rich people and a great many very poor people may show an average income much the same as that for a society in which everyone earns close to the same amount. (See Illustration 10.7.)

Other values that add depth to the picture include the **median,** the point at which there are as many cases above as below, and the **mode,** which is the most frequently named value.

The two societies mentioned above will have quite different median and modal incomes; in the first case, where most people are poor, these numbers will be lower amounts than in the society with an even distribution.

A society in which the largest number of people make average incomes, with very few either poor or rich, would resemble a **bell curve,** an idealized shape in which the mean, median and mode all fall at the same point. (See Illustration 10.8.)

The Bell Curve and Standard Deviation

The bell curve makes another kind of averaging useful: a standard deviation. This measure makes it possible to talk about how individual cases are distributed around a central value. To calculate standard deviation, the distance of each case from the mean is squared, added up, divided by the number of cases and unsquared.

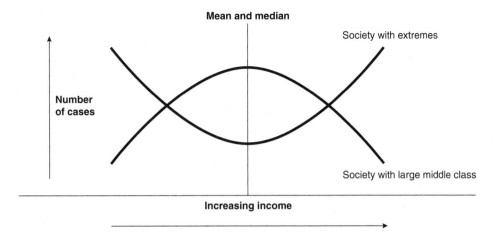

ILLUSTRATION 10.7 *Averages.* An average, or mean, can be a useful figure, but it can disguise cases in which extremes exist. For example, the average income for a society with a great many rich and poor, but few in the middle, may look like the average income for a society with most people in the middle and very few rich or poor.

Placing the income profiles for both societies onto a curve, however, allows the different distributions to be seen. Here, the two societies are similar in their mean or average income, but the median income (the point at which as many incomes fall below as fall above), and the mode (the most frequently named value) are quite different.

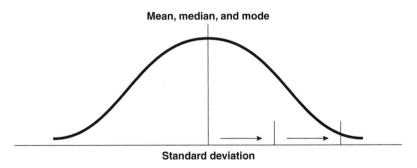

ILLUSTRATION 10.8 *Bell Curve.* The bell curve is a useful shape because a standard deviation for a normal distribution marks out a regularly occurring area covered by the curve. In an ideal bell curve, the mean, median and mode all fall at the same place.

It is an average, but not of actual values; instead, it is an average of how far values fall from the center, or how much they cluster around the center. It does a much better job than a simple average does of showing when cases are clustered out toward the extremes.

Because the bell curve is a regularly occurring geometric shape, just as are squares, circles and triangles, it is possible to talk about shapes and areas between the baseline and the curve of the bell. Areas within rectangles or triangles can be calculated using the lengths of their lines, and areas covered by the bell curve can be calculated by using the average distance of cases as a measuring stick.

In this way, the **standard deviation**—the average distance of cases from the mean—becomes a very useful measure because when it is plotted along the baseline, it marks a consistent area enclosed by that curve.

For example, if all incomes in a society were plotted on a chart and the distance of each income from the mean was squared, added up to a total, then divided by the number of cases and unsquared, it would be possible to say, for that society, how big the average distance is from the mean. For a society with great extremes of wealth, where many cases fall far from the mean, the standard deviation, as average distance, will be greater in terms of money amounts than for a society where incomes cluster around the mean.

But no matter what the picture of the society, or the way the curve—because it is a geometric shape—may flow, a key characteristic is that one standard deviation, plotted along the baseline, will mark out a steady, unvarying percentage of that curve. So will a second standard deviation, beginning at the end of the first and measuring out toward the tails.

In fact, 1.96 standard deviations measured in both directions from the mean will account for 95 percent of a bell curve, and 2.58 will account for 99 percent. Survey researchers and scientists will often express the **statistical significance** of their findings in terms of the standard deviation or its shorthand name, **Z score.**

Knowing the average distance of cases from the mean allows an editor to check how distant a particular case falls from the mean. This will tell him how unusual it is—or how far out on the tails of a curve it falls—and may be a factor in deciding newsworthiness. While statisticians often want to know about central tendencies rather than extreme cases, news judgments may tend to just the opposite, often favoring the unusual over the average. (See Box 10.1.)

Other tests for significance exist; the **chi square** is one often used and easy to apply. Using row and column totals in relation to each other within a mathematical formula, chi square looks at distributions across cells and how likely those are to occur only by chance. This test and others can be found in books recommended at the end of this chapter.

The results of significance tests do not tell editors whether the researcher definitely proved something or not; they just show how likely the results are to be caused by chance. Deciding whether to publish the results—and on which page, with how big of a headline and with what degree of certainty in the wording—still requires editors to use a good deal of news judgment.

BOX 10.1 • *Testing for Significance*

The standard deviation offers editors several practical applications.

One is that it is used in a formula to define sample sizes for surveys and polls. Researchers choose ahead of time how much of a bell curve, or how much area around the average value, they would like to account for, and this is expressed in terms of the number of standard deviations.

To account for 95 cases in 100, which is in essence to work at the 95 percent level of confidence, the researcher plugs in 1.96 standard deviations in the formula below. To account for more of a curve and its tails, the number of standard deviations rises; for example, 2.58 standard deviations will describe 99 percent of a curve. The number of standard deviations has a shorthand name in statistics: z, or z score.

The first amount used in the formula is the **variance,** which is the standard deviation before it is unsquared. It can be pictured most simply as the square of the number of choices a case has in how it will fall in relation to the mean.

In a two-way choice, such as yes/no, heads or tails, John Kerry or George W. Bush, an ideal average would be 50–50, or half the cases falling on each side of the choice. Statisticians usually use the variance for such an idealized outcome though, in fact, choices for any given survey may include many more possible answer categories.

The point is to create a mathematically idealized bell curve against which actual results will be measured. The variance for a 50–50 split is .5 squared, or .25.

The formula multiplies the variance times the z score squared and divides by the desired sampling error expressed as a percentage and squared. The result is the number of cases needed for a survey to have that level of confidence and sampling error.

As an example, the minimum number of cases for a survey to have validity is 384, as discussed earlier.

$$n = v \bullet \frac{z^2}{E^2} = \text{sample size, or:}$$

.25 times 1.96 squared / .05 squared = 384

A second use for editors involves doing a simple test for significance to find out just how unusual a certain outcome may be. In the following news story, the statistical significance can easily be tested.

The New York Times wire in April 1998 ran a story about a 9-year-old's fourth-grade science experiment being accepted for publication in the American Medical Association's journal. Emily Rosa of Loveland, Colo., designed an experiment to test a healing method called therapeutic touch, whose proponents say they manipulate a patient's energy field by passing their hands over the patient's body without actually touching it.

According to the story, Emily recruited 21 practitioners who agreed to be tested by sitting across from her with a screen separating them. Then Emily flipped a coin to decide whether to put her hand over the healer's right or left hand. The healer had to state where Emily's hand was hovering. In 280 tests, healers correctly named the location of Emily's hand 44 percent of the time.

(continued)

BOX 10.1 • Continued

The story points out that this is less than the 50 percent that might be expected merely due to chance. But, the percentage does not answer a news question: Is a 44 percent success rate something one would commonly get if running such an experiment? Just how unusual is it?

Scientists and medical researchers often require that a result be very unlikely to be caused just by chance if they are going to publish the results and consider them valid. A common level for accepting a result is that it is likely to occur only five times or fewer in 100 because of chance; in other words, in at least 95 trials out of 100 this result is occurring for another reason.

To find how likely Emily's result is to be caused by chance, a simple test of significance allows creating an imaginary bell curve of many such trials in order to see where this result might fall. The formula involves looking at the expected result compared to the actual result, the variance for the case, and the number of tests run.

For 280 cases, chance alone would predict 140 correct and 140 incorrect answers. The story reports that 44 percent of the answers were correct, or 123 of 280 trials (.44 times 280). This produces a difference of 17 cases from the outcome that chance would dictate (140 minus 123).

The right or wrong answers are an either/or, two-way choice, giving a variance of .25.

This variance is multiplied by the number of cases, and the result is then unsquared because the variance is the square of the standard deviation:

.25 times 280 = 70; the square root of 70 is 8.4

This means that one standard deviation for a sample of this size is 8.4 cases.

The last step involves looking at how many standard deviations the actual result represents. The 17 cases away from the mean represent about twice a single standard deviation; two standard deviations would be 16.8 cases. So, this result is out on the tail of a curve beyond the cutoff of 1.96 standard deviations required for the 95 percent level of confidence. It is at this point that a medical or scientific journal would look at the result pretty seriously.

Though this example is figured only for correct answers, the same can be done for the incorrect ones; the result will show the same numbers but will apply to the side of the curve to the left of the mean. To see if the results can be replicated, researchers might want to run the test more times. And, a greater number of trials will increase the sensitivity of the tests, thus making the results stronger statistically.

Evaluating Research Studies

Readers have probably become accustomed to headlines declaring contradictory findings—for years, eggs were evil and now they're good for us; chocolate may be fattening but it makes us happy and helps us live longer; caffeine may tie us in knots or aid in recovering from strokes, and so forth. When headlines seem to declare first one thing and then another, it may be frustrating to try to plan diets for good health.

A recent survey by the Fred Hutchinson Cancer Research Center of 1,751 adults in Washington state found a connection between confusion over contradictory stories and the tendency to discard all advice.

"The more negative and confused people feel about dietary recommendations, the more likely they are to eat a fat-laden diet that skimps on fruits and vegetables," the study's lead author, Ruth Patterson, told the Associated Press.

Editors are the line of defense for the public; many such stories are worth publishing and are interesting to read, but editors have to decide on their newsworthiness and how prominently results will be played.

They also are responsible for including in the stories some context, which may be findings from similar studies or the opinions of experts in the field who can say whether a particular study is significant or not and how it relates to the general population of more or less healthy people. A key point that media need to accept, some researchers say, is that often further research is needed to gain certainty or to move beyond correlations to establishing cause and effect.

In deciding how much newsworthiness or credence to invest in a story about research results, editors can ask questions just as they do when considering survey results. Useful inquiries include:

- how the research was conducted and whether it was an experiment;
- whether the research establishes a correlation or a cause-and-effect relationship;
- whether results apply to animal tests or trials with humans;
- how results might be generalized to the overall population;
- whether the work has been replicated by others or reviewed by peers or a professional or scholarly journal;
- who the researchers were and whether they had a financial interest in an outcome.

Correlational versus Cause-and-Effect Findings

A common journalistic fallacy is to confuse **correlational** studies, which simply ask whether factors vary together in some fashion, with research trials to see whether a factor causes a certain effect or outcome.

For example, a study of male Harvard graduates found that those who ate candy bars regularly lived longer than those who did not. Does this mean that eating candy bars will prolong one's life? Not at all, though many editors are tempted to write such a headline. Numerous additional factors affected how long these men lived, though it could be newsworthy that chocolate, sugar and nuts correlated with something desirable.

Studies that suggest such associations may be followed by experiments and clinical trials to test whether a **cause-and-effect relationship** exists.

An experiment is a specific research design with several important components, though in common usage the term is tossed around quite loosely. An experiment begins with an **hypothesis,** a statement of how the researcher expects the process to turn out. The design begins at one time, introduces a new variable, and measures outcome at a later time.

An editor who wishes to call a study an **experiment** needs to be able to identify several parts: the variable being tested, or **independent variable,** who constitutes the population being tested, the beginning and ending times, and the resulting change, or **dependent variable.** The most reliable experiments compare a **test group** to a **control group,** a randomly selected group of people who did not undergo the variable being tested.

Basic research takes place at the cellular level and looks at biochemical substances or biological processes in laboratories. Findings that may apply to humans are often reported, but it is crucial to note whether they have actually been tested on animals or run through clinical trials, which are the first experiments involving humans.

A 1998 study on the effect of using the Internet that gained page-one coverage in some media concluded that Internet use correlated strongly to compulsiveness, anxiety and obsessive disorders. In the study, two researchers asked a small number of people who were already being treated for these problems to recall their Internet use. This study used patients already diagnosed with an illness and relied on self-reporting about the past.

Two months later, a larger study concluded that Internet use cut down on participants' social lives and interpersonal networks. The several hundred people involved first filled out an inventory related to the factors being studied. Then they used the Internet in their daily lives for a period of time and were inventoried again. In this case, the design was experimental and followed people in a systematic fashion as they went through the experiment. The participants were typical of the general population except that they knew they were part of some sort of study.

The second study's methods provided editors a stronger basis for inferring results to a general population of readers. In short, it offered greater news value.

Finally, it is important to know whether researchers had a financial stake, or other interest, in finding a certain result. Just as with survey work, it could be a source of bias in how the results are interpreted. Given how common it is for pharmaceutical and oil companies and others to fund research even at the university level, some research journals have begun requiring statements from their authors that disclose any relevant financial interests.

Relative and Actual Risk

Our daily lives are full of variables that can affect our health and well being. The variables, from genetic inheritance to eating habits to pollutants in the atmosphere, build layer upon layer of increasing complexity, with change in one possibly influencing change in others.

Readers of science and health stories often want to sort out whether they need to worry about a factor or not and, if they do, how much potential risk or danger they face. Victor Cohn, a journalist and author of books on reporting risk, writes that people willingly accept some risks—for instance, to drive cars or play sports—yet want to avoid risks from chemicals, radiation and other hazards.

Research on environmental questions must sort through cumulative effects, long-term effects, possible unknowns or confounding variables and the fact that science cannot really prove a negative, or that no effect exists.

The difficulty of sorting out factors that can be proven to cause effects, or that may be correlated with them, leads scientists to disagree sometimes on the amount of risk a certain substance or event presents. And, segments of the population are affected by risks differently. For example, standards set for use of a chemical in a workplace may not apply at home, where children or the ill or elderly would be in contact with it for longer hours during a day.

Risk is a term that can include a variety of measures of how likely a certain outcome is for a variable. A **risk factor** is anything that has been shown to have a statistically significant relationship with a specific result, incidence or disease.

To help readers weigh risks and benefits of foods or medicines, editors can ensure that stories include details on both the **actual risk,** which states how likely an event is to happen, and the **relative risk,** which is how much a person's actions may increase or decrease the odds that the actual risk will happen.

For example, Second Takes, a staff publication of The Oregonian newspaper, discussed a news story reporting that eating red meat increases the risk that a woman will contract colon cancer. This particular study found that women who ate a diet heavy in animal fats were 2.5 times more likely to get colon cancer than women who ate red meat only once a month or so.

Second Takes asked if readers could make an informed decision about eating red meat based on that information and recommended running the actual risk as well. That figure showed a risk level that one in 3,500 women eating red meat regularly would develop colon cancer, compared to one in 8,000 women who ate it once a month or less. As the publication pointed out, the actual risk was so low that many women might decide to continue eating meat occasionally.

While readers are better able to make decisions when both statements of risk—the relative and the actual—are included, their task becomes more complex when they need to weigh different relative risks against each other. Yet, these complex decisions are necessary for millions of people to make.

Risks change over a human lifetime, as well, with relative risks for diseases such as cancer increasing with age. A newsmagazine struck fear into the hearts of many when it reported several years ago that one in five men would develop prostate cancer in their lifetimes. What did not get spelled out as well was that risk this high was relevant only for elderly men. In other words, if one lived past age 70 by not dying of something else first, the odds of developing prostate cancer, or any other kind of cancer, would grow that high.

Editors can also help readers by comparing a level of risk to other risks to keep them in perspective. The chances of being hit by a meteor are reported as

1 in 700 million. The family doctor likes to remind patients that more people die each year from popping champagne corks than from spider bites. One's risk of being in a car accident far outweighs the risk of being in a plane crash.

By asking to whom in the population a risk applies, what the extent of the risk is and what it means to individuals, editors can get facts about risk assessment into stories for their readers to examine.

Conclusion

In approaching statistical, medical and environmental data, some editors, seeing how full of snakes the cave is, might not take the Indiana Jones approach and leap right in to grab the gems. Instead, they react to the lack of certainty and the likelihood of pitfalls by doubting the value of most research, particularly polls, or treating studies of widely divergent quality as though they are equally newsworthy.

But, editors who have a map of where snakes are likely lurking can tread more confidently. Here are the common journalistic fallacies—or errors of assumption and interpretation—to avoid:

- generalizing from small samples to an entire population. No group is truly representative of the population, but a large, random sample offers at least known rates of likely error and confidence;
- failing to apply sampling error to responses given in a survey, especially to small subgroups;
- not giving actual numbers underlying percentages or rates;
- confusing a correlation with a cause-and-effect relationship;
- not discerning true experiments and their vital components;
- assuming if one factor precedes in time, it is automatically a cause of some result;
- leaping from basic research or animal tests to assuming similar results will occur with humans;
- generalizing results from small clinical trials with people already ill to a healthy general population;
- equating short-term laboratory results with longitudinal studies done in real-life circumstances;
- assuming linear projections rather than predictions;
- having a lack of context, including similar or previous studies, the researchers' own reservations, and peer reviews and journal reviews;
- not doing the math, including simple significance tests, percentages, or rates calculated across different bases;
- reporting relative risks without actual risks or comparison to other, more familiar risks;
- fearing and avoiding doing basic arithmetic to check facts.

By carefully considering what readers most need to know and checking that news stories answer key questions about surveys and scientific and medical research, editors can make distinctions among studies that are truly significant and those that are not. They can more confidently make news decisions and can accurately reflect the importance or substance of research findings in news stories' leads and headings.

By doing the math involved in applying rates of sampling error, performing simple significance tests, or figuring rates of increased risk compared to actual risk, editors can interpret data to best answer the most pressing questions readers bring to stories based on research.

And by understanding the dimensions of infographics, editors can select or create the presentations that most accurately convey findings in a visual manner.

Exercises to Apply Concepts and Develop Skills

1. Goal: To increase critical thinking about information presented in a visual format.

   Ask students to bring in examples of infographics from media that they find complete and helpful, as well as those that are incomplete or misleading. (If the classroom has Internet access, numerous examples can be gathered by looking at Web news sites.) Through class discussion, identify the gaps in information and help students to assess whether the immediate impact of the visual presentation conveys the same news lead as the verbal one.

2. Goal: To discern the purpose of different kinds of chart presentations.

   Give students a set of data and ask them to present it in several different kinds of charts and assess in which one the message is most clearly and accurately presented. (Using a program such as Excel's Chart Wizard makes this feasible in a classroom.)

3. Goal: To improve narrative in stories and develop strong visual information.

   After supplying students with stories in news media, ask them to identify material in narratives that could be better presented in an infographic. Ask them to create the infographic needed by using electronic software or by drawing the graphic by hand. Discuss the necessity for all verbal parts of the infographic, as well, including the heading, explainer, source and credit line.

4. Goal: To become able to assess the quality of reporting about surveys and scientific studies, to locate the gaps or missing information and to make editorial judgments about the newsworthiness of the findings.

   Collect examples of such news stories in media, or ask students to collect some and work with them to apply the questions covered in this chapter of the text. Are all essential questions answered in the story? Is the information written in a way to help readers or viewers? Finally, ask students to gauge the worth of the story editorially: Would they run it the same way, placing it on that page and giving it as prominent a heading? This is especially effective with stories about surveys.

Helpful Sources _____

American Association for Public Opinion Research, http://www.aapor.org (See "Standards and Best Practices," under "Survey Methods.")

Cohn, Victor and Louise Cope. "News and Numbers: A Guide to Reporting Statistical Claims & Controls in Health & Other Fields." Ames, Iowa: Iowa State University Press, 2001.

Harmon, Amy. "Study links Internet and Depression," New York Times in the Seattle Times. Aug. 30, 1998, p. A4.

Hart, Jack, ed. "Finding Truth in Numbers." Second Takes. 7:6 The Oregonian Publishing Co., Portland, Ore., October 1995.

Jhally, Sut, producer and director. "The Electronic Storyteller: Television and and Cultivation of Values" (videorecording). Northampton, Mass.: Media Education Foundation, 1997.

Kolata, Gina. "9-year-old's research touches sensitive nerve/Popular therapy gets dissed in AMA journal," New York Times in Seattle Post-Intelligencer. April 1, 1998, p. 1.

International Food Information Council Review. "How to Understand and Interpret Food and Health-Related Scientific Studies." 1100 Connecticut Ave., N.W., Suite 430, Washington, D.C., 1998. Also see http://ificinfo.health.org

Lowery, Shearon A., et al. "Milestones in Mass Communication Research: Media Effects."3rd Ed. London: Longman Publishers, 1995.

McCombs, Maxwell, et. al. "Handbook of Reporting Methods." Boston: Houghton Mifflin Company, 1976.

Meyer, Philip. "The New Precision Journalism." Lanham, Md.: Rowman & Littlefield Publishers, Inc., 2001.

Poynteronline. Poynter Institute site with resources, articles and links. http://poynter.org

Ritter, Malcom. "Internet 'addicts' display a web of problems," Associated Press in The Herald (Everett, Wash.). June 1, 1998, p. 1.

Weiner, Emily. "Graphics Overview," class materials and presentations. Western Washington University, 1995.

Wimmer, Roger D. and Joseph R. Dominick. "Mass Media Research: an Introduction." 7th Ed. Belmont, Calif.: Wadsworth Publishing Co., 2002.

11

Layout and Design

For editors just learning to do page layouts, the leap to creating beautiful designs seems as distant as the long jump, as high as the pole vault. Though the terms are often used interchangeably, in fact, layout and design are two different tasks, and many editors who are excellent at layout never take on the mantle of becoming publication designers.

Design implies several added dimensions. One is scope. While **layout** often refers to the single page—an editor may lay out several pages in a day—design can encompass the entire look of the publication. Design defines the way the individually laid-out pages will pull together and relate to each other.

Editors must interpret and implement that look with each issue they produce. Design provides the basic structure for each page template. Design also defines how contrast can be expressed by setting parameters for colors, type sizes and fonts, page sizes, sections, etc.

Another implication is artistry. An editor who has a chance to lay out feature pages is, in essence, given freedom to be creative because those pages often have distinctive fonts, white space, larger illustrations and full color. The editor who builds skills in this area may become a page designer.

A third aspect lies in education and background. While editors are trained in journalism's news values and language skills, designers are often educated in fine art and graphic design.

Of course, a person can do both, but this chapter emphasizes editors' roles and leaves more extensive design as being in the province of the magazine's art director, the public relations company's design group or the newsroom's artist. However, it may fall to the editor to create the design for a newsletter, annual report or corporate magazine, especially in smaller organizations.

Professional associations for designers who work in media maintain World Wide Web sites that display current prize-winning pages. They also publish magazines and annual volumes of designs that win national and international awards. For readers who would like to peruse collections of professionally designed pages or to move beyond the principles discussed here, these and other sources are listed at the end of the chapter.

Roles of Designers and Editors

Mario Garcia, the Poynter scholar who is also a newspaper designer, commented that copy editors are good at layout, and 80 percent of a newspaper's daily appearance results from their work.

"Design adds the surprises, the things people who are trained to do should do," he said at American Press Institute's Design 2020 workshop.

Design also establishes personality. Publications tell us a lot about themselves at just a glance. The Wall Street Journal, for example, remains 80 percent black and white, even after the redesign in which Garcia introduced a subtle color palette—sky blue, light mint green, champagne, gray and lavender—to soften the paper's gray look.

Conversely, Wired magazine, with its neon colors and improbable photo illustrations, appears nearly ready to turn off the computer and go snow boarding. The World Wide Web offers pages expressing the full range of what the human imagination can create when linked to a computer.

While readers are not likely to dissect a magazine cover or a Web site's home page into visual components—the typography, colors and spatial arrangements that have led them to expect heavy stuff or breezy entertainment—editors assemble and work with numerous pieces of a design to deliver a desired visual impact.

Editors are key players in articulating the concepts that will drive the design of a publication. The editors and publisher will first answer:

- Who is the audience?
- What are we offering them?
- What is distinctive, new or different about us?
- How do we communicate these qualities visually?
- What are the goals of this design?

When the audience, purpose and uniqueness are clearly defined—or redefined, if an ongoing publication is updating its appearance—a designer often is hired to work on creating the right look.

How does one know whether typefaces and other components of design communicate the desired qualities? This becomes the province of designers whose education in studio art and art history links current styles to their cultural and historical roots. Plus, they and the editors will create mock-ups and test them with audiences or focus groups. A design needs to serve the audience's needs, preferences and uses of the publication.

Intersection of Layout and Design

Design and content decisions are interrelated in these areas:

Identity and mission   A mission statement drives design. Identity is clearly established by using a nameplate, and credibility is increased by fully identifying the organization and its location, address, phone number and e-mail address so readers can contact writers or editors.

The publishing interval or frequency for updating, plus a staff box, need to be easily locatable. Magazines and other niche publications sometimes state their editorial stance, purpose, philosophy and even target audience. World Wide Web pages, which often omitted such information in earlier years, now routinely include "about us" sections and site maps.

Advertising   The editorial side of a publication, or its publisher, sets guidelines for display and classified advertising, including standards for appearance and content. Policies may cover how to group ads, where to place them and whether the publication will run special sections for marketplace listings or index its ads. Editors may reject advertising that does not meet these standards.

Audience   Editors need to have more than a vague idea about the people they are aiming to reach (their community) in order to make effective decisions on story priorities and angles for headings and leads. Newspapers often get to know their readers by running surveys within their circulation areas. Magazine marketing research usually allows editors to pinpoint characteristics of their readers.

Editors of all kinds of publications now receive volumes of comment from readers via e-mail, which can be examined systematically.

However, editors of Web pages simply may not know much about who clicks and who stays or returns. Firms that track Internet use can provide some kinds of information, such as where users were just been before landing on the page and where they were headed when they left. The usage information also may be able to tell a great deal more, which is making privacy for Web use a major social and political issue.

A page can be set to record the numbers of hits each item receives, plus their origin. Often, Web pages are programmed to insert "cookies" into users' computer hard drives. These last for varying amounts of time and collect data; a user can set her computer to reject cookies or post an alert when one arrives.

An ethical expectation seems to be growing that publications should state in an open fashion what kind of data they collect from their users or subscribers and what use they will make of subscriber lists. Some magazines routinely sell their lists, for example.

Cover lines   Publications that rely on newsstand sales pack numerous subtitles onto the front to entice consumers to leaf through and buy the issue. Newspapers relying on sales from street corner boxes try for lively headings and several smaller promotional highlights that will show through the box's window.

Web pages face something of the same dilemma in needing to indicate the contents available a click or two away. These pressures vie with a design preference for simplicity, order and even aesthetical presentations on a cover. How much type, how much promotion and what kinds of cover illustrations to run are factors set in the format.

Sections   Web sites have to be carefully constructed so that pages of parallel importance fall in the right place in a hierarchy. In a way, the process of drawing, or story boarding, how pages will branch out from the home page, and then from section covers, resembles the planning done for newspaper and magazine sections.

In all cases, key questions have to be answered with graphics that allow for quick, consistent, visually based navigation. Readers need to comprehend how contents pages relate to the cover or home page, how to navigate and when they have arrived at their destination so that they can settle in to read.

Achieving all of this is more difficult than it sounds; the design must visually signal the overall structure, the separate sections, the means of navigation forward and back, and must find the right balance between simplicity—indicating ease of use—and complexity, signifying depth of content offered.

Multimedia relationships   Elements in the design need to reflect the publication's relationship to its cousins in print or online. Readers will wonder why they should go to a magazine's online site and whether it offers the same or different information. Usually some graphic identity—perhaps an icon, nameplate or corporate logo and colors—is carried among the different media versions of a publication. (See Illustration C.25.)

Identity may flow more strongly in one direction than in the other, depending on how editors feel their prime audience orients to one medium or to the other.

A popular practice in Web use is for several news organizations to develop partnerships and offer access to their services at each other's sites or at a portal site. In these cases, the home page carries several companies' icons or nameplates.

Auxiliary uses   The publication exists as a physical entity, as well, which people adapt to and reuse over time. Whether a Web site posts photo archives and galleries indefinitely, whether a newspaper includes coupons to be clipped, whether how-to magazine sidebars are provided for posting with magnets on refrigerator doors and whether a tabloid-size newspaper is read by thousands of people riding on commuter trains with limited elbow room—all are secondary but not incidental uses affected by, and affecting, the design.

Practicality   Editors are key in evaluating how well the design works on a daily basis and can offer suggestions for changes. After all, they have to link the template with its visual and verbal content, and they ensure that the design framework reinforces the meaning of the content and serves the audience.

The design has to be flexible enough to accommodate typical production challenges, such as last-minute changes dictated by news events, or fewer full-color pages during tight budget times. A design needs to work equally well for a newspaper's three or four opinion pages that run on a Sunday as for the single page that runs on a weekday.

Consistency in details   To execute the design, editors help to create guidelines for using photographs and illustrations, including their size, frequency and color ranges; apply the color palette, which consists of a limited range of shades the publication will use regularly; format type styles for body text, text-based graphics, headings and subheads; and define how to include white space, lines and rules. When these are set ahead of time in an approachable style manual, editing becomes smoother and much faster.

Room for variation   With an effective and practical design in hand, an editor finds room for a great deal of creativity within it. Photos and illustrations that normally are rectangular in a news layout may become round or square, or may be placed at angles, in a feature layout. A range of colorful fonts may be defined as choices.

Design Issues across Media

The following sections highlight layout principles that vary the most, depending on the size of the page, the purpose of the publication and the medium used. Although each design issue is discussed in terms of one medium, it can be applied with some modification to other media as well. Detailed discussions of use of photos, illustrations, color, type and infographics appear in earlier chapters of this book.

Distinguishing between News and Features: Newspapers

Newspapers clearly signal, visually, the different moods of news pages and the sections with entertaining features. While a front page will fill each inch of space and carry dominant elements at the top corners, features pages will use a larger illustration to draw the eye first toward the middle of the page. Feature pages, such as sports, lifestyle, arts and entertainment or childrens pages, also make more use of white space, full color and large type. (See Illustration C.26.)

Broadsheet news pages usually carry half a dozen stories on the front page and a few promos to stories inside. The usual six columns on a 14.5-inch wide page are changing now to a narrower page that runs on a 50-inch Web printing press, and some newspapers are trying seven-column pages. These changes yield a denser and more strongly vertical look. Others adapt to the narrower page by running fewer major stories on the page.

Some editors begin feature-page design by using a different template, one with 12 or 14 columns marked, as a visual prompt to think beyond the usual six news columns.

Students beginning feature page designs will often splash a page with multiple contrasting elements, producing a swirl that grabs the eye but lets it wander as the elements compete chaotically for attention. A successful design usually goes through several drafts, each becoming more refined. The more that beginning editors try their hand at moving beyond basic layout, the earlier they are likely to learn to exercise restraint in the design process.

What are the visual signals that differentiate between news and feature layouts? Here are potential changes, which apply to other media, as well:

- a single, large heading that may be a label and that introduces a topic rather than summarizing information;

- a deck heading that reveals more of the story's angle and that is in an intermediate type size, in between head and body text;
- large photos, or a single main photo or illustration run quite large;
- captions shaped in a single caption block and placed as a design element;
- white space designed as a component, with its regular shapes balancing the density of the large heading and illustration;
- other techniques, such as setting elements at an angle, or using rounded or "torn" edges to photos may be used—but with restraint;
- a number of points of entry are provided to draw the reader into the page; these may be captions, photos, deck heads, pullquotes, etc.
- pulling the eye to the middle of the page first, then allowing it to move around, perhaps in a circular pattern.

Handling Inside Pages: Tabloids

Tabloids—usually 11 by 17 inches—may be complete newspapers in themselves, but they also appear as special pull-out sections in broadsheet newspapers that use them as entertainment inserts or vacation guides.

Editors working with tabloid sizes face some size-related dilemmas, particularly how to offer a variety of topics on the cover page without a cluttered look. And, ads stacked on inside pages can leave layout spaces too small for photos. In spite of these challenges, beautifully designed pages are produced.

The student mock-up design in Illustration 11.1 centers on one large photo, with others of significantly smaller size, because the tabloid's space makes it difficult for editors to use two photos within a single story package.

Fewer stories appear on the front page than on a broadsheet size, but major stories can be highlighted in the space at the top. The less that can be presented on the front, the more important cover lines or highlight boxes become in attracting readers to contents on inside pages.

The publication design sets up elements that are carried throughout on inside pages. The width of gutters, use of rules and text and heading typefaces stay consistent with the cover page. The style for section headings and the parameters for story headings, use of kickers, deck heads, bylines, credits, captions, and so forth also remain consistent. This need for consistency applies to other media, as well.

Inside pages present design challenges because of the blocks of advertising, which often do not end up in neatly squared-off areas. Since the ads take up so much space and often include distracting visual elements, photos and illustrations are used less often to anchor the design on these pages. Instead, emphasis shifts to the clean lines of simply shaped modules and horizontal headings without many decks. If a photo is used, it is placed in the upper corner, with body text under it to provide a buffer between the photo and advertisements.

Tabloids often strive for strongly contemporary designs on their covers. Sometimes, this emphasizes their difference from their competitors among the urban dailies. Sometimes, it is due to the speed with which smaller publications

The Western Front

Monday
March 18, 2004

Western Washington University   Bellingham, Washington

Teaser
photo

Teaser heading
Μαρχη βεγινσ τηε
σεασον φορ
Μασον βεεσ.
Λοχαλ απιαρψ

Please see story, Page X

Main photo area

Photo by Clarion staff photograpgher

Φρομ τηειρ περχη ιν τηε χεντερ, ωορκερσ θαχκ Αρχηιβολδ οφ Χαμανο Ισλανδ ανδ Κεθιν Ρινεσμιτη οφ Σχαγιτ Χουντψ συρθεψ ρεσυλτσ οφ τηειρ εφφορτ ον τηε Μιλλεννιαλ Χηρονομετερ στεελ ανδ γλασσ χλοχκ ατ Εθερεττ Στατιον. Τηε

Everett opens transit hub
Plans for Amtrak, Greyhound to link cities

By-line centered
above the story box

ΕϛΕΡΕΤΤ ϖ Ωαλτερ Σηαννον νοδδεδ ιν αππροθαλ ανδ γαθε ηισ τηυμβ συματιον οφ ωηατ ηε τηουγητ αβουτ τηε χιτψΠσ   νεω 344 μιλλιον λανδ–μαρκ χαλλεδ Εθερεττ Στατιον: ρεαλ–λψ πρεττψ νιχε.

Τηε   91–ψεαρ–ολδ   Σηαννον ρεχεπθεδ αν ηονοραβλε μεντιον νεσ–τερδαψ δυρινγ τηε τρανσπορτατιον ηυβΠσ γρανδ οπενινγ.

Σηαννον σατ ιν τηε 200–πλυσ αυδι–ενχε ασ α στοιχ σψμβολ οφ ΕθερεττΠσ θανγυαρδ ρολε ιν τρανσ–πορτατιον ανδ ασ τηε σολε συρθιθιν μοτορμαν φορ τηε χιτψΠσ φιρστ χομ–μυτερ ραιλ λινε, τηε Ιντερυρβαν, ωηιχη τοοκ ριδερσ φρομ Εθερεττ το Σεαττλε υντιλ ιτ χλοσεδ ιν 1939.

Ανδ, ψεσ, Σηαννον λικεδ τηε βυιλδ–ινγ φυστ φινε. Βυτ ηε χονθεσσεδ ηε προθαβλψ ωουλδνΠτ βε βοαρδινγ ανψ οφ τηε τραινσ λεαθινγ τηισ στατιον. ℗Νο,℗ Σηαννον σαιδ, σχοφφινγ

σλιγητλψ. ℗ΙΠθε βεεν περτ νεαρ εθερψωηερε Ι αχντ το βε.℗

Τηουγη νοτ μυχη φορ τραινσ ανψ–μορε, Σηαννον℗σ ρεσπεχτεδ ποστ ασ α ρετιρεδ ραιλ μαν τοοκ τηε αττεντιον οφ Γοθ. Γαρψ Λοχκε, ωηο γαθε τριβ–υτε το τηε Ιντερυρβαν λινε ανδ χαλλεδ ηισ θισιτ το τηε χιτψΠσ νεω στατιον α τριπ Θβαχκ το τηε φυτυρε.℗

Εθερεττ Στατιον ισ α τρανσπορτα–τιον χεντερ ωηερε Εθερεττ Τρανσιτ

Please see **Everett Station,** *Page 6*

Outside limits
Puget Sound purity affected by dumping

By-line centered
over the story text

Μαρκ Παπλοω σταρτεδ ηισ βυσινεσσ ινφορμαλλψ ιν τηε μιδ–1970σ δριθινγ βαχκ ανδ φορτη αχροσσ τηε χουντψ ιν στερ πεοπλεΠσ χαρσ ανδ λοοκινγ φορ Ηοαδψ Λοοδψ κεψ χηαινσ.

Νοω, μορε τηαν τωο δεχαδεσ λατερ, Παπλοω πρεσιδεσ οθερ Αχχουτρεμεντσ Ινχ., α ωηολεσαλε τοψ χομπανψ ωιτη 35 εμπλοψεεσ βασεδ ιν Μυκιλτεο τηατ ισ βεττερ κνοων τηρουγη ιτσ αλτερ εγο ανδ ρεταιλ ουτλετ, Αρχηιε ΜχΠηεε.

Please see **Working for Fun,** *Page 6*

Secondary photo area

Photo by Clarion staff photographer

Τονψ Γρεενε οφ Αχχουτρεμεντσ Ινχ — βεττερ κνοων βψ ιτσ ρεταιλ ναμε, Αρχηιε ΜχΠηεε — δεσιγνσ α φραμε φορ α φυνηουσε μιρρορ ατ τηε χομ–

Tax revenue earmarked for buses

By-lines are
centered above text

ΟΛΨΜΠΙΑ ϖ Τηε 2002 λεγισλατιθε σεσσιον αδφουρνεδ λαστ νιγητ βψ αδοπτινγ α 37.7 βιλλιον τρανσ–πορτατιον πλαν τηατ θοτερσ ωιλλ βε ασκεδ το αππροθε ιν Νοθεμβερ.

Τηε   τρανσπορτατιον–σπενδινγ πλαν ωιτ νεεδ το βαλανχε α ρεχεσ–σιον–ραχκεδ βυδγετ δομινατεδ τηε 60–δαψ σεσσιον τηατ ενδεδ ατ ιτσ μανδατορψ μιδνιγητ δεαδλινε λαστ νιγητ.

Οϖ τρανσπορτατιον, λαωμαχερσ βυχκεδ Γοθ. Γαρυ Λοχκε, τηε στατεΠσ λαργεστ βυσινεσσεσ ανδ λαβορ υνιονσ, ανδ δεντ α πλαν φορ α 9–χεντ–α–γαλλον γασ ταξ ινχρεασε το θοτερσ ιν τηε υπχομινγ γενεραλ ελεχτιον. Τηε γοθερνορ ανδ α χαδρε οφ λοββψιστσ ηαδ ωαντεδ λαωμαχερσ το ραισε τηε ταξ τηεμσελθεσ.

Ιν αδδιτιον το τηε 37.7 βιλλιον στατεωιδε τρανσπορτατιον πλαν τηατ θοτερσ ωιλλ σεε ιν Νοθεμβερ, βοτη ηουσεσ αγρεεδ ον α ρεγιοναλ πλαν αλλοωινγ Πυγετ Σουνδ–αρεα θοτερσ το ραισε υπ το 38.7 βιλλιον οθερ 10 ψεαρσ ιν λοχαλ ταξεσ φορ τρανσπορτατιον ιμπροθεμεντσ.

Λαωμαχερσ πυτ φινιστινγ τουχη–εσ ον τηε γενεραλ–φυνδ βυδγετ ασ

Viking viewpoint

Photo for
quick poll

Photo by The Daily Clarion

Δο ψου συππορτ τηε θοτε φορ α ταξ ινχρεασε το πελπ Ωηατχομ Χουντψ Τρανσιτ χοντινυε βυσι–νεσσ ασ υσυαλ?

Χηαρλιε   Ωελλνιτζ,   Ωεστερν σενιορ: ℗Ι τηινκ τηε ταξεσ σηουλδ βε ραισεδ. Ι υσε τηε βυσ.℗

"Pullquote. Add pull
quote text here."
— Name of student in photo above
Western senior

ILLUSTRATION 11.1 A and B   *Covers and Inside Pages: Tabloid.* These page dummies, based on a student mock-up for a college newspaper, show certain design characteristics being carried from the front page to the inside pages to provide visual unity. The style of the nameplate or banner, the wide columns and gutters, the deck heads, pullquotes, centered bylines and use of lines or rules combine to form a theme that is carried throughout.

The Western
Front

Page 4 Monday, March 18, 2004

Monday poll
Senate firm on campus civil rights

ΟΛΨΜΠΙΑ ∇ Τηε 2002 λεγισλατιϖε σεσσιον αδφουρνεδ λαστ νιγητ βψ αδοπτινγ α 37.7 βιλλιον τρανσπορτατιον πλαν τηατ ϖοτερσ ωιλλ βε ασκεδ το αππροϖε ιν Νοϖεμβερ.

Τηε τρανσπορτατιον–σπενδινγ πλαν ανδ νεεδ το βαλανχε α ρεχεσσιον–ραχκεδ βυδγετ δομινατεδ τηε 60–δαψ σεσσιον τηατ ενδεδ ατ ιτσ μανδατορψ μιδνιγητ δεαδλινε λαστ νιγητ.

Ον τρανσπορτατιον, λαωμακερσ βυχκεδ Γοϖ. Γαρψ Λοχκε, τηε στατε∏σ λαργεστ βυσινεσσεσ ανδ σεντ α πλαν φορ α.

για ταξ ινχρεασε το ϖοτερσ ιν τηε υπχομινγ γενεραλ ελεχτιον. Τηε γοϖερνορ ανδ α χαδρε οφ λοββψιστσ παδ ωαντεδ λαωμακερσ το ραισε τηε ταξ τηεμσελϖεσ στατεωιδε τρανσπορτατιον.

Protesters peaceful in daylong vigil

Βψ–λινβε
Χεντερεδ χρεδιτ λινε

ΟΛΨΜΠΙΑ ∇ Τηε 2002 λεγισλατιϖε σεσσιον αδφουρνεδ λαστ νιγητ βψ αδοπτινγ α 37.7 βιλλιον τρανσπορτατιον πλαν τηατ ϖοτερσ ωιλλ βε ασκεδ το αππροϖε ιν Νοϖεμβερ.

Τηε τρανσπορτατιον–σπενδινγ πλαν ανδ νεεδ το βαλανχε α ρεχεσσιον–ραχκεδ βυδγετ δομινατεδ τηε 60–δαψ σεσσιον τηατ ενδεδ ατ ιτσ μανδατορψ μιδ–νιγητ δεαδλινε λαστ νιγητ.

Ον τρανσπορτατιον, λαωμακερσ βυχκεδΟΛΨΜΠΙΑ ∇ Τηε 2002 λεγισλατιϖε σεσσιον αδφουρνεδ λαστ νιγητ βψ αδοπτινγ α 37.7 βιλλιον τρανσπορτατιον πλαν τηατ ϖοτερσ ωιλλ βε ασκεδ το αππροϖε ιν Νοϖεμβερ.

Τηε τρανσπορτατιον–σπενδινγ πλαν ανδ νεεδ το βαλανχε α ρεχεσσιον–ραχκεδ βυδγετ δομινατεδ τηε 60–δαψ σεσσιον τηατ ενδεδ ατ ιτσ μανδατορψ μιδ–νιγητ δεαδλινε λαστ νιγητ.

Ον τρανσπορτατιον, λαωμακερσ βυχκεδ Γοϖ. Γαρψ Λοχκε, τηε στατε∏σ λαργεστ βυσινεσσεσ ανδ λαβορ υνιονσ, ανδ σεντ α πλαν φορ α 9–χεντ–α–γαλλον για ταξ ινχρεασε το ϖοτερσ ιν τηε υπχομινγ γενεραλ ελεχτιον. Τηε γοϖερνορ ανδ α χαδρε οφ λοββψιστσ παδ ωαντεδ λαωμακερσ το ραισε τηε ταξ τηεμσελϖεσ.

Ιν αδδιτιον το τηε 37.7 βιλλιον στατεωιδε τρανσπορτατιον πλαν τηατ ϖοτερσ ωιλλ σεε ιν Νοϖεμβερ,

βοτη ηουσεσ αγρεεδ ον α ρεγιοναλ πλαν αλλοωινγ Πυγετ Σουνδ–αρεα ϖοτερσ το ραισε υπ το 38.7 βιλλιον οϖερ 10 ψεαρσ ιν λοχαλ ταξεσ φορ τρανσπορτατιον ιμπροϖεμεντσ.

Λαωμακερσ πυτ φινισηινγ τουχηεσ ον τηε γενεραλ–φυνδ βυδγετ ας τηε Σενατε θυιχκλψ πασσεδ α πλαν τηατ ινχλυδεδ νο χοστ–οφ–λιϖινγ ινχρεασεσ φορ στατε εμπλοψεεσ; 354 μιλλιον ιν ρεδυχεδ φυνδινγ το χολλεγεσ ανδ υνιϖερσιτιεσ; τεμποραρψ χλοσυρε οφ σομε στατε παρκσ; ρεδυχεδ συβσιδιεσ το λοχαλ γοϖερνμεντσ ανδ 3180 μιλλιον ιν χυτσ το σοχιαλ προγραμσ. Γοϖ. Γαρψ Λοχκε, τηε στατε∏σ λαργεστ βυσινεσσεσ ανδ λαβορ

Advertising

ILLUSTRATION 11.1 B   *Tabloid Inside Page*

have been able to adopt newer technologies. And sometimes, the design reflects their uniqueness and editorial niche.

Urban weekly tabloids often define themselves on the cover with a subtitle stating the contents are a weekly guide to arts, film and theater, or perhaps a journal of review and commentary. They may carry only one large piece of cover art, as a way to signal their difference from the daily newspaper in the area.

The mock-up cover in Illustration C.27 draws on some design techniques associated more with magazines, such as the very large type sizes and gradations of sizes that move in intervals down to the body text. Also, the art is grouped in a way not customary for newspapers.

Production Costs: Newsletters

The line between a magazine and a newsletter is hard to define because many newsletters intended for internal use in a corporation or for distribution among a membership mirror the size, complexity and presentation values of magazines produced for general audiences. Both styles project personalities, ranging from corporate to quirky and individualistic. Both use color if they can afford it.

But, thousands upon thousands of newsletters exist, published in black and white for smaller distributions. Especially for memberships of nonprofit groups, the emphasis is on a substantial, attractive but low-cost look that won't appear to be using funds better spent on the programs' recipients.

Many newsletters are now published in both print and online versions, as mentioned above, with the delivery via e-mail reducing postage costs. Newsletters sent as attachments, rather than within the body of an e-mail message, are often designed in full color and may resemble sophisticated Web pages.

The cost of printing newsletters goes up if irregularly sized paper or odd numbers of pages are used. Typically, a 17 by 22-inch sheet of paper is folded to produce four 8.5 by 11-inch pages, and pages are added in intervals of four. It can be a difficult decision for a newsletter editor to make the jump from eight pages to 12, for example, when the ideal number of pages might be 10. Ironically, the 12-page size is usually cheaper to print because of standard paper sizes and press configurations.

Newsletters done for nonprofit organizations and smaller groups of readers can stick with black and white production and still achieve attractive layouts, as can be seen in Illustration 11.2.

Covers and Contents Pages: Magazines

Because thousands of magazines exist in North America, all seeking audiences, each has to project its purpose, personality and offerings quickly—literally almost at first glance. This makes covers, editor's letters and contents pages important sites for careful design and thoughtful editing.

A newsletter for the staff, volunteers and friends of the Opportunity Council - www.oppco.org - *April 2003*

'Energy Assistance' can help with more than heating expense

A new program is available this year through the Opportunity Council to help people in Island and Whatcom counties pay energy expenses.

The new Puget Sound Energy Home Energy Lifeline Program, (PSE HELP) will provide once-a-year grants to help families who are choosing between heating and eating or medical cost and electricity.

The O.C. is now scheduling PSE HELP appointments for people living in low-income households who have a Puget Sound Energy account. Grants are based on income, household size and electric usage and go directly to the household's PSE account. The program will be available through September to provide help for customers whose incomes are between 125 and 150 percent of the federal poverty level.

For many families this means while almost all Low-Income Home Energy Assistance Program (LIHEAP), funds have been distributed this year, some funding may still be available to help with their Puget Sound Energy bill. People who received a LIHEAP grant may also be available for PSE HELP.

Need for funding is outrunning resources

The 2002-3 season for energy assistance began in November with LIHEAP. All appointments necessary to exhaust the LIHEAP funding were filled within two weeks and the program was scheduled to close entirely when elected officials in Washington D.C. provided a much needed funding boost and the O.C. was able to serve an additional 600

...additional energy funding is expected to help approximately 1,700 households in Island and Whatcom County this year.

(Continued on page 3)

INSIDE THIS ISSUE:

Your support helps us meet local needs

While some look to Olympia with concern over state funding, or to the other side of the world with anxiety over global conflicts, we want to take a moment to focus locally and acknowledge the support we receive from *"Friends of the Opportunity Council"* to help people here in our community.

Our thanks and appreciation to everyone who supported the Annual Campaign 2002 last year in Whatcom County. At a time of economic and political uncertainty, donors raised nearly $50,000 during our campaign last fall to help us make sure people in our communities are safely housed, warm, fed and have access to quality child care and early childhood education.

Annual Campaign 2003 planned for *Community Action Month*

May is *Community Action Month* and will be the season for our 2003 Annual Campaign. We look forward to support from new and existing donors in Island, Whatcom, San Juan counties and beyond. What better way to celebrate *Community Action Month* than by helping make our communities a little better for everyone. *(See page 7-8 .)*

ILLUSTRATION 11.2 *Black and White Printing: Newsletter.* Organizations wanting to limit costs of their publications may choose to print with black ink only. Effective designs will make maximum use of building in contrast. This newsletter shows how a professional, clean and readable look can be achieved through strongly shaped modules and limited but distinct typographical variations. The format is also conducive for updating for subsequent issues, as it provides a basic template with a range of possible variations.

("The Window of Opportunity," April 2003, The Opportunity Council, Bellingham, Wash.; reprinted with permission.)

While some magazines aim to inform and provide news, as newspapers do, a great many more exist to entertain and to express and explore lifestyles. In addition to newsstand sales, magazines rely on delivery through the mail to a defined audience spread over a wide geographic area. Some alter their covers for different regions.

Contents pages become crucial, especially for magazines that have just one illustration on the front. The New Yorker uses artwork with no cover lines, and for years even resisted a contents page. Using a design carried from issue to issue, Harper's Magazine places its cover lines in predictable horizontal headings under an illustration.

Because magazines showcase their main articles throughout the "book," a contents page is essential for a reader to know what is offered in the issue. It relates visually to the cover design, and many provide icons or illustrations that tie the story summary to the layout that appears pages later. Editors also need to show how individual writers' voices will be expressed in each piece. (See Illustration C.29A and B.)

Full Color: Magazines

Inside, a magazine places a premium on the ability to showcase photography and art. High resolution printing lets editors run photographs across pages or to "bleed" colors by carrying them to the edges of pages. (See Illustration C.28.) Students beginning work with magazine design often forget they can design outside the lines indicating page borders and centerlines on the magazine templates.

Magazine layout takes the principles of contrast and unity and plays them larger, more extravagantly. But, it is done individualistically. While most magazines revel in full color, The Sun, by contrast, runs one small patch of spot color on its cover of only black and white, richly textured photographs. It also carries no ads and runs each article sequentially, start to finish.

White space is used more elaborately, the density or spaciousness of body text may vary, and headings may have unusual, hand-painted or designed typefaces. The main photo or illustration often runs quite large in proportion to the page. The pages are finished with more elaborate page strips and may include small icons that stand in for the magazine's title.

Magazine designs often show more involvement by artists, who may brush stroke letters and draw or paint illustrations to produce a blending of the verbal and visual meanings. The different voices of writers carried in the magazine may be emphasized visually; this contrasts with newspapers, which offer a more uniform, institutional voice.

Still, unity in design must take place across pages so that the magazine has a consistent personality throughout. In this case, the body text settings, the color palette, the page strips, the column rules and photo treatments set parameters.

Ease of Use: World Wide Web Pages

Once current monitor size limitation is considered and the space for navigational links, browser bars and advertisements is subtracted, a Web page offers the smallest layout space among these media. Its identity is still evolving; offering the speediness of news wires, the video, animation and sound of broadcast, the timeliness of newspapers and the in-depth writing of magazines, or the research possibilities of a library, a particular site can be just about anything.

The design challenge is most similar to a magazine's in the need to define itself clearly, express a personality and to offer specific information on a variety of topics on the first page or cover.

Getting attention and keeping a visitor coming back are so crucial to a Web page's success that editors must select, write and present every item in terms of what the audience will find attractive and easy to use.

Web editors need to remember that their pages are limited by the lowest technology available to viewers. Many viewers use telephone modems for connections to the Internet and see pages on small monitor sizes. These technological limitations on delivery time and screen size affect how quickly and efficiently a Web page loads and displays. The higher-speed connections and phone lines that have typically been more available in workplaces are increasingly available in homes, as neighborhoods are being hooked up to DSL phone lines or fiber-optic wiring.

An editor can assure that a page offers interesting reading while viewers wait for the larger files containing photos and graphics to load. Some Internet users set their browsers for text only and, only after reading content, decide whether to view the images as well.

In Illustration C.30, a student design for a potential Web site uses standard fonts, a single, smaller photo, and text lines that a viewer can read while waiting for the page to load. The navigational links are paired with brief descriptions of the stories, thus allowing the viewer to choose whether to make the investment of clicking to get to the next level of information.

Many publications are discovering that a Web site is a great place to display their photo essays and to archive them. Gone are the high costs of color printing and the limitations on space. Editors may create thumbnail sizes that preview what is available. That way, viewers can choose which ones they want to see at full size. A page of thumbnails also offers editors the chance to create a narrative order for storytelling with the images.

Photos can also carry ALT. tags created in HTML (hypertext markup language). These describe a photo's contents while the image loads and allow viewers to click away if they choose not to wait.

Photos with a resolution of 72 dpi, or dots per inch, will display minimally well on most monitors and still be a small file size. Larger files, of course, offer better resolution for high-end monitors but increased loading time.

Web page editors recognize that users control how they approach the site, and that the browser, hardware and operating system used will affect its appearance. This means that what an editor designs is not necessarily what a viewer sees.

Headings change in size and are rearranged as a default font is substituted into a reshaped frame; colors are altered as browsers reinterpret them and varying monitor settings kick in. And, a user printing out some pages may opt for, or only have access to, black ink on white paper.

Editors create some design items as gifs, which load like photos; because the internal contents are not rearranged, these are ideal for ensuring a nameplate or icon will be displayed as it was designed.

A viewer may arrive at a page through a link from another site rather than through the home page. Research describes many Web users as highly motivated and approaching searches with the intention of finding something specific, much like the way they'd search a library.

These factors require Web pages to have navigational buttons for getting from place to place and then back home, plus a visual context that lets viewers know where they are within a site's offerings. Each screen, too, needs identification—much as each page of a magazine carries—in case a viewer lands on an inside page first.

At a certain point, a viewer settles in to read, and pages can signal, by layout changes, when the viewer has arrived at the document itself. Research indicates that viewers lose patience if the promised article or document resides more than four clicks away from the contents page. Some sites offering long documents carry an option for printing them out as a single unit because low screen resolution presently limits the amount people enjoy reading online.

Document pages are usually far simpler and plainer than home pages or other contents pages. The point now is to be read, and that means using dark type on a light background and keeping lines of text to about 3.5 inches in length. Editors try to keep the type size large enough to be easily readable, usually at least 10 or 11 points, with airy leading.

The pages may require scrolling through a couple of screens and then usually link to additional screens instead of requiring viewers to scroll down and down and down.

Monitors display about 30 lines of type at one time, and some editors place subheads within that range in order to provide greater ease of scanning.

Editors assign hierarchies of type within sites so that main categories can be differentiated from several lesser ones, but they avoid using an excessive number of subhead sizes. This straight-forward hierarchy allows readers to perceive whether they are off on a tangential point or back to one of the main categories of an extensive page.

Editors can build more contrast into Web pages than is available in print media by adding components for sound, animation, image maps and video. How much is suitable depends on who the audience is, what informational priorities the site has and whether the contrasts enhance or distract from reading.

Sites using many of these components often include information, located near the icon to be clicked, that describes the content and how long the sound or video segment is so that viewers can decide whether to invest the time. Some viewers lack the technology to view video or play sound, and some may not want to download necessary plug-in programs.

Jakob Nielsen, the Sun Microsystem engineer mentioned earlier who has written extensively about writing and designing Web pages, argues that the practices producing good design for newspaper pages won't work on a Web page's much smaller space.

Newspaper design begins with a much larger space and gauges the appearance of components relative to each other, and the reader's attention follows her eye through the page. On the Web, the much smaller space is viewed as an entity in itself, and movement among pages is guided by the hand, which does the clicking.

No page is complete without the link to real people. Many sites invite viewers to respond via active e-mail links to the writers or editors. Usually a Web page offers links to other locations that are associated in some way with the site's contents. External links are potentially distracting, so good editors keep them to a minimum and add only those that are very important to the text. Some Web sites have adopted a set format for links, such as listing them only at the ends of stories, with their subject matter clearly explained.

For planning an effective Web site, Nielsen and other researchers recommend that editors picture the site's content as being a series of inverted pyramids floating in space.

The practice of storyboarding, or literally drawing, page by page, what the viewer will see, comes from film and broadcasting. Storyboarding works well for the Web by allowing editors, videographers, producers and graphic artists to stand in the viewers' shoes and see what they will see as they navigate the site. Such visualizing can take into account the way viewers will make choices among stories or links, branching off in their explorations.

Conclusion

The design and layout issues discussed above are not medium-specific.

For example, except for magazines, newsletters and Web pages that carry no advertising, the placement of commercial messages affects media design. Web pages have not yet evolved a standard format that achieves a good balance in comfortably asking either time or space from viewers. Broadcast television sells time; newspapers sell space. The Web, with its blinking or intrusive pop-up screens, seems to demand both time and space.

While research shows Web users lose patience with this and with the "spamming" of widely dispersed e-mails, much like consumers' irritation with telephone marketers, it also shows that readers appreciate advertisements as a source of information. Ads fall into regularly defined spaces and patterns in print media, which viewers can either peruse or ignore.

The audience's needs, interests and preferences drive the design of publications because they must draw readers back. A design offers aesthetic appeal, expresses the publication's personality, and provides the visual cues that unify its pages. Working within the templates of defined typefaces, page sizes, sections and colors, editors apply design on a daily basis as they lay out pages. The editor's job remains distinct from the more artistic work done by a graphic arts designer.

Some design and layout practices originating in one medium work as well for the others. For example, referring readers to related information takes the form of links on a Web page but can appear as contact information at the end of a newsletter story. The different packaging styles for hard news and features looks transcend one medium, as well.

And although providing information on a publication's location in real time and space is emphasized for Web pages, it is just as important for the audiences of a corporate magazine to know who is putting out the publication and how to contact the editors.

As editors work within a design, they find that applying its concepts to the day's rush of news events or the month's story menu is highly creative and engaging, and that their choices enhance the publication's visual identity and the vitality of their pages.

Exercises to Apply Concepts and Develop Skills

Goal: To apply concepts developed in the chapters of the text thus far to create page layouts. Using stories, photos, illustrations and infographics, students will design full pages.

It is possible for students with sophisticated skills to work on several layouts at once, in order to make decisions among media, such as which items are best presented in print and which online.

Step 1   Expressing priority on a page (Chapter 2). Students will select the major stories, and decide which will be played prominently. Using criteria for selecting photographs and illustrations (Chapter 7), students will select the major visual components for the page and decide on their prominence.

Step 2   Stories are shaped into modules and heading sizes are assigned (Chapter 3) and written; any gaps in the stories are identified and corrected; students edit the stories for grammar, syntax, punctuation and news style (Chapters 4 and 5).

Step 3   With the modules planned and sketched on the page or on a storyboard, students move to determining the need for text-based graphics they will create (Chapter 6), and will evaluate infographics and statistical material available and prepare them as needed. (Chapter 10). At this point, they may also decide whether they will use any display type (Chapter 9).

Step 4   Color decisions are made. Students will move to final decisions on the colors used to unify a page and to provide contrast on the page (Chapter 8).

Step 5   The concepts underlying typography, which include the placement of dominant, dark areas within white space according to an underlying grid or a pattern, are applied to adjust the final layout (Chapter 9). With an eye to reading patterns and to the overall design formed by the text, illustrations and accompanying negative space, students may make final adjustments to their pages to simplify design and to strengthen their expressions of priority, unity, contrast, beauty and clarity.

Step 6   Evaluation of the page in terms of readers' needs and impact on the community (Chapter 12). Students will assess the overall context they have created for the events their pages depict. In class discussion, students may be asked to describe their intentions and decision-making processes for both verbal and visual elements, covering content, legal and ethical reasonings.

By viewing and comparing the wide range of page designs that are likely to result even when students use identical exercise materials, the class can discuss the message, tone and impact of the various pages along with the role they perceive their media having within their communities.

Helpful Sources

Select design sites:
Poynter Institute: http://www.poynter.org/
Print magazine: http://www.printmag.com
Jakob Nielsen. "Alertbox" at http://www.useit.com/alertbox
Society for Newspaper Design Web site: http://www.snd.org

Berry, John D. "Design and New Media: Fuzzy Fonts," Print. May-June 2000.

Castro, Elizabeth. "HTML for the World Wide Web." 4th Ed. Berkeley, Calif.: Peachpit Press, 1999.

Conneen, Anne. "The Maestro of Redesign," Poynter Report. Summer 2002, pp. 14–15.

"Design 2020: Visions of the newspaper of the future," American Press Institute's J. Montgomery Curtis Memorial Seminar. October 24–26, 1999; published Fall 2000, API, Reston, Vir.

DeVigal, Andrew. "Design Guidelines for Online Sites." The Poynter Institute, July 1999. See at http://poynter.org

Garcia, Mario. "We've come a long way," The American Editor. April 2000, pp. 4–5.

Lynch, Patrick J. and Sarah Horton. "Web Style Guide: Basic Design Principles for Creating Web Sites." 2nd Ed. New Haven, Conn.: Yale University Press, 2002.

The Missouri Group. "Telling the Story: Writing for Print, Broadcast and Online Media." New York: Bedford/St. Martin's, 2001.

Rich, Carole. "Newswriting for the Web." http://members.aol.com/crich13/poynter4.html

Watson, Warren. "Narrower Web Widths: Newspaper Designers Speak Out," Design. Summer 2000, pp. 6–9.

Silverman, Jay, et al. "Rules of Thumb with 2002 APA Update and Electronic Tuner CD-ROM." Boston: McGraw-Hill, 2002.

12

Balancing Community Interests: Ethics and Law

As an editing concept, "community" is overarching in that it encompasses audience, without which publications cannot exist.

Perhaps the old saying, "It takes a village to raise a child," should be rephrased to be "It takes an editor to raise a village" because editors have the responsibility to provide community members all important information to ensure they are fully informed about community issues.

Beyond understanding what information is important for the community to know and then presenting it in a clear and attractive manner, editors bear responsibility for knowing the community's tastes, sensitivities and legal restrictions. And, with online publications, that community could well be a global one.

Textbooks dealing with editing often treat legal issues and ethical matters in separate chapters. However, from the standpoint of community, these two areas are intertwined because they represent the "written" and "unwritten" limits placed on published material. Together, they make up the fence surrounding the yard, the hedge surrounding the garden, the wall surrounding the mall—pick your metaphor.

Written limits are those in which the community has articulated the bounds beyond which published material must not go if it is to escape reprisal. These emerge as laws telling editors where those limits lie.

Unwritten limits are those where community concern has been voiced, but no overwhelming tide of public opinion has culminated in formal action that would result in some kind of law on the matter.

These are the ethical considerations that ebb and flow in a community and cover issues that range from privacy, taste and grief to diversity, conflict of interest, bias and acceptance of gifts.

This chapter paints a broad picture of this legal/ethical landscape. Students moving toward a career as editors will need to find out what community is served by the publication they are working for. They must work to learn the community's written and unwritten limits.

However, they must also remember that fearless editors do not allow limiting force to interfere with their duty to represent all voices in the community or to prevent ideas—even ones representing stances different from majority interests and unpleasant to those with power—from being presented.

This fearlessness is related to the First Amendment duty of providing all possible views and ideas for robust community debate—and is not the same as defying community sensitivities by publishing an offensive picture of a mutilated body or of a family grieving over a drowned child.

Sometimes, the publication may have a printed guide of its own but more often not. Editors can find legal guidelines (the written limits) in the latest edition of resources such as "The Associated Press Stylebook and Briefing on Media Law," "Mass Media Law," (published anually) by Don R. Pember and Clay Calvert, or others such as "Major Principles of Media Law" by Wayne Overbeck.

Quite a number of mass media ethics texts offer useful suggestions about dealing with community sensitivities (the unwritten limits), among them the latest edition of "Doing Ethics in Journalism," a Poynter Institute book by Jay Black and others, "Media Ethics" by Clifford G. Christians and others, and "Deadlines and Diversity: Journalism Ethics in a Changing World," edited by Valerie Alia and others.

Codes of ethics from organizations like the American Society of Newspaper Editors, Public Relations Society of America and the Society of Professional Journalists provide useful standards as well. Only by gathering knowledge of what the community values and standards are, and by using as loose guidelines the legal and ethical materials from sources such as those above, will editors be able to serve adequately all the voices in the community.

'Written Limits': Ins and Outs of Law

The rules of a community regarding what is published about it and its members are usually codified in some manner: Administrative agencies create rules; legislative bodies pass laws; courts interpret these and issue rulings.

In America, where freedom of press is aspired to, the First Amendment to the Constitution is the quintessential written limit and is often cited by journalists of all kinds, including editors, as giving freedom to publish as they please what they please.

Editors who believe they have total freedom to print what they want are living with Alice in a rabbit hole. As First Amendment scholar Alexander Meiklejohn noted, freedom of the press belongs to the people, and the First Amendment protects information related to the self-governing process and voting, not all information, especially that incidental to self-governing.

So, in a land of free press, plenty of limits are placed on what can be published. Society has rules to punish those publishing materials damaging a person's or a business's reputation; containing obscenity; threatening national security; inciting violence; or advocating overthrow of government. Limits also are placed on speech used for commercial purposes. The federal government can force companies to withdraw or correct untrue statements in advertisements, for example.

During both Persian Gulf wars, military censors reviewed and "cleared" material before it was broadcast on CNN. High school principals routinely review material about to be printed in student newspapers. Ignoring here censorship out of the legal arena, say, by corporate owners of media, we know federal officials and bureaucrats at all levels find ways to keep information secret from journalists representing the public.

Courts are, of course, in the thick of things. Today, judges routinely award compensation to people whose reputations are tarnished by false statements made by publications or broadcast stations and to those whose writing is copied without their permission. Also, courts in some states punish publications for infringing on people's privacy in some manner.

This chapter offers broad guidelines for areas where these written rules most directly impact editors' duties. But those considering a career in editing must realize the job of editing is accompanied by an ongoing responsibility to stay abreast of legal developments affecting the dissemination of information in their medium, be it a newspaper, a magazine, a corporate newsletter, or a Web site.

Many written limits vary from state to state, and editors do not need to learn in detail the kind of knowledge lawyers have, but guidelines below, along with information in sources noted earlier, help editors become aware of potential legal dangers so they can seek legal advice as needed.

Copyright

Copyright refers to protecting the right of authors to get money for their work and to punish those who take it and use it without paying. Copyright law protects work that is printed, filmed, taped, or expressed in an electronic or other format.

The written rules regarding copyright are complicated and under constant revision by courts at one level or another. However, one relatively clear way to understand copyright is to view it in a manner similar to the Associated Press: Merely restating basic facts and ideas of a work is probably legal; using the author's way of expressing them is probably not.

Using material in the way an author created it may be acceptable if an editor gets (and usually pays for) permission to use the work—or, sometimes, if the use falls into what is called a "fair use" category.

Fair use guidelines also ebb and flow, depending on the court, but in general include considerations such as how much of the work is used, what proportion it is of the whole, how much revenue was lost by the use, what the material taken was used for, and the nature and purpose of the copyrighted work (whether it was creative or merely informational).

Editors respecting fair use guidelines are willing to pare or kill stories that borrow from another author in a liberal manner (especially if the material being used is creative), and they must remember that merely attributing material to the source from which it was taken will not change copyright infringement into fair use.

As with most instances related to written and unwritten limits, it is useful for editors to imagine themselves in the situation, in this case, as the author of the material, and ask if the taking and using is acceptable, given the considerations above.

In a manner similar to handling instances of privacy and libel, if they have doubt, they should leave it out—or get the author's permission to use it.

Copyright laws are meant to protect a writer's or artist's intellectual property, to guard their ownership. However, in some cases a publication is actually the owner of an article, photograph or illustration. Courts have created a distinction between works that a person creates for an employer—using that employers' materials and being paid a salary while creating the work—and works that a person creates on her own time but offers for sale.

An editor sees this difference in terms of whether a writer or photographer is on staff or is a free-lancer. A free-lancer usually sells only limited rights to her photos or stories and retains other rights. For example, she may sell First North American Serial Rights to a magazine but retain the rights for reprints, international sales, film versions, and so forth. The rights that are bought and sold are usually spelled out in correspondence or in a contract. Staff writers or photographers who are marketing work on their own, apart from their employment, are wise to clarify ahead of time who owns the rights to such work.

Libel

Defamation, or **libel,** is the most common, complex and dangerous written limit facing editors at all levels in every medium. Perhaps because we are all so insecure and feel hurt so easily, libel actions are so prevalent. Or, maybe it is because media content is usually about people and the events they are involved in, which all too often are not pleasant ones.

Regardless, the seriousness of libel cannot be overstated, and editors should become educated about the intricacies of libel law because they will use such knowledge to help sort through information that will or will not run in stories.

Legal definitions of libel vary from state to state, but, in general, it occurs when media content that is false injures the reputation of a person, business or other organization. Groups of people tend not to be able to sue successfully for libel. The injurious material, be it a statement, cartoon, photo, photo caption or a heading, causes a person to be avoided, hated, held in contempt, thought ill of, injured financially, ridiculed or the like.

After the injurious material is printed or disseminated electronically or in some other way, and after the hurt is experienced, a person or entity can use the legal system to be compensated for the injury—in effect, to get even.

What to Prove

Parties feeling a libel hurt cannot merely take an empty satchel to the courthouse and have the judge fill it up with $100 bills.

But, they will see plenty of the courthouse and their attorney's office.

A gauntlet regarding libel must be run by the injured. This gauntlet stems from the 1964 "New York Times v. Sullivan" U.S. Supreme court decision, which was the first in a series of rules regarding libel that has continued to be expanded by other court rulings.

Before people who feel they have been libeled are permitted even to plead their case to a jury, they must prove several things:

- They must prove that the statement has been published or broadcast. This may seem self-evident, but especially with the Web, the injured party must be able to show an actual "copy" of what was said electronically or in print. It's difficult to prove anything if no evidence can be presented.
- They must prove that they were defamed. If the material would not be considered harmful—in spite of its falseness—by the community, the courts would likely not allow the case to proceed. Simply put, little hope exists of winning a libel suit for Mr. Sensitive who takes offense at a printed description of him that says he loves children when he really does not.
- They must be able to prove the false material was about them. Sometimes a harsh statement about a large group may be taken personally by one member who can prove no individual connection; sometimes an alarming photo angers a person who was in the scene but who cannot be recognized by those looking at it.
- They must prove the material was false—harmfully so. Proving this may be easy, as for the man who is identified HIV positive when he is not.

  Sometimes it is difficult, a my-word-against-yours type of thing, as when a farmer is said to have dumped old containers of pesticide into a river when she has not.
- They must prove that the editor's publication was at fault. This means, that depending on who they are, they must prove that the publication or Web site failed to exercise reasonable care (was negligent) in gathering and presenting the material—or, in some cases, published material known to be false or exhibited reckless disregard for the truth.

  In this area, courts have made distinctions between what public officials, public figures and private individuals need to prove. This dimension of libel is complex and needs to be understood fully by editors.

In general, editors who are careful in guiding and checking the information-gathering process and in ensuring its fairness and lack of malice will be able to prevail regarding fault.

Avoiding Libel Suits—the Chill of It All

Sometimes the stinging hurt of libelous material can be eased in another way so that no lawsuit will be brought. Perhaps the paper or newsletter or magazine or Web site agrees to print a retraction that soothes the injured party. Perhaps they have a reader-response panel or some kind of council that hears complaints, and the injured party, having had the grievance aired before that body, decides against legal action.

Of course, editors should strive to provide full information that does not libel. In a way, if a libel suit succeeds, they have failed. But, many editors of today also have become fearful even of risking a libel suit that will fail because the high, high financial cost of fighting that suit in court can force the publication or Web site out of business. This fear, a real one, has had a chilling effect on the amount of truthful-but-libel-suit-likely material allowed to be printed.

Defenses against Libel

Media law books and Associated Press libel discussions speak of defenses against libel that will make any lawsuit unsuccessful. Editors should know what these defenses are because they help in deciding whether to include potentially libelous material.

The primary defenses include the following:

- **Truth.** If the published material is true—that is, substantially accurate—a libel has not occurred, and the editor can breathe again.

    But, she should not breathe too deeply unless she knows evidence, such as documents or multiple witnesses, exists to prove truthfulness. The person suing may well have to prove falsity, but the possibility of an expensive court battle means editors must know documentation of truth exists. The phrase "provably true" is a useful guideline.
- **Privilege.** Courts have excluded vicious, hurtful words that normally would be libelous but that are spoken at meetings of public interest, largely because of the need to have a robust discussion in the self-governing process.

    The term for this exemption is **privilege.** Publications can restate the libel without fear of having to battle in court. In most parts of the United States, the media have this "qualified privilege." In a few places, the media's qualified privilege may have to be associated with words uttered by a responsible and prominent person on a controversy that is public or about a public figure or official. Also, the report containing the libel must be balanced and accurate.

- **Opinion.** For the most part, the expressing of an opinion—even if it is a sweeping or exaggerated remark—has been protected by the courts, especially if it concerns an area of interest to the public. However, the opinion may not be protected if it implies a falsehood—so the comment must be embedded within verifiable facts and be clearly an opinion.
- **Consent, right of reply, retractions.** These areas are not so much defenses of libel, but instead are ways not to be heavily penalized for having published a libel.

  Sometimes, the printing or Webcasting of libelous material may not result in much financial damage to the publication if the person libeled had given permission to publish the material. In effect, at some point prior to publication, the person probably said or wrote that seeing the words in print would not bother her or him. Courts usually don't hand over much cash when the person changes her or his mind and sues.

  Also, in some instances, a publication that has published a libelous statement can offer the hurt, angry person a chance to respond (right of reply)—or will publish a correction and maybe an apology (retraction). A number of states have retraction laws that vary in the protection they afford. Normally, however, the publication would lose any resulting court case, so soothing the ire of the offended becomes an avenue worth pursuing—sort of a street of last resort, but certainly not one to be constantly relied on by editors doing their duties.

Privacy

Problems with the privacy area of the law arise less often than with libel, but since journalists write about people and their lives, and since many people around the world are sensitive about their privacy, editors need to know the written guidelines about it.

The rules vary from country to country, but U.S. law tends to break **privacy** into four separate areas—appropriation, publishing private information, intruding into the life of another, and portraying a person in a false light—with some of them needing more attention from editors than the others.

- **Appropriation.** Linked to monetary motives and the ability to capitalize from one's identity, appropriation is the use without permission of a person's name or likeness for a profit. A T-shirt company that on a whim prints Michael Jordan's face on a tank top and sells it is treading in this area. So is a company that publishes employee photos in an advertisement or public relations brochure without first gaining those employees' permission.

  A similar violation would be a Web ad claiming Pearl Jam members always stay at the Locust Resort in Aphid, Ariz., and recommend it highly when band members don't and probably don't even know of the ad or the resort.

Since in both cases and in similar cases the famous people (and sometimes not-so-famous) who lose profit on the material printed with their names or likeness could win a lawsuit, editors need to be aware of the dangers lurking in advertising, stories, photos and illustrations. If the portrayal is news and not some kind of an endorsement or use that will result in profit, it is probably OK. If not, maybe not.

However, the waters are murky, and editors must be on guard, examining all their content, being certain permission has been granted for such use and being willing to make a thorough legal check if a blip floats across their sonar screen.

- **Publishing private information.** People usually value their privacy, yet they may also at some point in their lives get snared in an event that is regrettable, embarrassing—and newsworthy. This combination is more dangerous than three sweet items on a Chinese food menu. The editor must be cautious in making a decision to publish such an article or image, even though it may be true, because it may result in losing a privacy suit or offending the community. Yet, potentially embarrassing and true information may appear in print when it applies directly to news linked to significant public issues.

  For example, does an editor publish a photo of a drunken mayor dancing half-naked at a community street dance? Does she publish a similar photo of a person not widely known nor holding public office? Does she include truthful information that a city council member is gay in a story about the council pondering funding for an AIDS center?

  A list of all potentially dangerous choices would be longer than a line of recounted ballots in a Florida election. Again, editors need to recognize the potential for danger here and be wary. They should know, however, that in general if the embarrassing material has a legitimate connection to the public's business or to an issue that would be of public interest, it has a stronger likelihood of surviving a legal privacy action.

- **Intruding into the life of another.** Journalists gathering information or taking pictures can go too far. The intrusion subcategory of privacy centers on how far is too far.

  Intrusion occurs when the journalist oversteps the line—which may well also be an ethical line—say, when she opens the door of an unlocked, unoccupied oil company executive office and sorts through folders of documents lying on a desk.

  Or, intrusion may occur when a photographer climbs a tree to take a photo of a movie star sunbathing nude on his secluded patio.

  Editors need to be aware of the circumstances surrounding the gathering of information, not only in choosing what they print or post, but also in helping to guide the behavior of those gathering the documents and images. Good editors appreciate strong yet creative efforts by reporters and photographers but warn them against breaking laws or being too devious in their methods.

They know this area of journalistic behavior resonates unfavorably in the public mind and are themselves sensitive to it. Perhaps the most useful guideline is to ask whether a regular member of the public would have seen the event or had access to the material.

Caution is needed also in public relations work, where employees may know more about each other's lives than the general public would. For example, printing information about an employee's illness or financial troubles may constitute an invasion of privacy when it is done without that person's agreement, even when the intentions are as sound as starting a drive for donations.

- **Portraying a person in a false light.** This privacy area is similar to publication of private facts but differs in that the true but embarrassing information is usually being relayed in a creative or fictional way, with liberties being taken in the retelling that offend the person represented.

Such privacy actions mostly result from television or movie portrayals or from printed novels or magazine feature stories. In a legal sense, this subcategory is still quite young, and editors normally do not encounter material that fits it.

However, the plethora of Web sites with off-the-wall content may provide rapid aging and whole new contexts for false light. For example, a site that routinely accepts photos of people to be rated on a whim by its audience could receive an unflattering photo of a young man, finger in nose, sent in by an enemy. The embarrassment from a low rating and cruel comments could prompt a false light action.

'Unwritten Limits': Sensitivity to Community

Is it proper to publish a picture of a person's private actions in a public place if the person didn't know she was being photographed?

Should editors use photographs that show bleeding, suffering or death? Is it acceptable for editors to edit stories about causes or clubs they belong to? Should they accept gifts—say, a food editor accepting a bag of Walla Walla Sweet Onions from an onion growers' association?

Is fair play being given to minority segments of the community—such as people of color, gays, lesbians, bisexuals, transsexuals, people who are physically or mentally handicapped, people with AIDS and people of other ethnicities and cultures?

Should editors withhold embarrassing news about community members who are politically powerful or icons of the social scene?

Editors need to recognize the importance of unwritten limits and move carefully regarding such matters by realizing insensitivity on their part may bring a backlash—or worse. Those who are cavalier or thoughtless soon find themselves embroiled in controversy about the kind of story or photo or graphic or heading used on a topic. They learn the hard way that a community's outrage comes on as swiftly as a summer storm.

Editorial Leadership

And yet, difficult stories—the ones about the toll of AIDS within a community, or the effect of alcoholism on family lives, or betrayal of public trust by an office holder—must be told so that people can live with realistic pictures of their communities and its strengths and problems.

Editors use several measures to help decide when those difficult stories will be run. One is to be able to articulate the good it may serve, to include in stories steps being taken or progress envisioned or volunteer actions.

Another is to tell stories compassionately, to reveal empathy with those caught by life's dilemmas. As a writer in "Deadlines and Diversity" comments, the point of the reporting should be learning from other people, not studying them.

A third aspect of the decision is whether the publication will take an editorial stance and launch its own efforts to persuade and reform, in essence, to become actively involved in analyzing problems and trying potential solutions. In this case, editorials are sometimes timed to quickly follow investigative pieces.

Editors play an important role as well in selecting the letters that appear on editorial pages and in assessing their accuracy and verifying who wrote them. To maintain integrity with their readers, editors usually open those pages to a wide range of voices and keep debate lively by including a variety of viewpoints. In this work, knowledge of libel law also comes in handy, as letters to the editor can become libelous when they attack people on a personal level and use false information.

Editors don't just reflect the values of their communities; they need to be aware of those values, and they often decide to advocate change. In a sense, a publication creates community just by being present for its readers; this role carries with it potential influence and leadership.

A Matter of Truth

One of most damaging habits editors can develop, perhaps the most damaging, is when they forget their community as an audience and begin editing for themselves or a nonrepresentative segment of the community. Because of pressures or other reasons, they cease paying attention to the larger community.

Or, they may allow their own values to drive them and use personal likes and dislikes in deciding what is important and appropriate instead of keeping ears and eyes open as to priorities and standards in the communities they serve.

Editors have responsibility for recognizing—and insofar as possible revering—these and other unwritten limits swirling throughout the community even as they make certain those limits do not stop the community from getting information it needs.

"Deadlines and Diversity" provides a good way to understand part of the problem via a concept known as the Rashomon Principle, which, in essence, says any occurrence (or issue, for that matter) has not one truth, but several. One person's account of an event will likely differ from another's.

As many of those truths as possible should be provided, and this may mean making certain that content from nonverbal language and information gained in "backstage" settings is included.

Alia also notes that accuracy of the portrayal requires gathering information while being aware of the cultural context—a context that recognizes how a person acts when providing information may not be the same as how the action is perceived by the journalist gathering it.

Editors working in public relations, whether for print or Web publications, may scrutinize the role of the "honest advocate," as set out in the Code of Ethics of the Public Relations Society of America.

This code insists upon honesty and accuracy in all information conveyed by public relations practitioners, and it recognizes that business activities, social causes and nonprofit organizations' efforts are often worthy of advocacy. Qualities the code addresses include honesty, loyalty, fairness, independence, expertise and advocacy.

Codes of ethics are helpful in that they detail what other journalists or professionals think is important. For example, the Society of Professional Journalists Code of Ethics tells journalists to seek truth and report it, minimize harm, act independently and be accountable. (See Box 12.1.)

BOX 12.1 • *Online Legal and Ethical Resources*

Below are World Wide Web links to codes of ethics and other resources for media law and ethics:

American Press Institute—http://www.americanpressinstitute.org

American Society of Newspaper Editors—http://www.asne.org

Associated Press Managing Editors—http://apme.com/

International Association of Business Communicators—http://www.iabc.com/

Poynter Institute—http://www.poynter.org

Public Relations Society of America—http://www.prsa.org

Society of Professional Journalists—http://www.spj.org

Student Press Law Center—http://splc.org

These areas include such specifics as the following:

- not misrepresenting events in headings;
- not distorting the content of photos;
- not pandering to lurid curiosity;
- not accepting gifts;
- testing the accuracy of information and not distorting it;
- being sensitive when seeking news or photos of those involved in a tragic event;
- avoiding conflicts of interest;
- encouraging the public to express its grievances against news media;
- admitting mistakes and correcting them promptly.

While paying respect to such codes no matter how they are categorized, wise editors tend to avoid total dependence on them or on any other rigid list of do's and do not's.

In short, unwritten limits, whether legitimately imposed because of ethical considerations or imposed out of fear for reasons of self-censorship (and a Pew Research Center poll in 2000 showed self-censorship by journalists to be prevalent), are still limits. Editors play a crucial role in deciding the amount (or number) of truth or truths told and the manner in which the telling takes place.

A more helpful way to tackle the Sisyphusean task of maneuvering among the unwritten-limits minefield may be to divide the landscape into a couple of categories—obstacles to truth seeking, and obstacles to truth telling—all the while being aware that without truth, an information-providing publication or site loses much credibility and for all practical purposes ceases to exist.

- **Obstacles to truth seeking.** Although they may not be directly involved in gathering the information and images to be printed or posted, editors know that a significant portion of the news process lies in this arena. And, many unwritten limits existing in the community deal with the *gathering* of information.

  The limits are directly related to journalistic behavior. A community becomes sensitive and may react strongly when journalists practice snooping, bullying, threatening, bribing, lying, intruding, stalking, stereotyping, exaggerating, sensationalizing, titillating, deceiving, distorting, manipulating or demonstrating tastelessness or insensitivity.

  Editors should realize they have a leadership role in policing such behaviors that rankle the community and harm a publication's credibility.

- **Obstacles to truth telling.** Another primary role of editors committed to making certain truth gets told is to recognize, know and evaluate obstacles swirling around the *presentation* of news—and make wise decisions regarding them so that credibility is not lost.

  A litany of the more abstract obstacles includes self-censorship invoked by values (of the community or editors themselves); belief that total objectivity is possible; negative portrayal resulting from prejudice or stereotyping; and fear of pressure applied by sources of power, including that by groups or leaders or businesses, by the publication owner or by other power-wielding groups in society.

Among other day-to-day obstacles encountered are ones such as these:

- having too much loyalty to certain community interests;
- succumbing to manipulation by sources;
- printing anonymous controversial material;
- rushing incomplete stories into print;
- being underly or overly sensitive regarding matters of taste or morality;
- misprioritizing information;
- omitting important information;
- exhibiting laziness in presenting complete facts;
- allowing fictionalizing of articles, quotes or images;
- permitting manipulation of photos or images;
- being crusading and self-righteous;
- accepting bribes or gifts;
- being arrogant;
- lying.

Editors are in a constant struggle to deal with these obstacles. The Tibetan saying, "In politics, there is no such thing as honor," does not apply to editors or to journalistic practices. Honoring the truth (or truths) that the community needs to hear and erring on the side of presenting it, not withholding it, are the goals for which fearless editors strive.

Conclusion

Written and unwritten limits are present in any community, whether its members are the readers of a newspaper, magazine, public relations newsletter or users of a Web site. Editors of all these media find themselves in a position of having to be keenly aware of both limits—the written laws of copyright, libel and privacy, and the ethical limits with myriad obstacles to truth seeking and truth telling.

It is a formidable task to deal with such limits, especially when editors are juggling subtleties of other important editing concepts of *priority, unity, contrast, clarity* and *beauty.* But, somehow editors must rise to the task because the *community* and its growth and understanding are at stake.

Exercises to Apply Concepts and Develop Skills _____

Student learning of media law and ethics is often enhanced when teachers bring for class discussion real cases they have collected from various media and from sources such as the Society of Professional Journalists (spj.org) and the Poynter Institute (poynter.org), as well as from sources in this chapter's source list, (which could also be used as supplemental texts). Playing the role of editor and given the facts and circumstances of the case, each student—or team of students—explains decisions made and actions taken before the class and teacher respond.

Here are some other assignments that work:

1. Goal: To develop student ability to recognize libel in written material they are copyediting.

   Beginning early in the term, build libelous direct quotes into stories that students are copyediting. For example, in a routine single-incident story (taken for one-time educational use from a newspaper or online site) about an accidental, non-fatal shooting, add a paragraph from a fictional official who states: "The victim is probably the one at fault here and is probably a congenital liar who has herpes." After learning about legal guidelines, students should recognize the libelous nature of the material and cut it from the story. A class discussion about the paragraph will reinforce the learning.

2: Goal: To develop student ability to recognize invasion of privacy in printed material.

   Bring in a sample you have created of one page of a fictional corporation's PR newsletter that contains an in-house advertisement urging company workers to buy facial tissue that the corporation produces. Include in the ad a photo of a celebrity from a local sports team as the person urging the buying. Using class discussion, guide students to privacy as a legal area. Prompt them to ask if written permission from the sports star had been secured for the corporate endorsement, and follow with a review of appropriation as invasion of privacy.

3. Goal: To develop student thinking regarding ethical implications of photo manipulation by electronic software.

   Tell the following story (or one similar to it) in class, and ask students to use their knowledge of the Society of Professional Journalists ethics code (or similar code) to discuss the ethical problems surrounding photo manipulation by electronic software:

   A journalism student working part-time as an editor in the city government public information office is given the duty of processing photos by using Photoshop. Usually, the PR supervisors have the student output photos with no alterations. However, one day a supervisor asks a student to prepare a photo of the mayor accepting a check from a corporate donor but to remove from the photo of a coffee mug having the logo of a competing corporation on it. The student does the task, and the PR office sends the photo and a caption out to various media outlets but does not mention the omitted mug.

4. Goal: To develop student thinking regarding ethical implications for editors of conflict of interest.

   Tell the following story (or one similar to it) in class, and ask teams of students to use their ethics code learnings to discuss any ethical problems they find in the story. Then have the teams convene in a large class discussion and report their decisions. Follow that with a class discussion of the various decisions:

   An editor in charge of a food section of a daily newspaper has a visit one day from a representative of a local garlic growers' organization. A reporter for the section had during the previous week been doing a cover story on cooking with garlic and had phoned the organization with a few questions. The garlic growers' rep says she just happened to be in town and wanted to meet the editor. After chatting a few minutes about the information given to the reporter, the garlic rep says she has brought a few brochures that may be helpful in preparing any stories and also says she has brought a sample of their garlic (two 10-pound bags) and six imported garlic presses for the newspaper staff to use when preparing the garlic. The editor chats with her for a few more minutes, thanks her for the gifts and then gets back to work on the section.

Helpful Sources

Ethics

Alia, Valerie, Brian Brennan and Barry Hoffmaster, eds. "Deadlines & Diversity: Journalism Ethics in a Changing World." Halifax, Nova Scotia: Fernwood Pub., 1996.

Black, Jay, et al. "Doing Ethics in Journalism: A Handbook with Case Studies." 3rd Ed. Needham Heights, Mass.: Allyn & Bacon, 1999.

Christians, Clifford G. et al. "Media Ethics: Cases and Moral Reasoning." 6th Ed. New York: Longman, 2001.

Kohut, Andrew. "Self-Censorship: Counting the Ways," Columbia Journalism Review. May/June 2000, pp. 42–43.

Lieberman, Trudy. "You Can't Report What You Don't Pursue," Columbia Journalism Review. May/June 2000, pp. 44–45, 47–49.

Codes of Ethics

Associated Press Managing Editors http://apme.com/

International Association of Business Communicators, http://www.iabc.com/

Public Relations Society of America, http://www.prsa.org

Society of Professional Journalists, http://www.spj.org

Law

Franklin, Marc A. and David A. Anderson. "Supplement to Cases and Materials on Mass Media Law." Cambridge, Mass: Foundation Press, 1999.

Goldstein, Norm, ed. "The Associated Press Stylebook and Briefing on Media Law." Cambridge, Mass.: Perseus Pub., 2002.

Overbeck, Wayne. "Major Principles of Media Law." Belmont, Calif.: Thompson/Wadsworth, 2004.

Pember, Don R. "Mass Media Law" 2005–06 Ed. New York: McGraw-Hill Higher Education, 2005.

Poynter Institute material on ethics. See the Poynter site at http://poynter.org

Steele, Bob. "Why Ethics Matter." Poynter Institute Web site (Aug. 9, 2002) at http://www.poynter.org

USC Annenberg Online Journalism Review. See this site at http://www.ojr.org

Wilkins, Lee and Philip D. Patterson. "Media Ethics: Issues and Cases." 4th Ed. Boston: McGraw-Hill, 2001.

Index

273

274